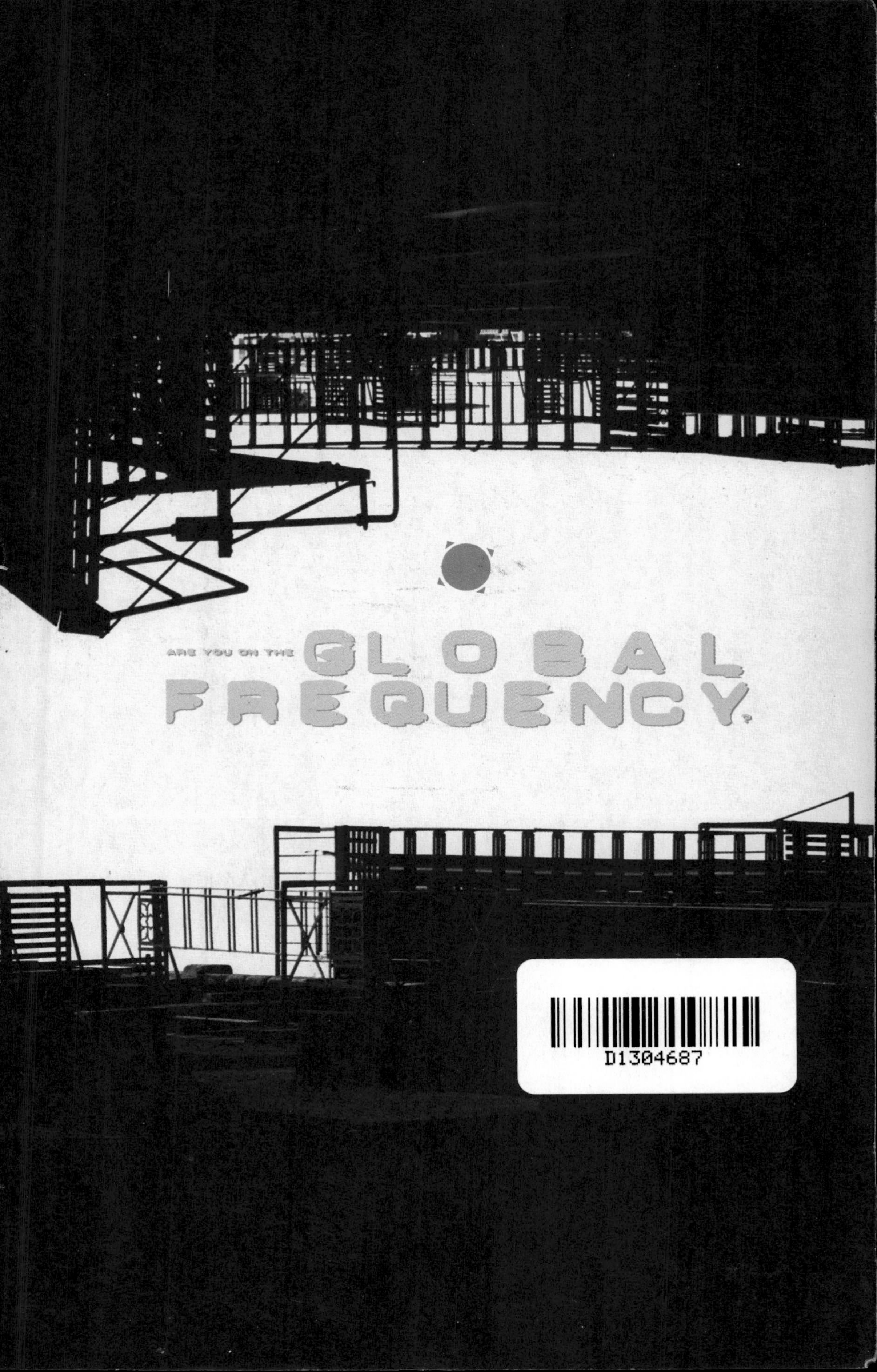
ARE YOU ON THE GLOBAL FREQUENCY?

Warren Ellis: writer

Steve Dillon, Glenn Fabry, Garry Leach, David Lloyd, Roy A. Martinez, Jon J Muth, and Liam Sharp: artists

GLOBAL FREQUENCY created by: Warren Ellis

Collected edition design: Larry Berry

GLOBAL FREQUENCY: PLANET ABLAZE, published by WildStorm Productions, 888 Prospect St. #240, La Jolla, CA 92037.
Compilation, cover and new material copyright © 2004 WildStorm Productions, an imprint of DC Comics. All Rights Reserved. GLOBAL
FREQUENCY is ™ Warren Ellis. WildStorm and logo are ™ DC Comics. Originally published in single magazine form as GLOBAL
FREQUENCY #1-6 copyright © 2002, 2003 Warren Ellis and DC Comics. The stories, characters, and incidents mentioned in this
magazine are entirely fictional. Printed on recyclable paper. WildStorm does not read or accept unsolicited submissions of ideas, stories
or artwork. Printed in Canada. Third Printing.
DC Comics, a Warner Bros. Entertainment Company.
ISBN-10: 1-4012-0274-8
ISBN-13: 978-1-4012-0274-3

David Baron: colors Michael Heisler: letters

Brian Wood:
Original series & collected edition covers

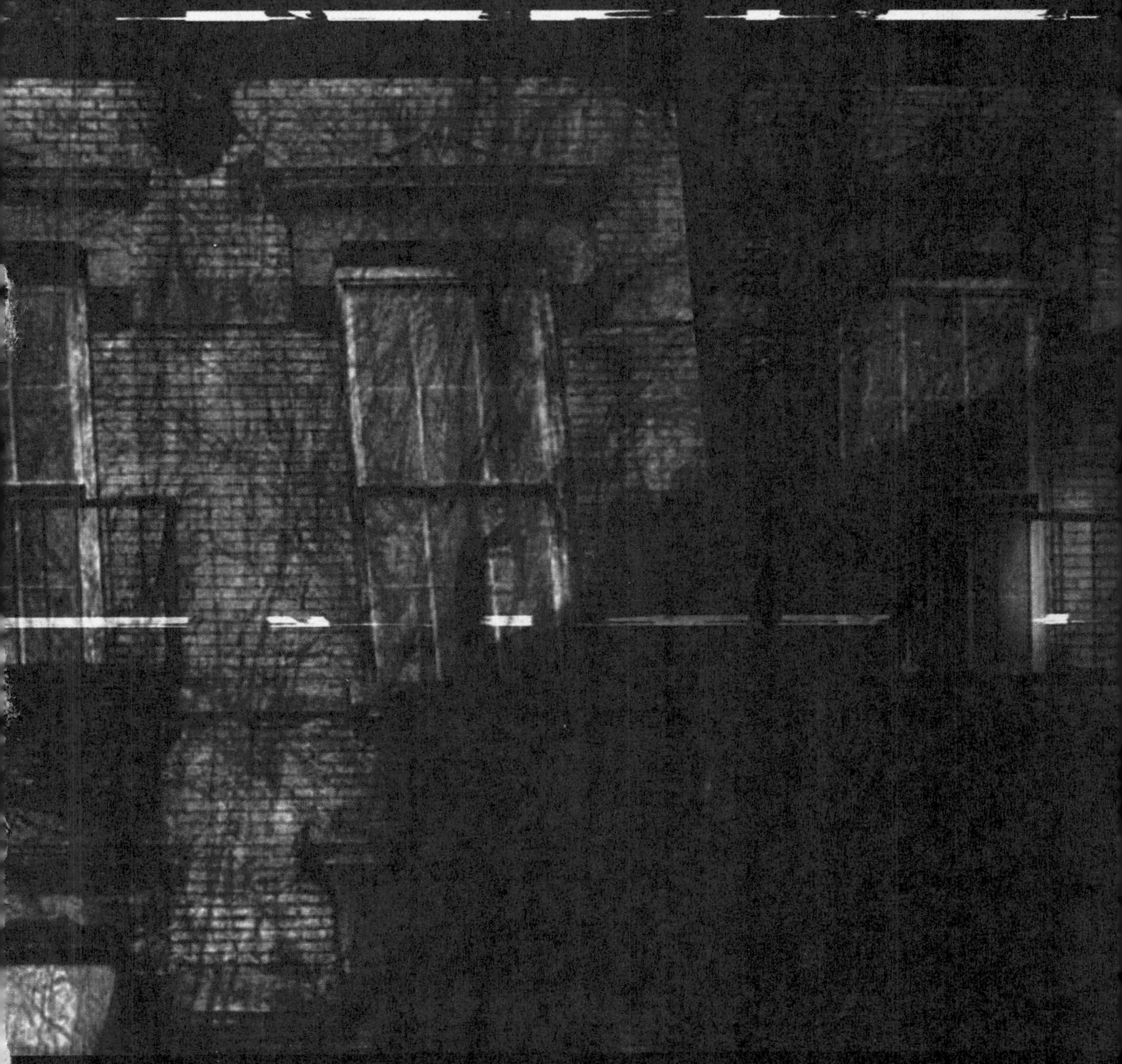

Jim Lee, Editorial Director ▸ John Nee, VP—Business Development ▸ Scott Dunbier, Executive Editor
Kristy Quinn, Assistant Editor ▸ Robbin Brosterman, Senior Art Director ▸ Ed Roeder, Art Director
Paul Levitz, President & Publisher ▸ Georg Brewer, VP—Design & Retail Product Development
Richard Bruning, Senior VP—Creative Director ▸ Patrick Caldon, Senior VP—Finance & Operations
Chris Caramalis, VP—Finance ▸ Terri Cunningham, VP—Managing Editor ▸ Dan DiDio, VP—Editorial
Alison Gill, VP—Manufacturing ▸ Rich Johnson, VP—Book Trade Sales
Hank Kanalz, VP—General Manager, WildStorm ▸ Lillian Laserson, Senior VP & General Counsel
David McKillips, VP—Advertising & Custom Publishing ▸ Gregory Noveck, Senior VP—Creative Affairs
Cheryl Rubin, Senior VP—Brand Management ▸ Bob Wayne, VP—Sales & Marketing

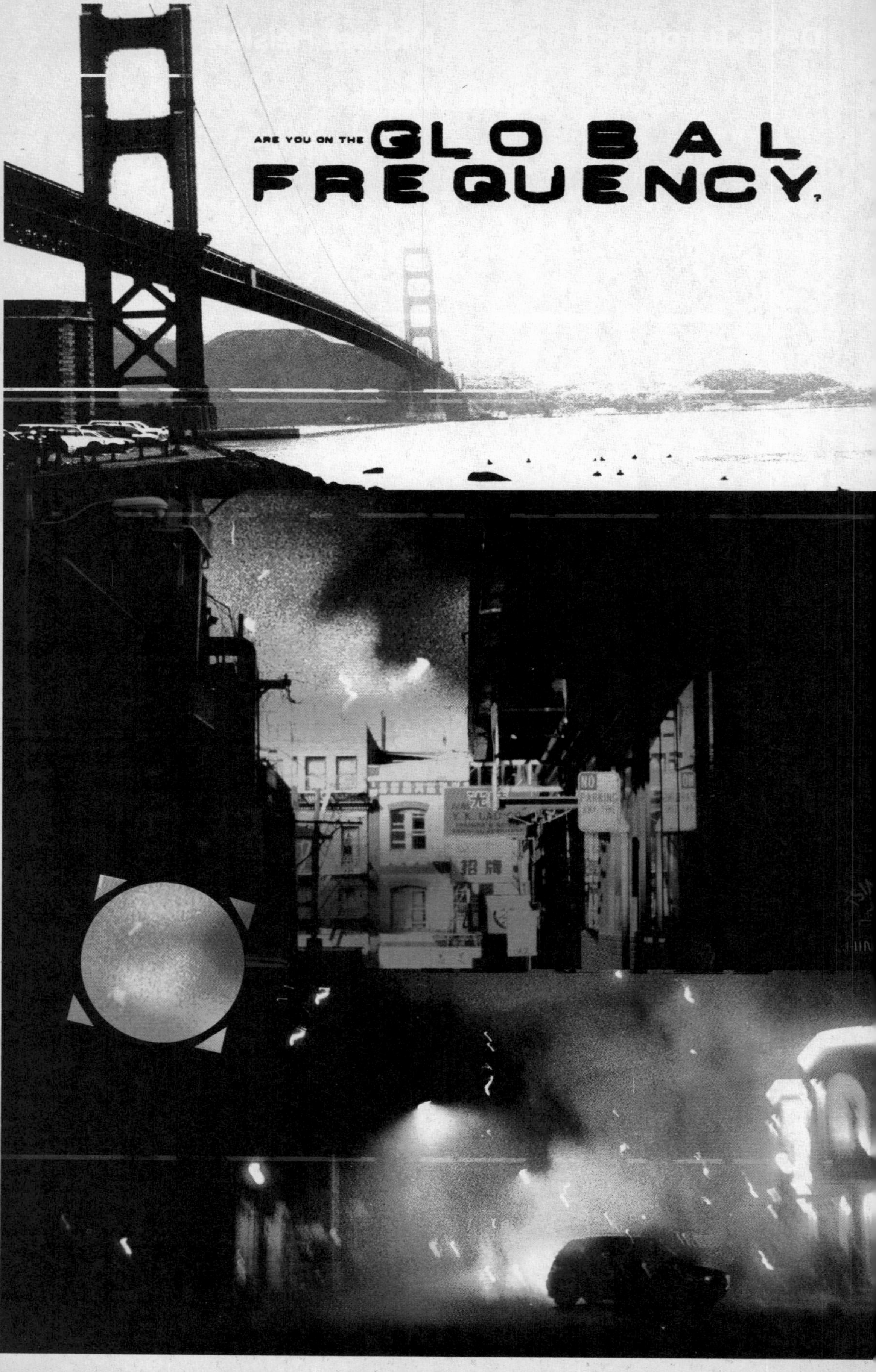
ARE YOU ON THE GLOBAL FREQUENCY?
NO PARKING ANY TIME
Y. K. LAU
招牌

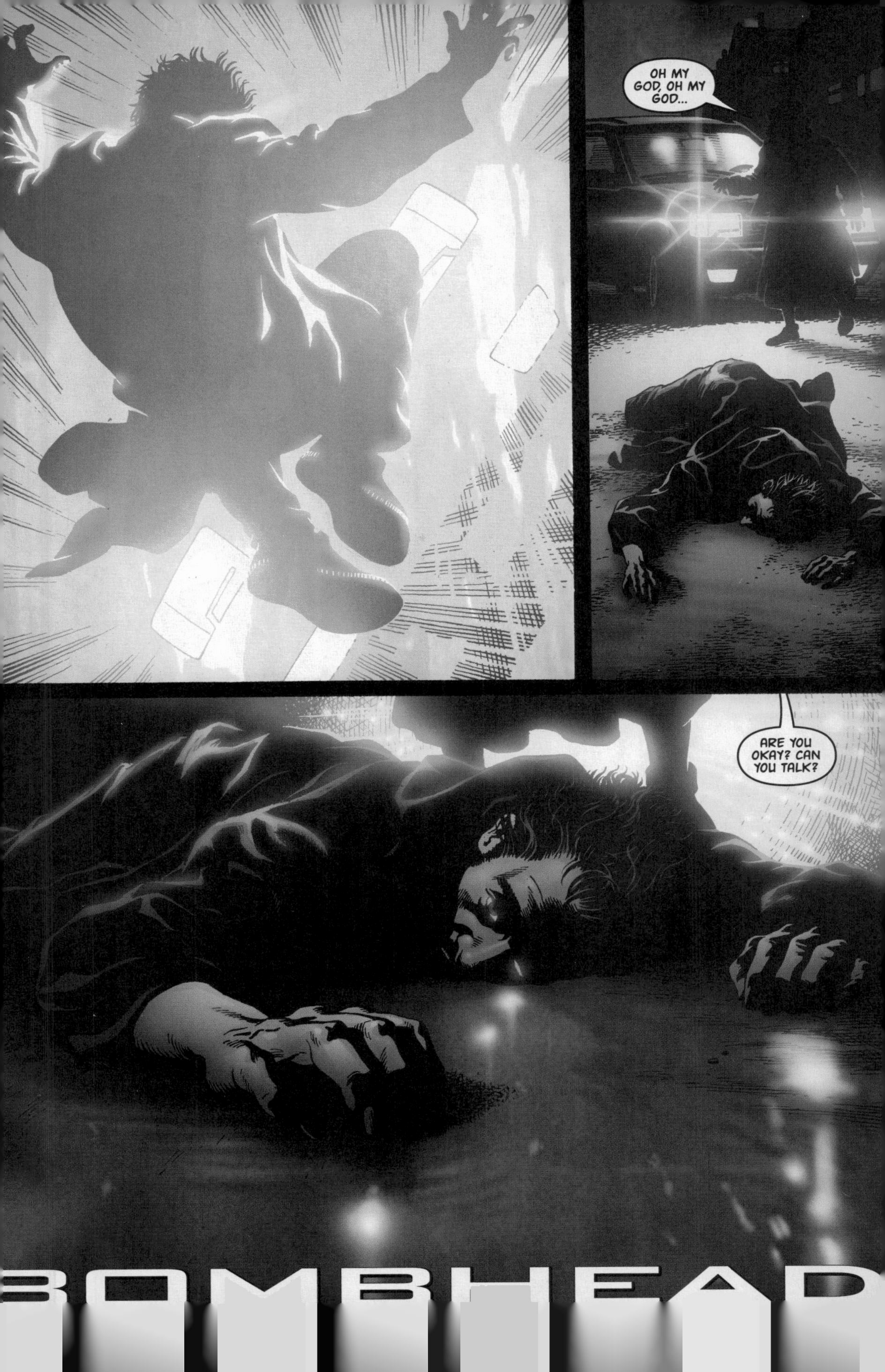
OH MY GOD, OH MY GOD...
ARE YOU OKAY? CAN YOU TALK?
BOMBHEAD

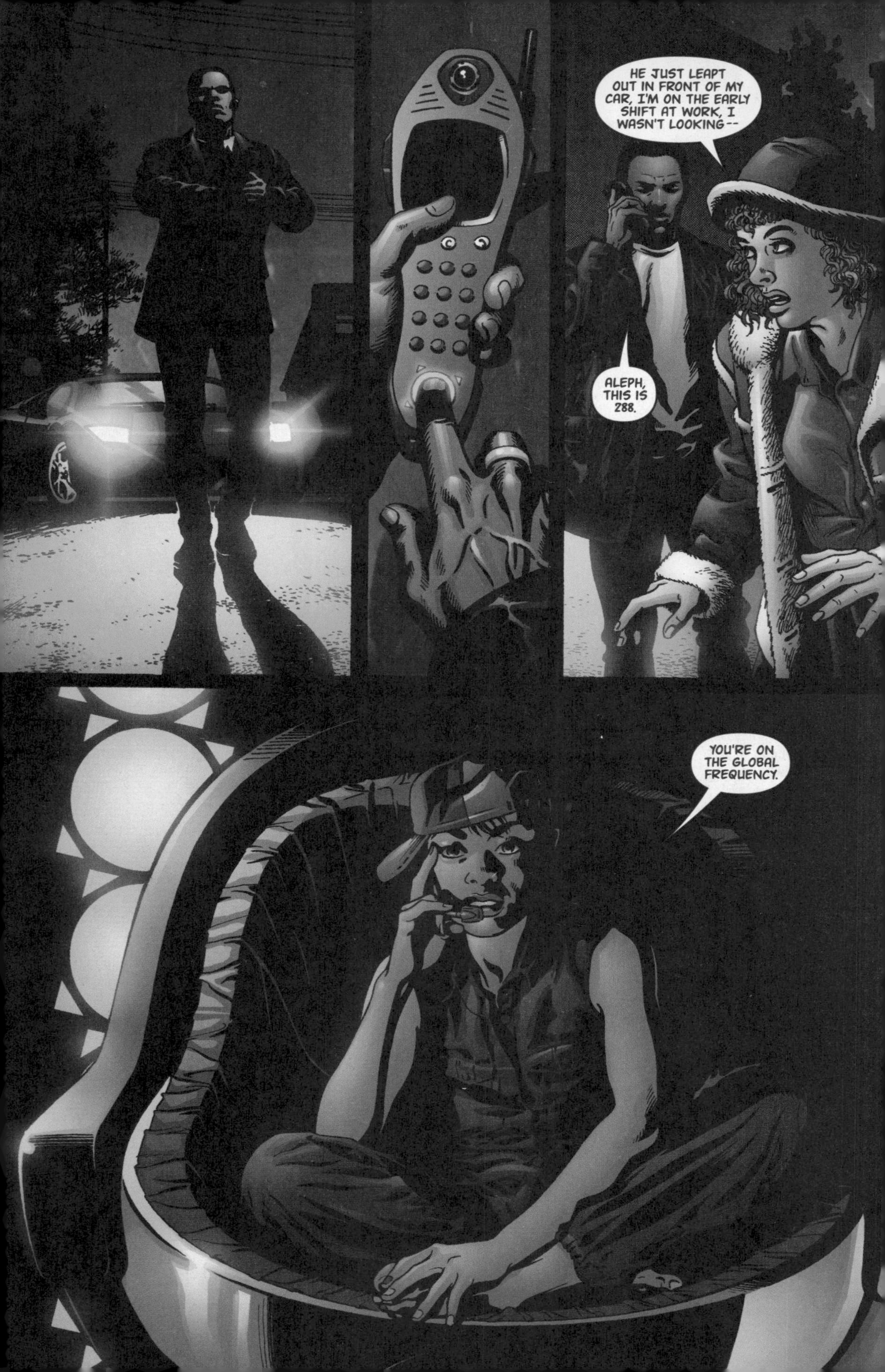
HE JUST LEAPT OUT IN FRONT OF MY CAR, I'M ON THE EARLY SHIFT AT WORK, I WASN'T LOOKING--
ALEPH, THIS IS 288.
YOU'RE ON THE GLOBAL FREQUENCY.

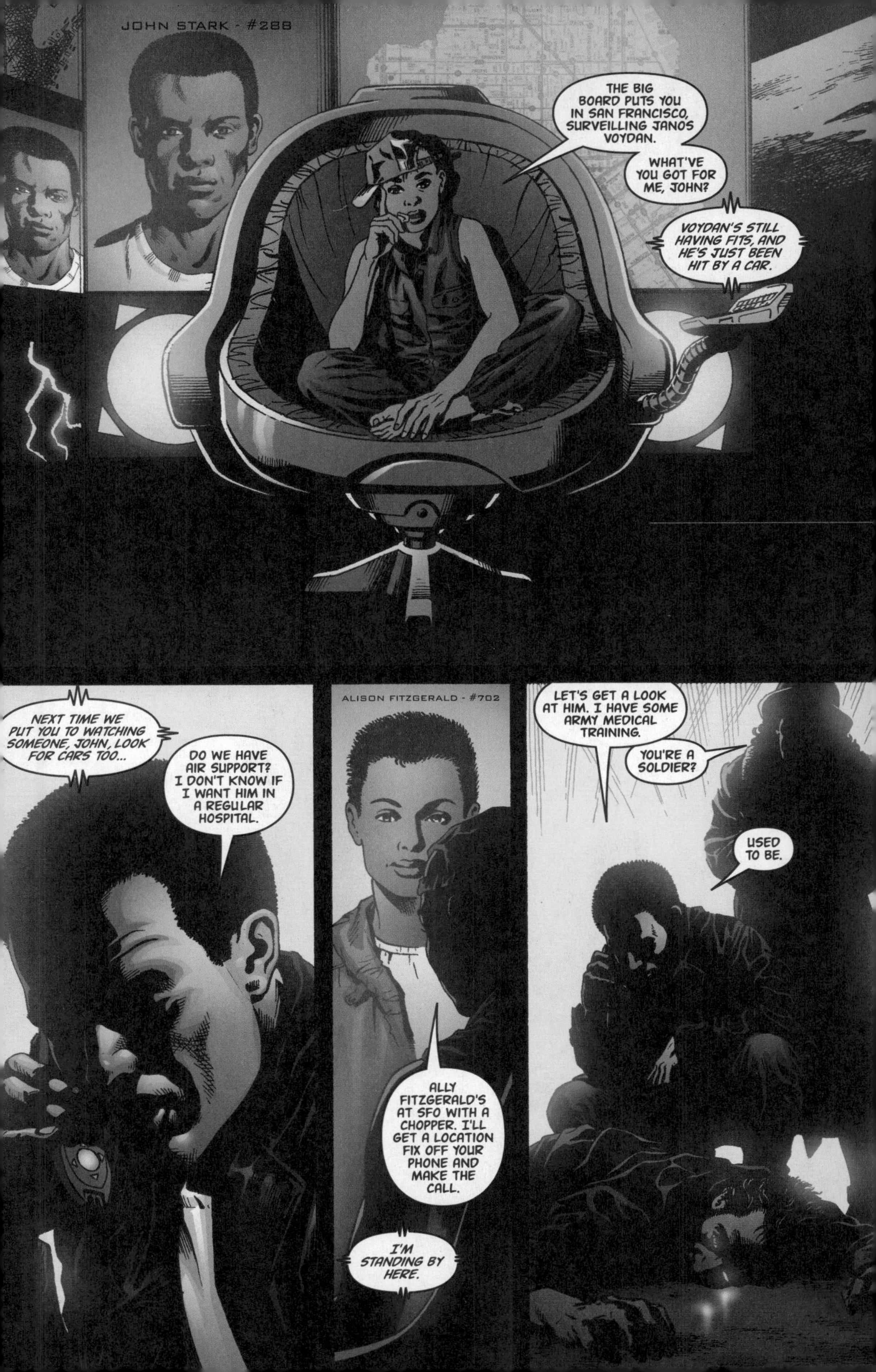
JOHN STARK - #288
THE BIG BOARD PUTS YOU IN SAN FRANCISCO, SURVEILLING JANOS VOYDAN.
WHAT'VE YOU GOT FOR ME, JOHN?
VOYDAN'S STILL HAVING FITS, AND HE'S JUST BEEN HIT BY A CAR.
NEXT TIME WE PUT YOU TO WATCHING SOMEONE, JOHN, LOOK FOR CARS TOO...
DO WE HAVE AIR SUPPORT? I DON'T KNOW IF I WANT HIM IN A REGULAR HOSPITAL.
ALISON FITZGERALD - #702
ALLY FITZGERALD'S AT SFO WITH A CHOPPER. I'LL GET A LOCATION FIX OFF YOUR PHONE AND MAKE THE CALL.
I'M STANDING BY HERE.
LET'S GET A LOOK AT HIM. I HAVE SOME ARMY MEDICAL TRAINING.
YOU'RE A SOLDIER?
USED TO BE.

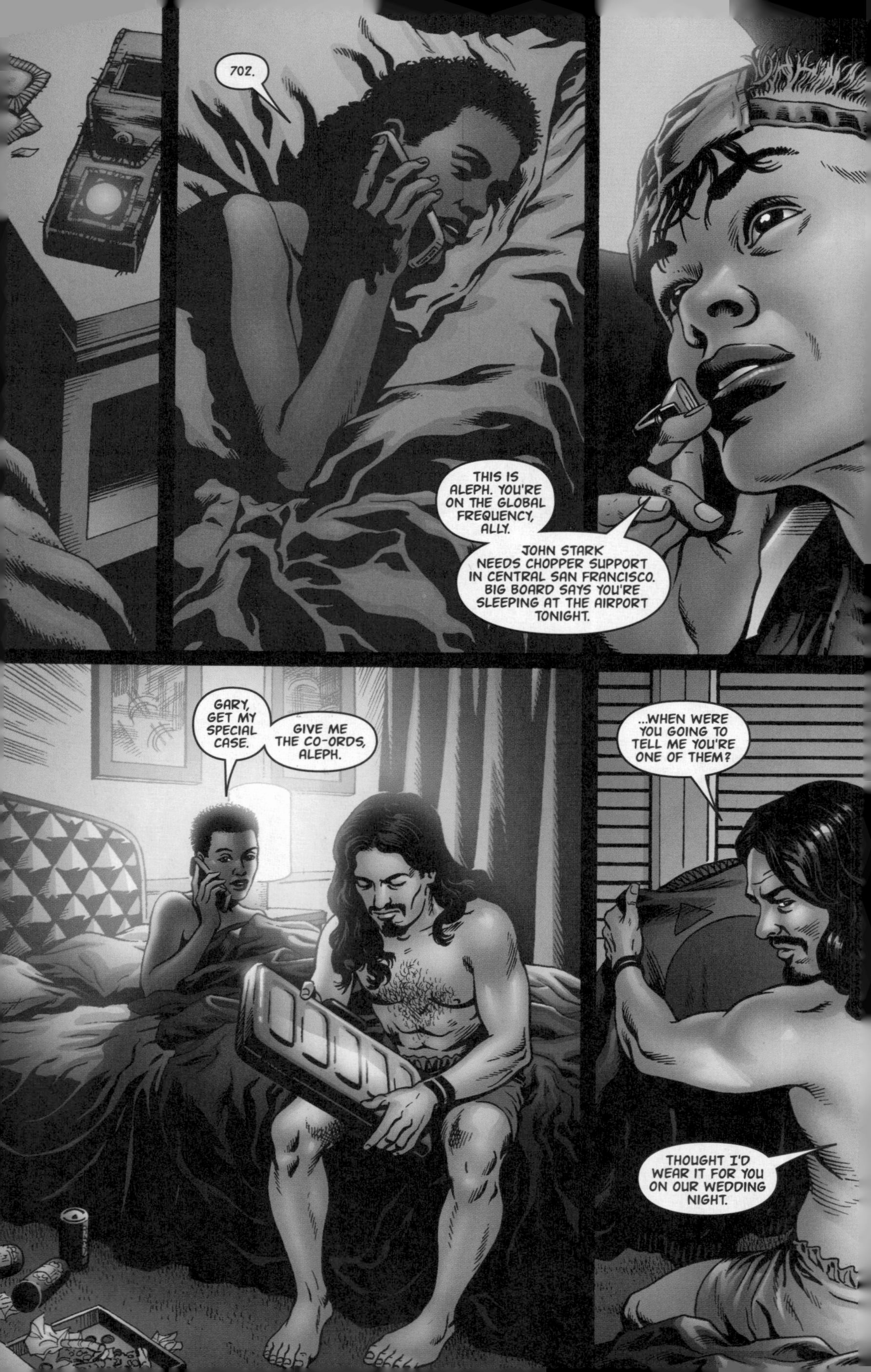
702.
THIS IS ALEPH. YOU'RE ON THE GLOBAL FREQUENCY, ALLY.
JOHN STARK NEEDS CHOPPER SUPPORT IN CENTRAL SAN FRANCISCO. BIG BOARD SAYS YOU'RE SLEEPING AT THE AIRPORT TONIGHT.
GARY, GET MY SPECIAL CASE.
GIVE ME THE CO-ORDS, ALEPH.
...WHEN WERE YOU GOING TO TELL ME YOU'RE ONE OF THEM?
THOUGHT I'D WEAR IT FOR YOU ON OUR WEDDING NIGHT.

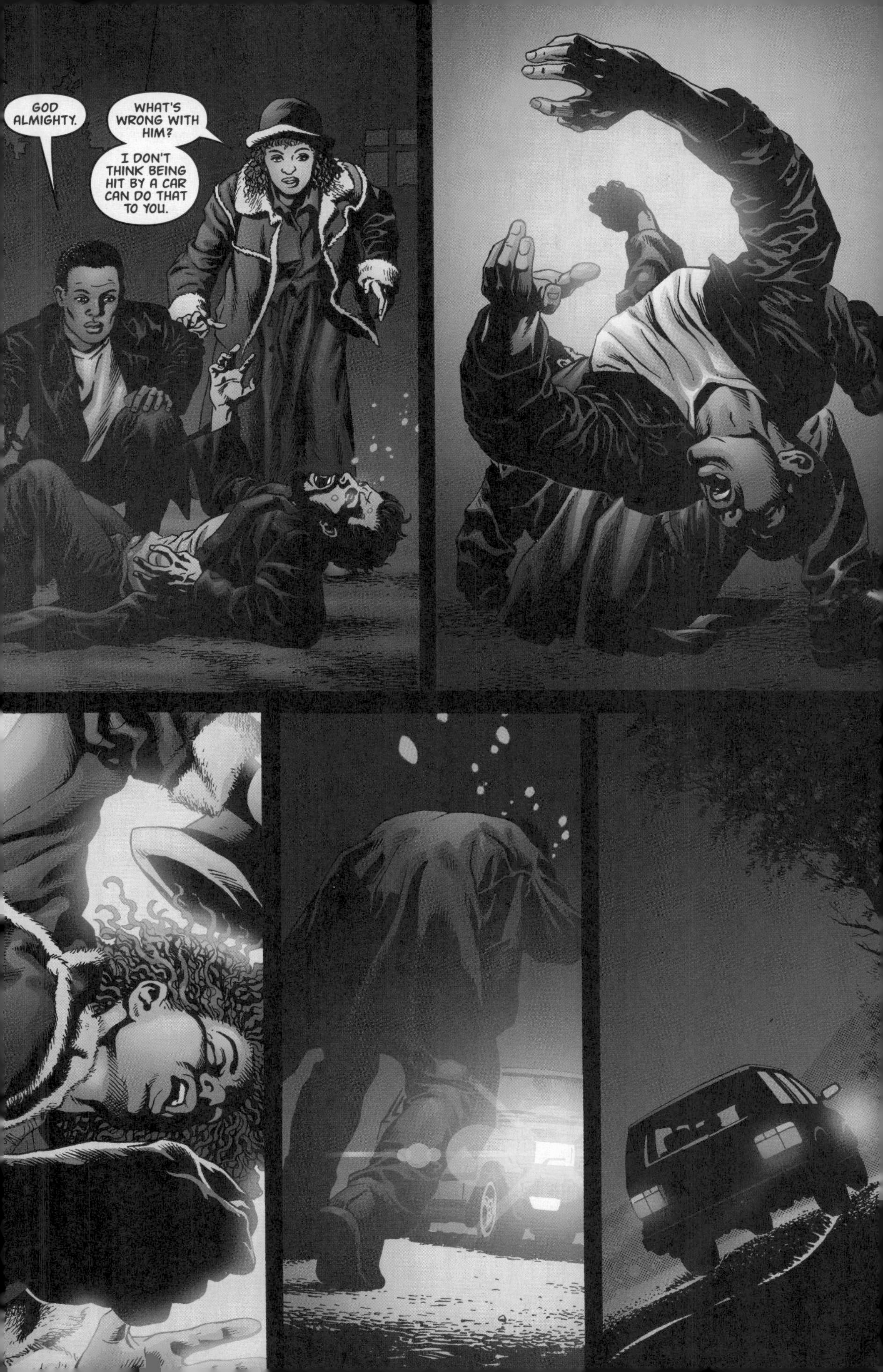
GOD ALMIGHTY.
WHAT'S WRONG WITH HIM?
I DON'T THINK BEING HIT BY A CAR CAN DO THAT TO YOU.

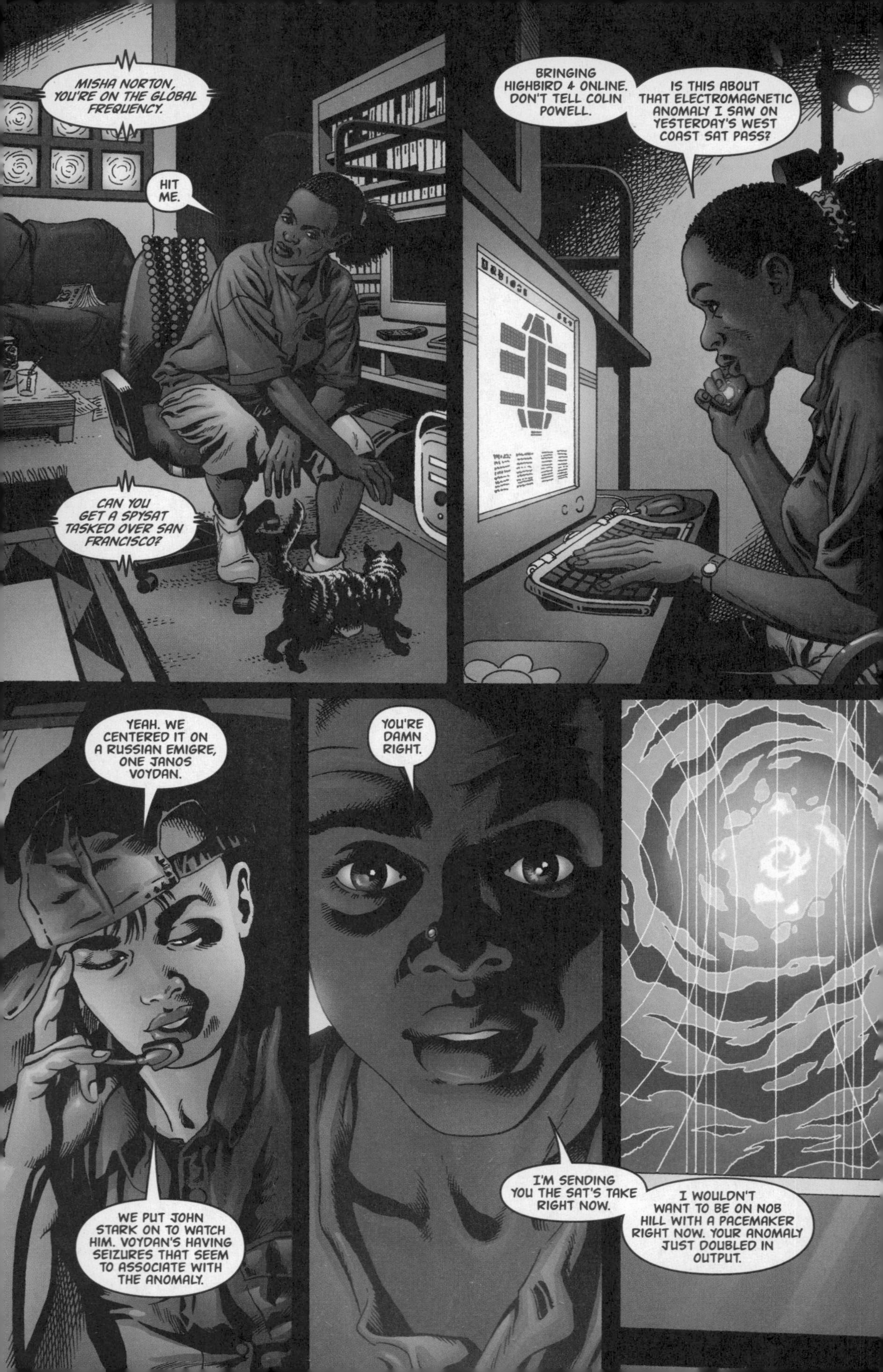
MISHA NORTON, YOU'RE ON THE GLOBAL FREQUENCY.
HIT ME.
CAN YOU GET A SPYSAT TASKED OVER SAN FRANCISCO?
BRINGING HIGHBIRD 4 ONLINE. DON'T TELL COLIN POWELL.
IS THIS ABOUT THAT ELECTROMAGNETIC ANOMALY I SAW ON YESTERDAY'S WEST COAST SAT PASS?
YEAH. WE CENTERED IT ON A RUSSIAN EMIGRE, ONE JANOS VOYDAN.
WE PUT JOHN STARK ON TO WATCH HIM. VOYDAN'S HAVING SEIZURES THAT SEEM TO ASSOCIATE WITH THE ANOMALY.
YOU'RE DAMN RIGHT.
I'M SENDING YOU THE SAT'S TAKE RIGHT NOW.
I WOULDN'T WANT TO BE ON NOB HILL WITH A PACEMAKER RIGHT NOW. YOUR ANOMALY JUST DOUBLED IN OUTPUT.

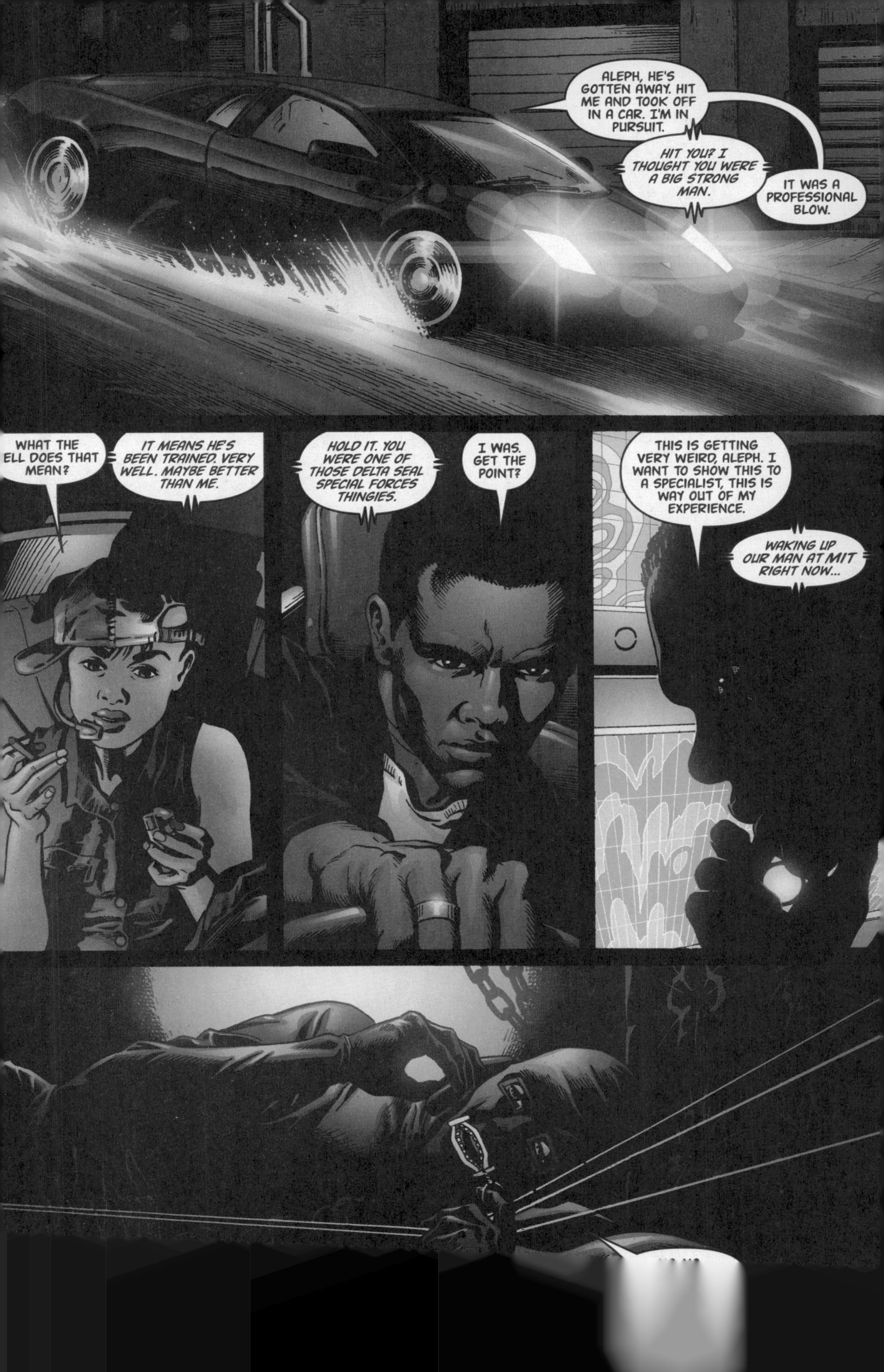
ALEPH, HE'S GOTTEN AWAY. HIT ME AND TOOK OFF IN A CAR. I'M IN PURSUIT.
HIT YOU? I THOUGHT YOU WERE A BIG STRONG MAN.
IT WAS A PROFESSIONAL BLOW.
WHAT THE ELL DOES THAT MEAN?
IT MEANS HE'S BEEN TRAINED. VERY WELL. MAYBE BETTER THAN ME.
HOLD IT. YOU WERE ONE OF THOSE DELTA SEAL SPECIAL FORCES THINGIES.
I WAS. GET THE POINT?
THIS IS GETTING VERY WEIRD, ALEPH. I WANT TO SHOW THIS TO A SPECIALIST, THIS IS WAY OUT OF MY EXPERIENCE.
WAKING UP OUR MAN AT MIT RIGHT NOW...

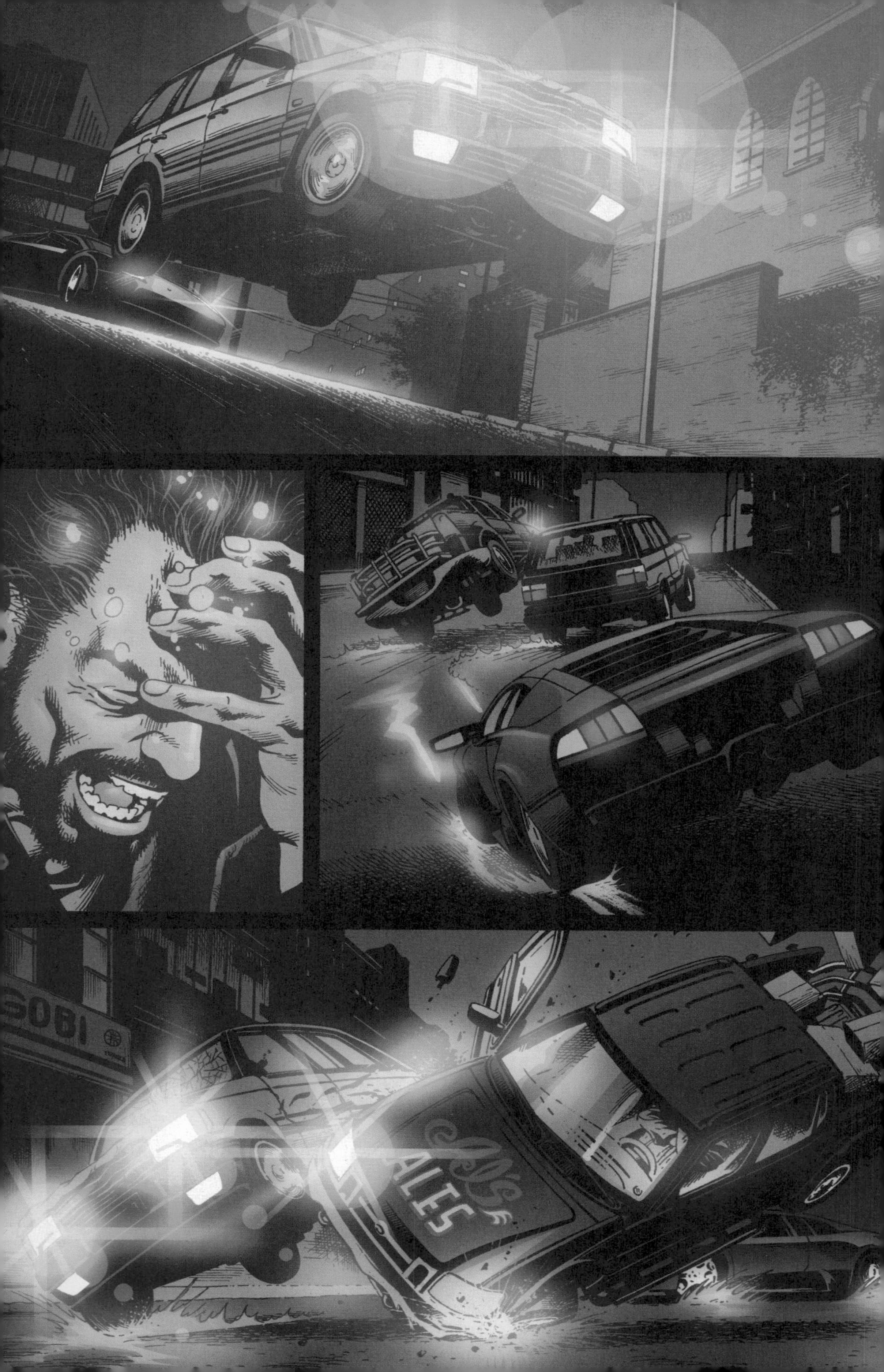
GOBI
ALES

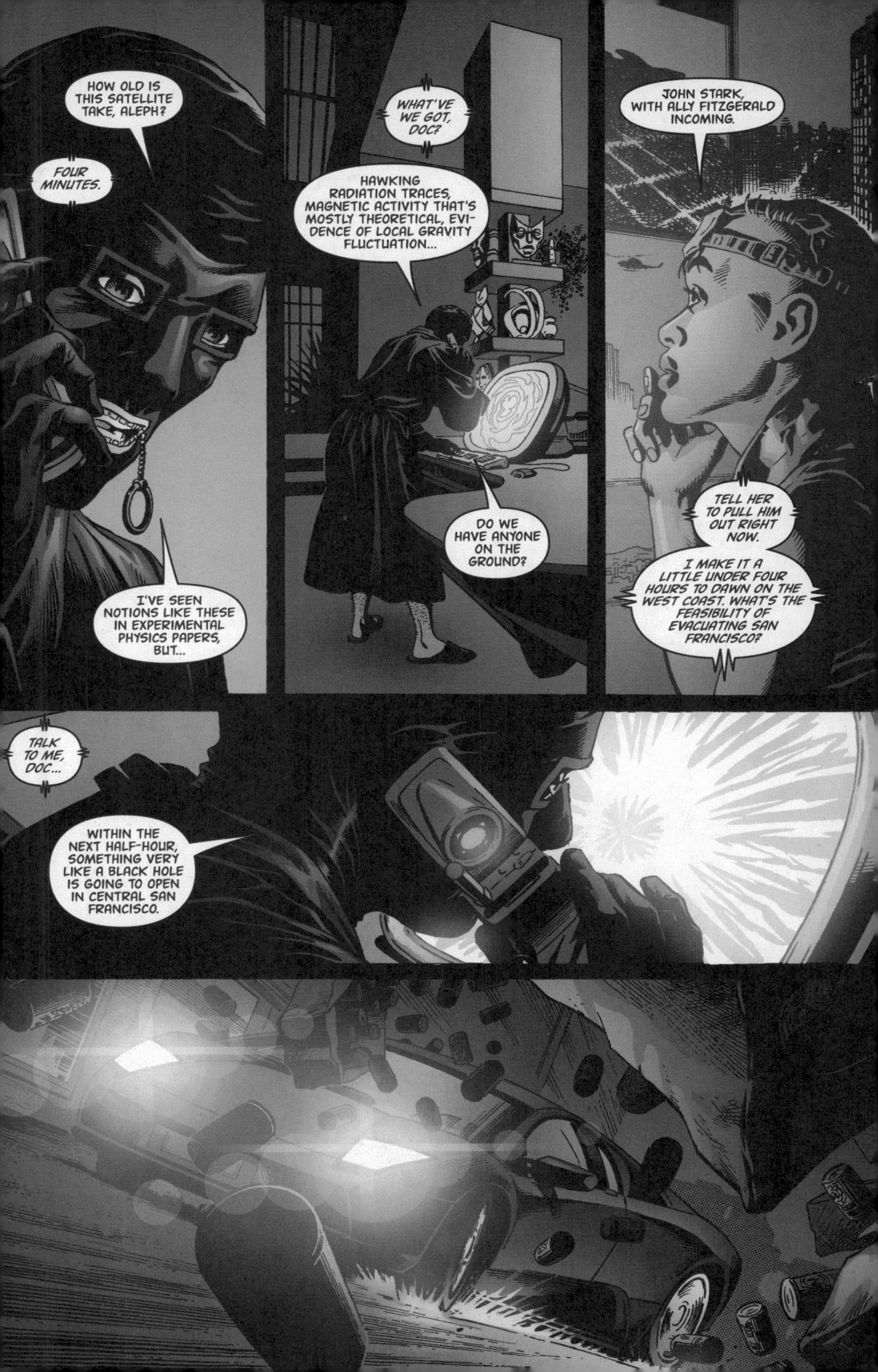
HOW OLD IS THIS SATELLITE TAKE, ALEPH?
FOUR MINUTES.
I'VE SEEN NOTIONS LIKE THESE IN EXPERIMENTAL PHYSICS PAPERS, BUT...
WHAT'VE WE GOT, DOC?
HAWKING RADIATION TRACES, MAGNETIC ACTIVITY THAT'S MOSTLY THEORETICAL, EVIDENCE OF LOCAL GRAVITY FLUCTUATION...
DO WE HAVE ANYONE ON THE GROUND?
JOHN STARK, WITH ALLY FITZGERALD INCOMING.
TELL HER TO PULL HIM OUT RIGHT NOW.
I MAKE IT A LITTLE UNDER FOUR HOURS TO DAWN ON THE WEST COAST. WHAT'S THE FEASIBILITY OF EVACUATING SAN FRANCISCO?
TALK TO ME, DOC...
WITHIN THE NEXT HALF-HOUR, SOMETHING VERY LIKE A BLACK HOLE IS GOING TO OPEN IN CENTRAL SAN FRANCISCO.

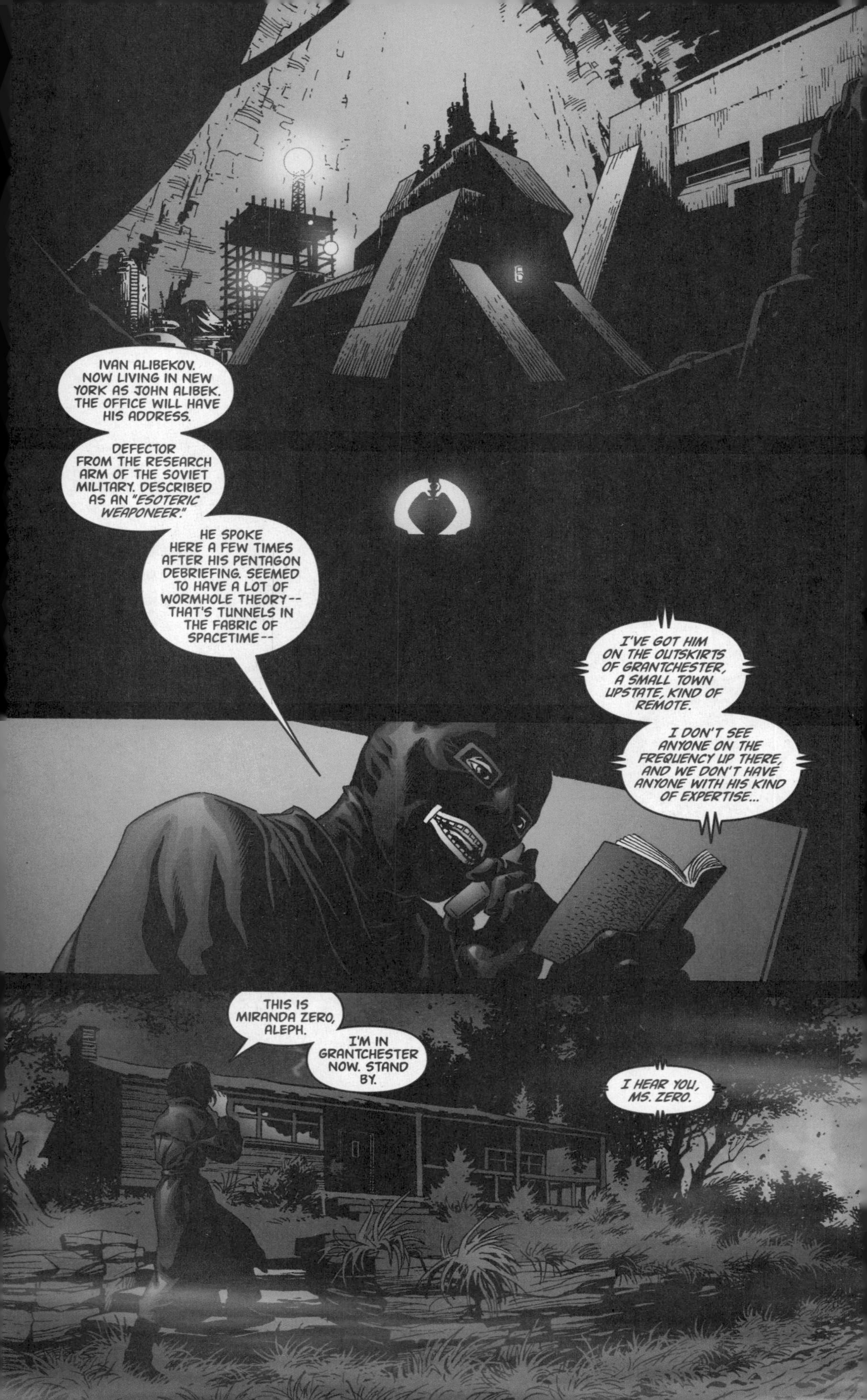
IVAN ALIBEKOV. NOW LIVING IN NEW YORK AS JOHN ALIBEK. THE OFFICE WILL HAVE HIS ADDRESS.
DEFECTOR FROM THE RESEARCH ARM OF THE SOVIET MILITARY. DESCRIBED AS AN "ESOTERIC WEAPONEER."
HE SPOKE HERE A FEW TIMES AFTER HIS PENTAGON DEBRIEFING. SEEMED TO HAVE A LOT OF WORMHOLE THEORY-- THAT'S TUNNELS IN THE FABRIC OF SPACETIME--
I'VE GOT HIM ON THE OUTSKIRTS OF GRANTCHESTER, A SMALL TOWN UPSTATE, KIND OF REMOTE.
I DON'T SEE ANYONE ON THE FREQUENCY UP THERE, AND WE DON'T HAVE ANYONE WITH HIS KIND OF EXPERTISE...
THIS IS MIRANDA ZERO, ALEPH.
I'M IN GRANTCHESTER NOW. STAND BY.
I HEAR YOU, MS. ZERO.

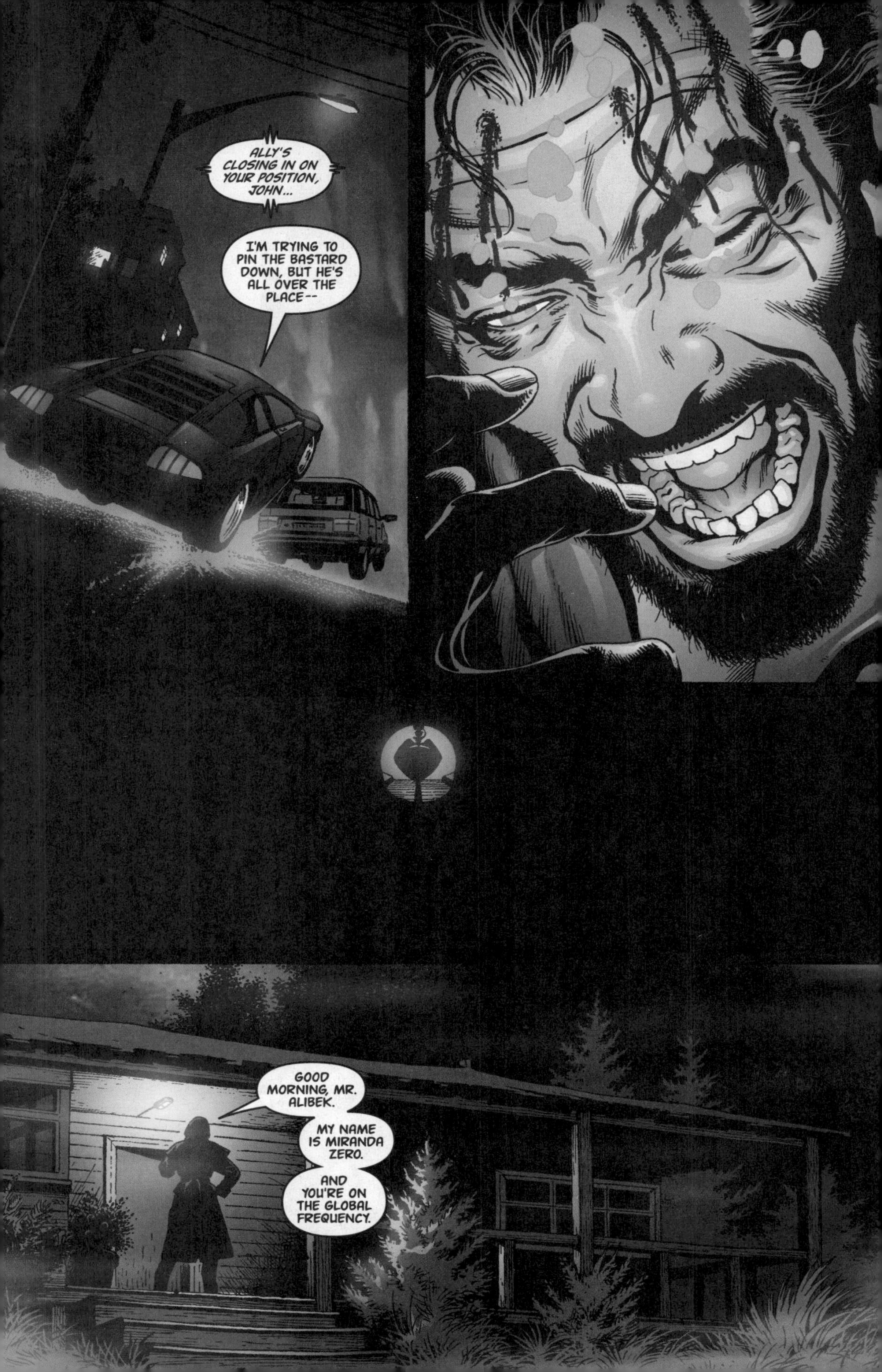
ALLY'S CLOSING IN ON YOUR POSITION, JOHN...
I'M TRYING TO PIN THE BASTARD DOWN, BUT HE'S ALL OVER THE PLACE--
GOOD MORNING, MR. ALIBEK.
MY NAME IS MIRANDA ZERO.
AND YOU'RE ON THE GLOBAL FREQUENCY.

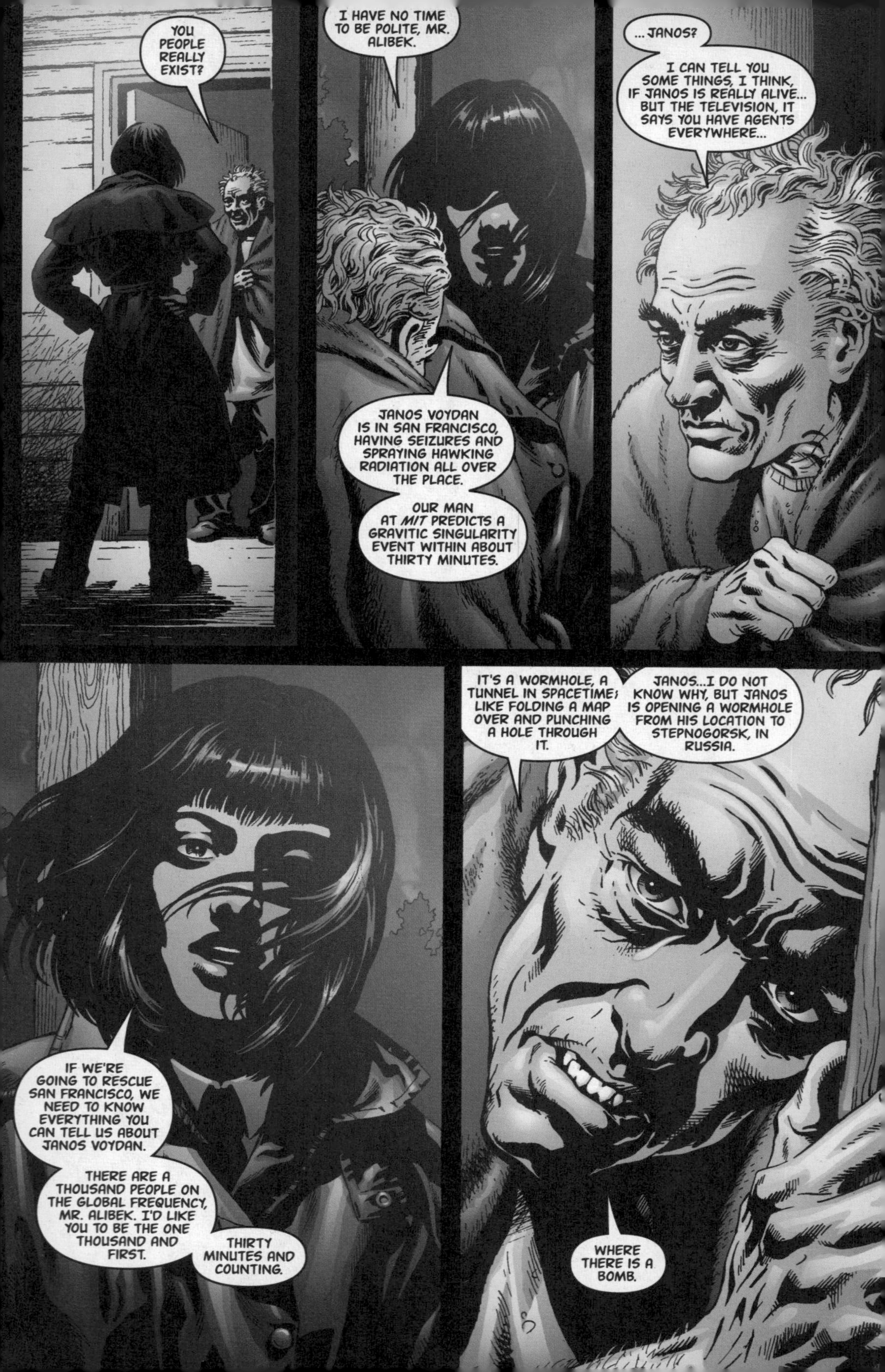
YOU PEOPLE REALLY EXIST?
I HAVE NO TIME TO BE POLITE, MR. ALIBEK.
JANOS VOYDAN IS IN SAN FRANCISCO, HAVING SEIZURES AND SPRAYING HAWKING RADIATION ALL OVER THE PLACE.
OUR MAN AT *MIT* PREDICTS A GRAVITIC SINGULARITY EVENT WITHIN ABOUT THIRTY MINUTES.
...JANOS?
I CAN TELL YOU SOME THINGS, I THINK, IF JANOS IS REALLY ALIVE... BUT THE TELEVISION, IT SAYS YOU HAVE AGENTS EVERYWHERE...
IF WE'RE GOING TO RESCUE SAN FRANCISCO, WE NEED TO KNOW EVERYTHING YOU CAN TELL US ABOUT JANOS VOYDAN.
THERE ARE A THOUSAND PEOPLE ON THE GLOBAL FREQUENCY, MR. ALIBEK. I'D LIKE YOU TO BE THE ONE THOUSAND AND FIRST.
THIRTY MINUTES AND COUNTING.
JANOS...I DO NOT KNOW WHY, BUT JANOS IS OPENING A WORMHOLE FROM HIS LOCATION TO STEPNOGORSK, IN RUSSIA.
IT'S A WORMHOLE, A TUNNEL IN SPACETIME; LIKE FOLDING A MAP OVER AND PUNCHING A HOLE THROUGH IT.
WHERE THERE IS A BOMB.

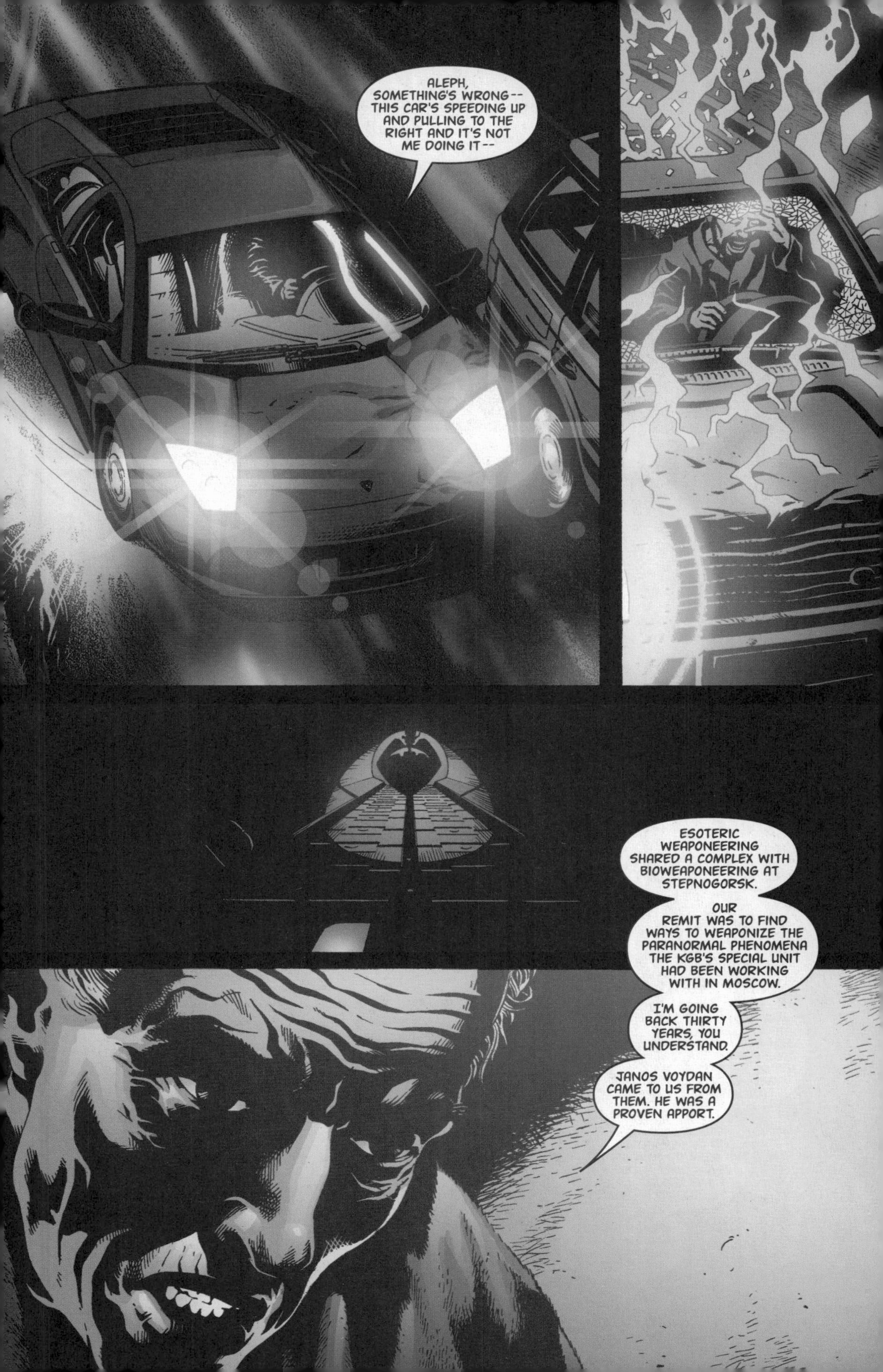

ALEPH, SOMETHING'S WRONG-- THIS CAR'S SPEEDING UP AND PULLING TO THE RIGHT AND IT'S NOT ME DOING IT--
ESOTERIC WEAPONEERING SHARED A COMPLEX WITH BIOWEAPONEERING AT STEPNOGORSK.
OUR REMIT WAS TO FIND WAYS TO WEAPONIZE THE PARANORMAL PHENOMENA THE KGB'S SPECIAL UNIT HAD BEEN WORKING WITH IN MOSCOW.
I'M GOING BACK THIRTY YEARS, YOU UNDERSTAND.
JANOS VOYDAN CAME TO US FROM THEM. HE WAS A PROVEN APPORT.

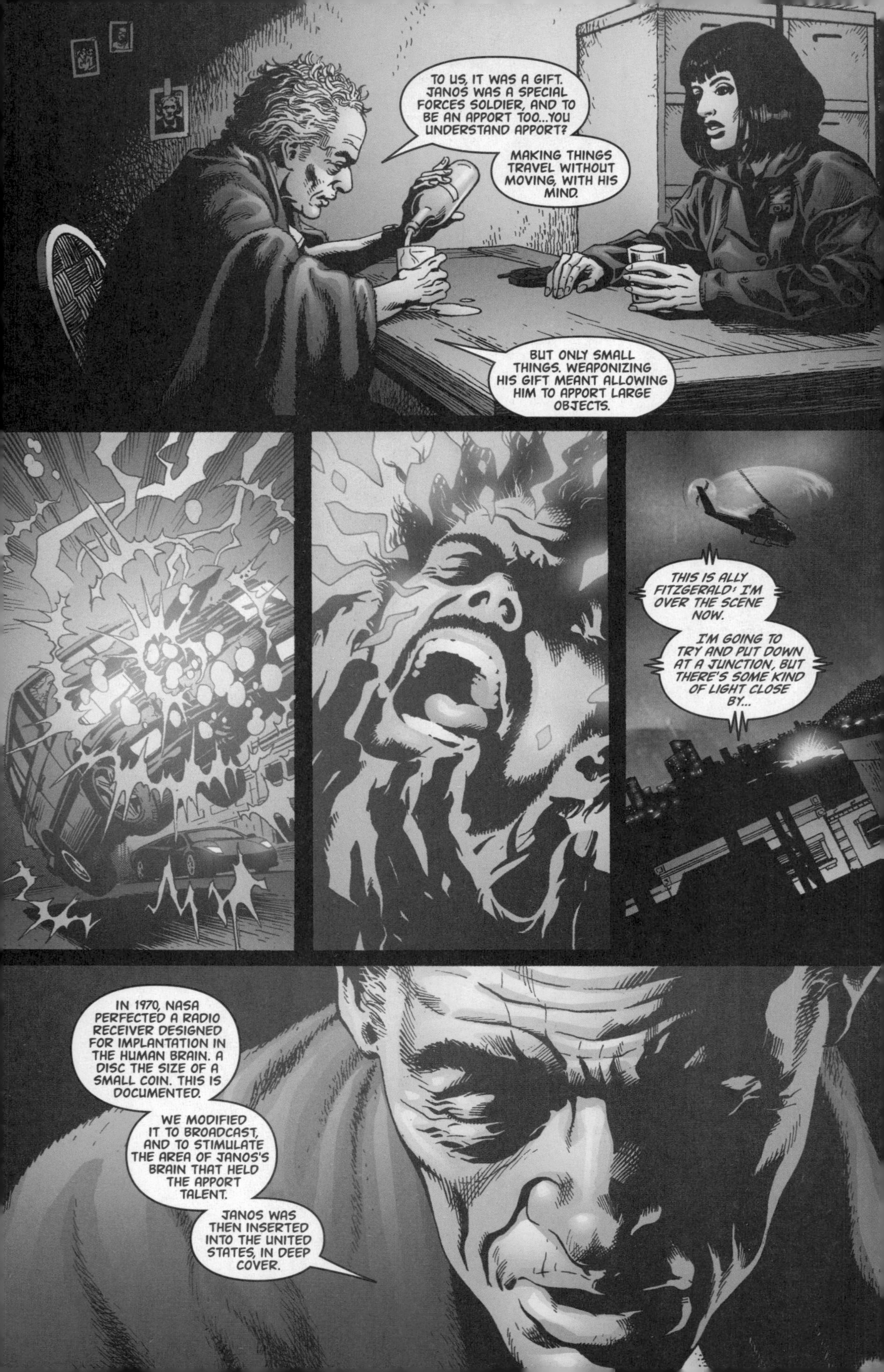
TO US, IT WAS A GIFT. JANOS WAS A SPECIAL FORCES SOLDIER, AND TO BE AN APPORT TOO...YOU UNDERSTAND APPORT?
MAKING THINGS TRAVEL WITHOUT MOVING, WITH HIS MIND.
BUT ONLY SMALL THINGS. WEAPONIZING HIS GIFT MEANT ALLOWING HIM TO APPORT LARGE OBJECTS.
THIS IS ALLY FITZGERALD: I'M OVER THE SCENE NOW.
I'M GOING TO TRY AND PUT DOWN AT A JUNCTION, BUT THERE'S SOME KIND OF LIGHT CLOSE BY...
IN 1970, NASA PERFECTED A RADIO RECEIVER DESIGNED FOR IMPLANTATION IN THE HUMAN BRAIN. A DISC THE SIZE OF A SMALL COIN. THIS IS DOCUMENTED.
WE MODIFIED IT TO BROADCAST, AND TO STIMULATE THE AREA OF JANOS'S BRAIN THAT HELD THE APPORT TALENT.
JANOS WAS THEN INSERTED INTO THE UNITED STATES, IN DEEP COVER.

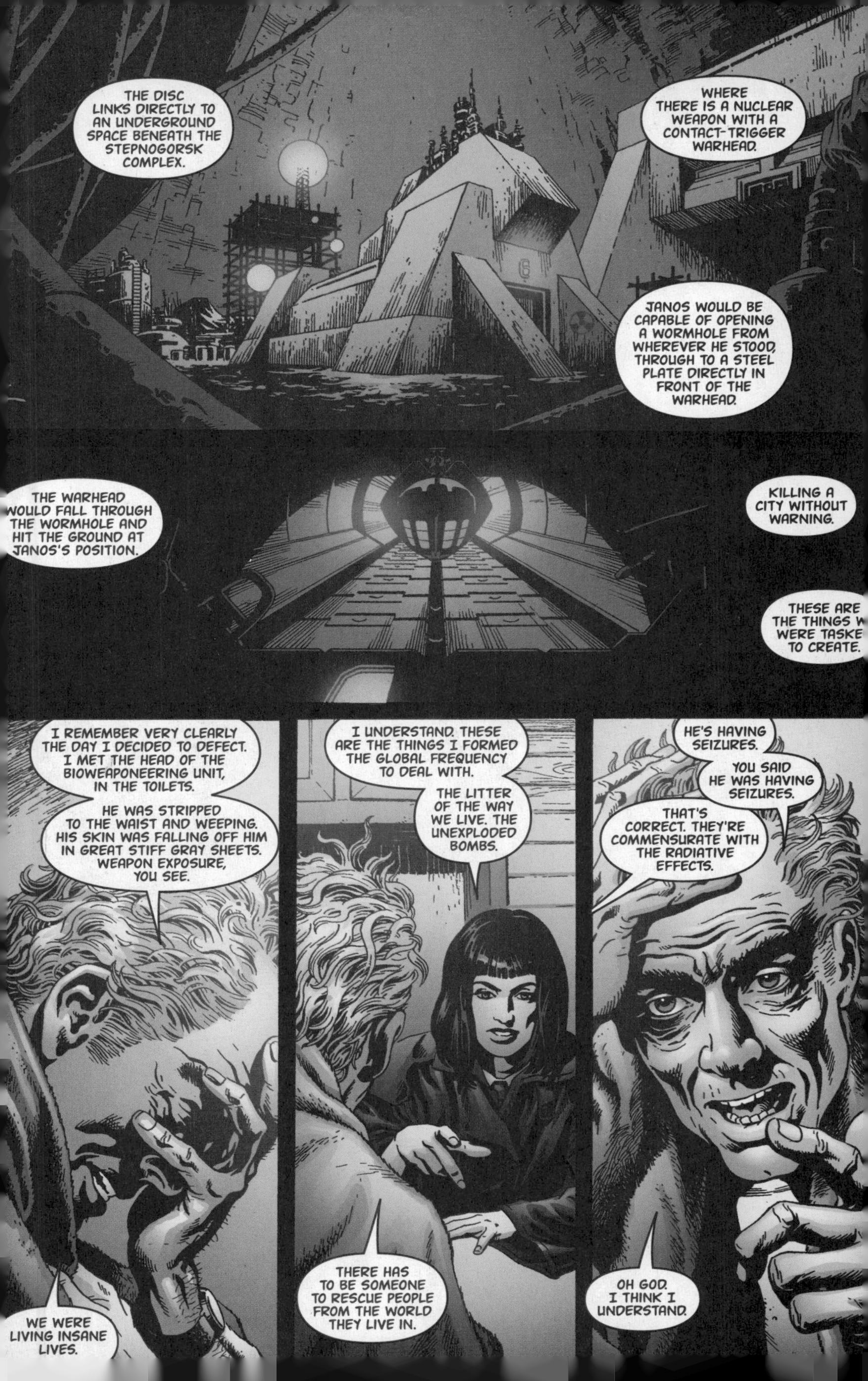
THE DISC LINKS DIRECTLY TO AN UNDERGROUND SPACE BENEATH THE STEPNOGORSK COMPLEX.
WHERE THERE IS A NUCLEAR WEAPON WITH A CONTACT-TRIGGER WARHEAD.
JANOS WOULD BE CAPABLE OF OPENING A WORMHOLE FROM WHEREVER HE STOOD, THROUGH TO A STEEL PLATE DIRECTLY IN FRONT OF THE WARHEAD.
THE WARHEAD WOULD FALL THROUGH THE WORMHOLE AND HIT THE GROUND AT JANOS'S POSITION.
KILLING A CITY WITHOUT WARNING.
THESE ARE THE THINGS W WERE TASKE TO CREATE.
I REMEMBER VERY CLEARLY THE DAY I DECIDED TO DEFECT. I MET THE HEAD OF THE BIOWEAPONEERING UNIT, IN THE TOILETS.
HE WAS STRIPPED TO THE WAIST AND WEEPING. HIS SKIN WAS FALLING OFF HIM IN GREAT STIFF GRAY SHEETS. WEAPON EXPOSURE, YOU SEE.
WE WERE LIVING INSANE LIVES.
I UNDERSTAND. THESE ARE THE THINGS I FORMED THE GLOBAL FREQUENCY TO DEAL WITH.
THE LITTER OF THE WAY WE LIVE. THE UNEXPLODED BOMBS.
THERE HAS TO BE SOMEONE TO RESCUE PEOPLE FROM THE WORLD THEY LIVE IN.
HE'S HAVING SEIZURES.
YOU SAID HE WAS HAVING SEIZURES.
THAT'S CORRECT. THEY'RE COMMENSURATE WITH THE RADIATIVE EFFECTS.
OH GOD. I THINK I UNDERSTAND.

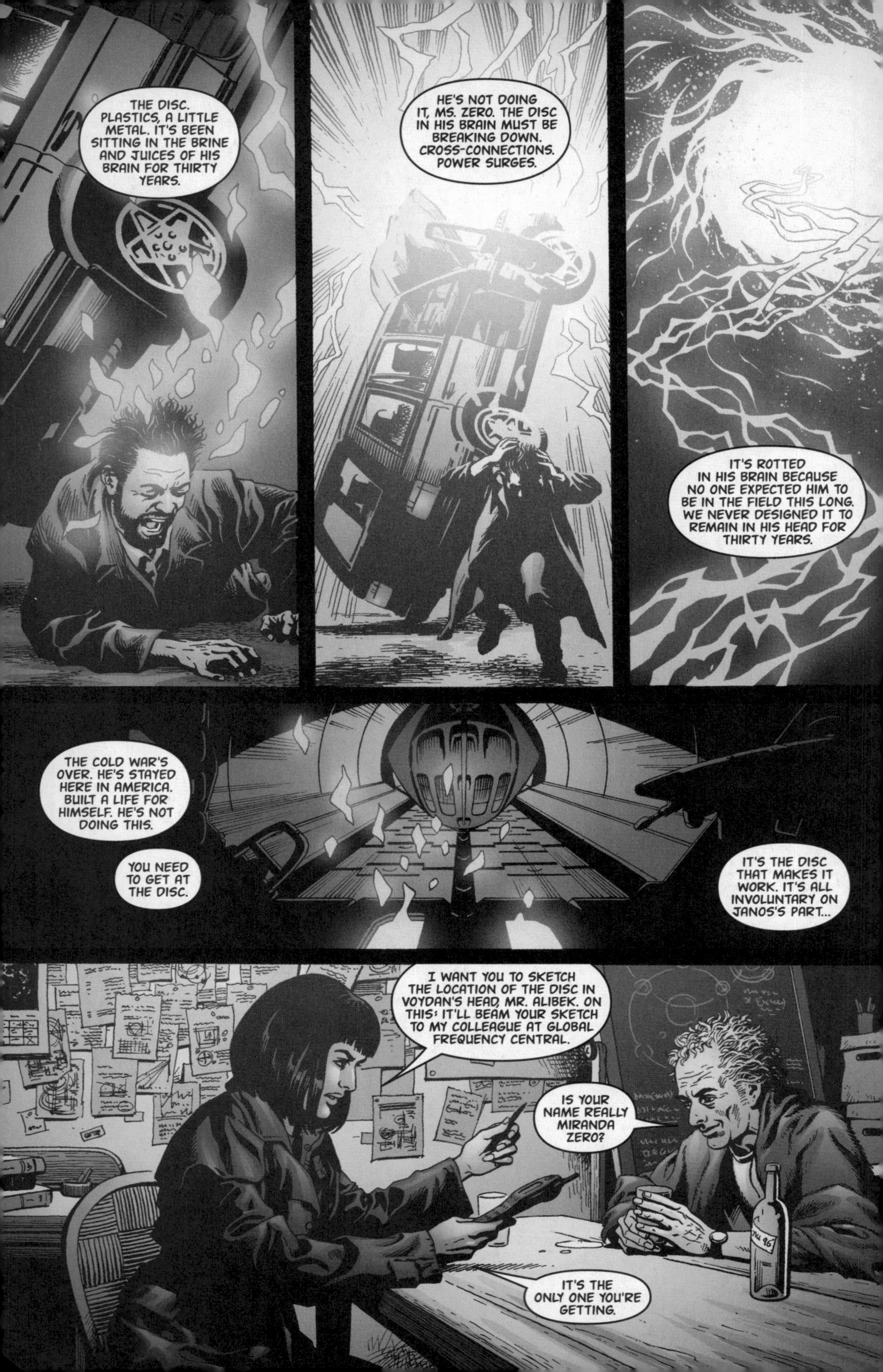
THE DISC. PLASTICS, A LITTLE METAL. IT'S BEEN SITTING IN THE BRINE AND JUICES OF HIS BRAIN FOR THIRTY YEARS.
HE'S NOT DOING IT, MS. ZERO. THE DISC IN HIS BRAIN MUST BE BREAKING DOWN. CROSS-CONNECTIONS. POWER SURGES.
IT'S ROTTED IN HIS BRAIN BECAUSE NO ONE EXPECTED HIM TO BE IN THE FIELD THIS LONG. WE NEVER DESIGNED IT TO REMAIN IN HIS HEAD FOR THIRTY YEARS.
THE COLD WAR'S OVER. HE'S STAYED HERE IN AMERICA. BUILT A LIFE FOR HIMSELF. HE'S NOT DOING THIS.
YOU NEED TO GET AT THE DISC.
IT'S THE DISC THAT MAKES IT WORK. IT'S ALL INVOLUNTARY ON JANOS'S PART...
I WANT YOU TO SKETCH THE LOCATION OF THE DISC IN VOYDAN'S HEAD, MR. ALIBEK. ON THIS: IT'LL BEAM YOUR SKETCH TO MY COLLEAGUE AT GLOBAL FREQUENCY CENTRAL.
IS YOUR NAME REALLY MIRANDA ZERO?
IT'S THE ONLY ONE YOU'RE GETTING.

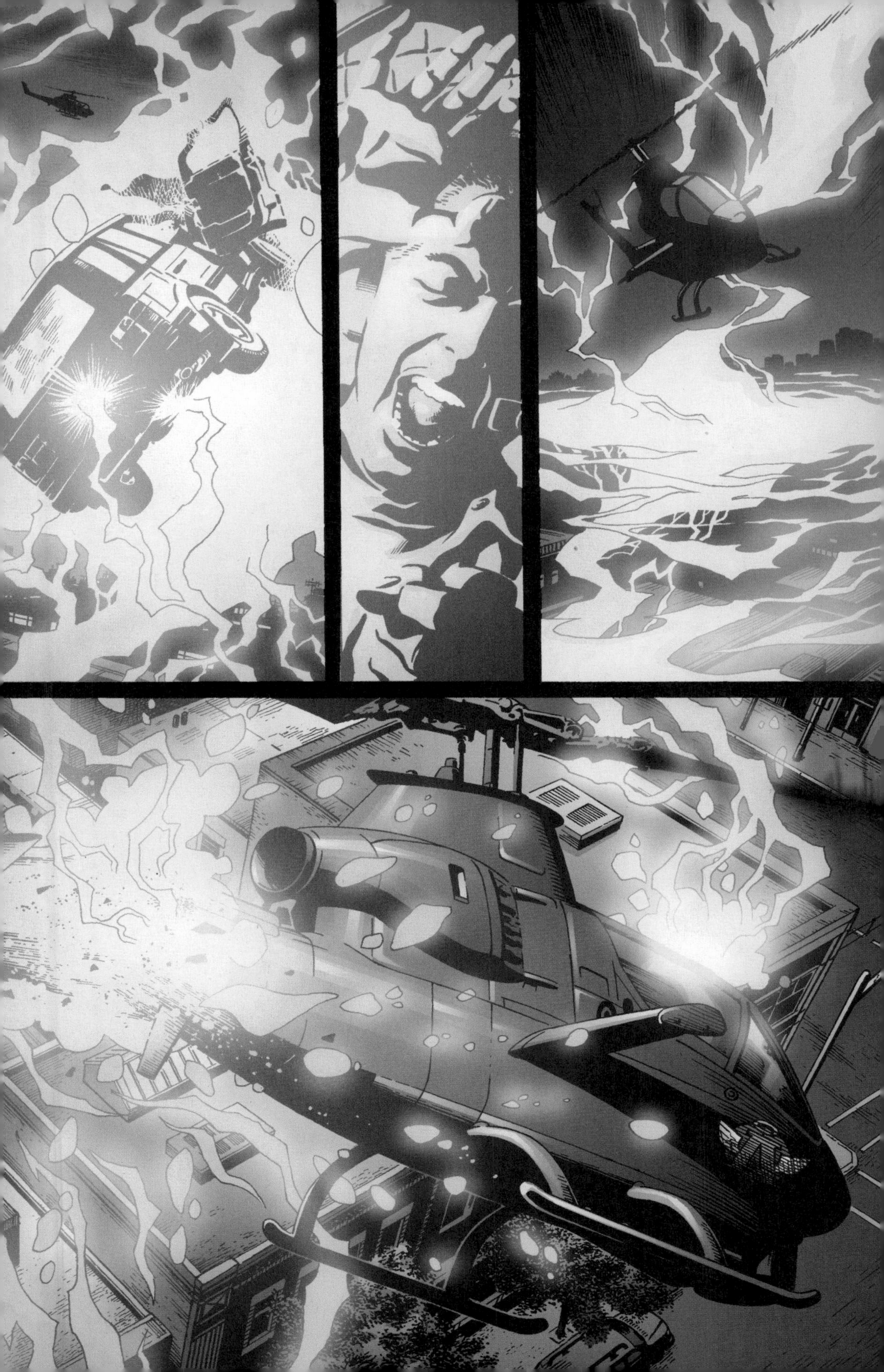

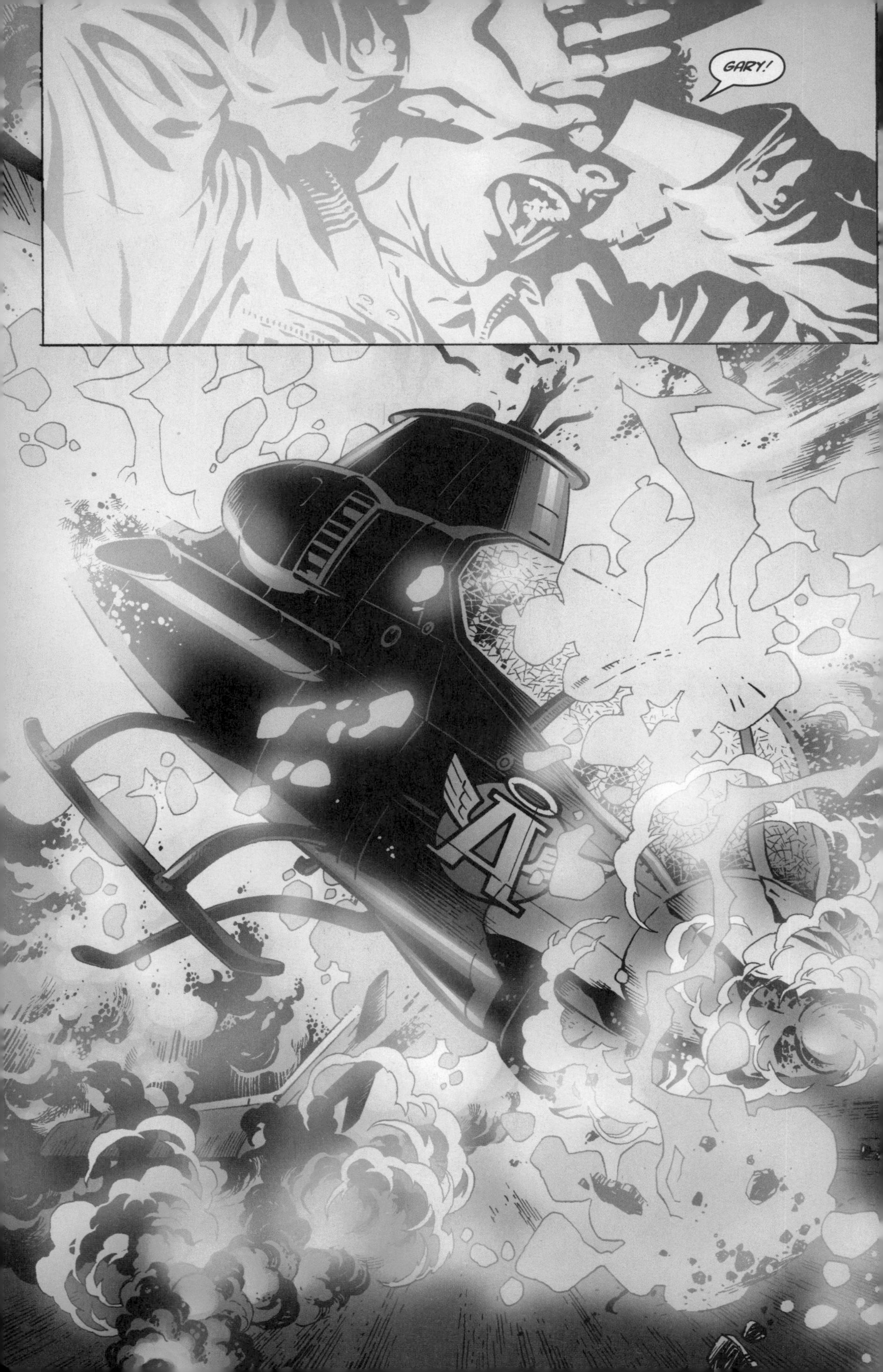
GARY!

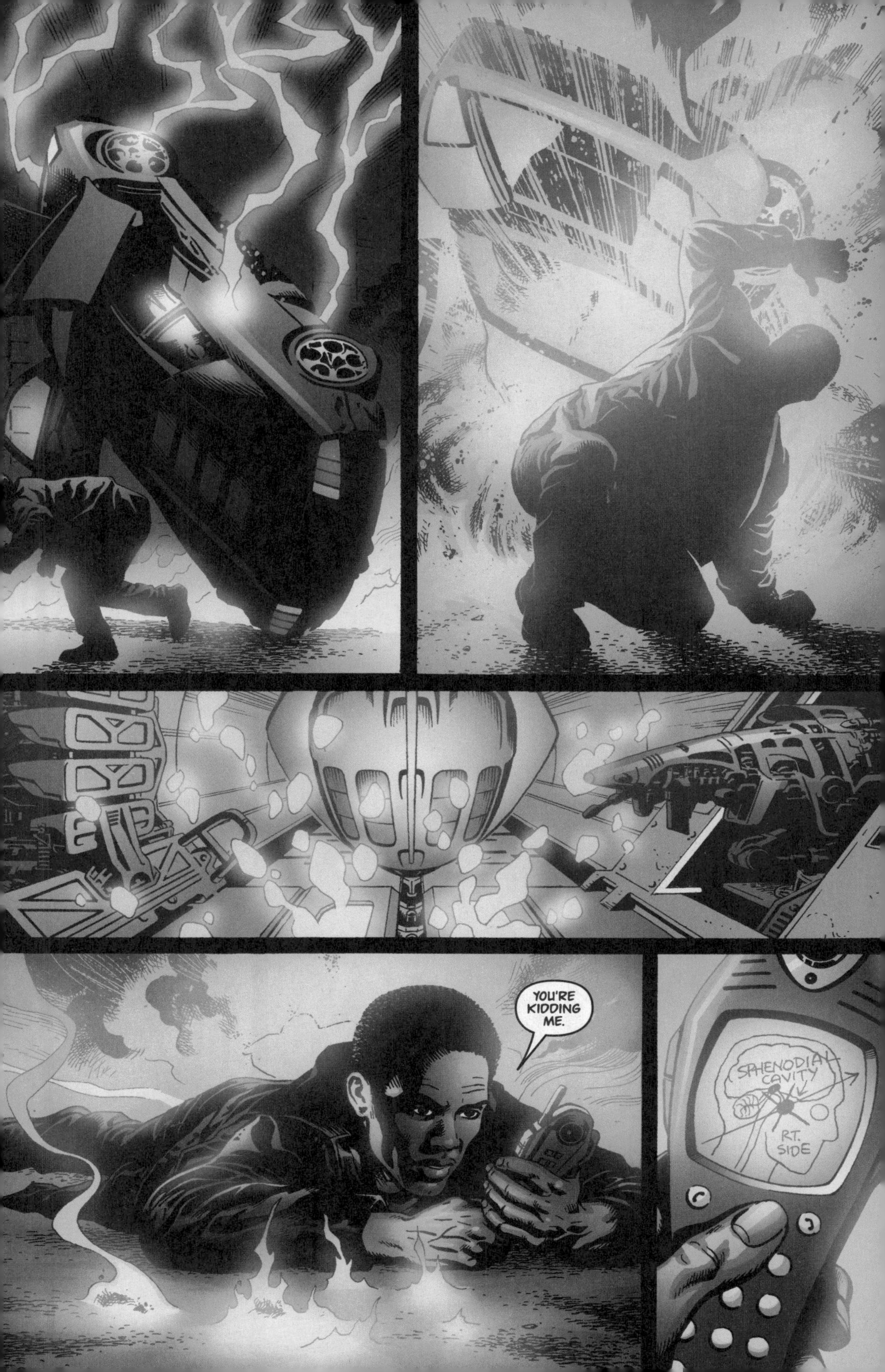
YOU'RE KIDDING ME.
SPHENODIAL CAVITY
RT. SIDE

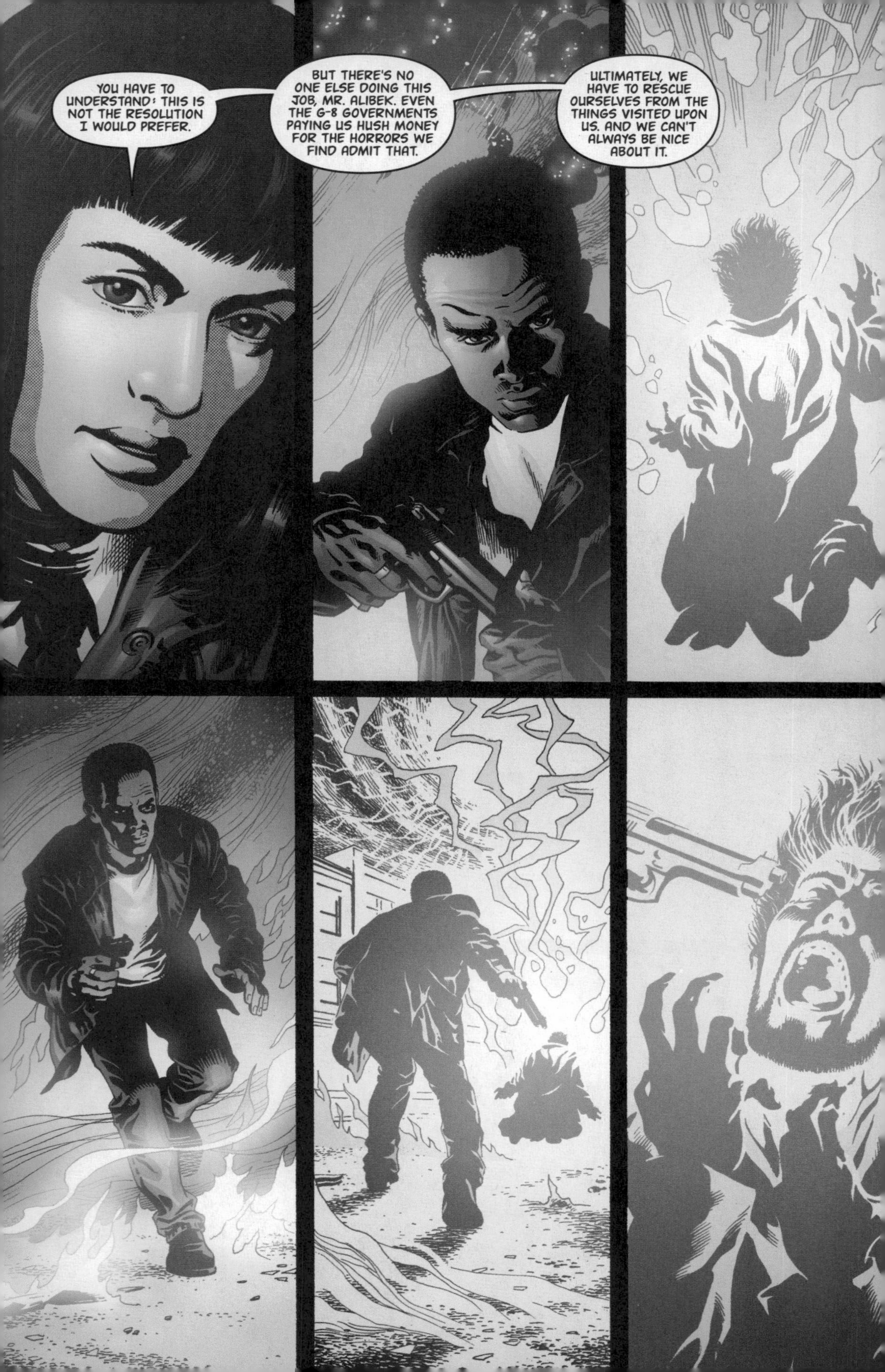
YOU HAVE TO UNDERSTAND: THIS IS NOT THE RESOLUTION I WOULD PREFER.
BUT THERE'S NO ONE ELSE DOING THIS JOB, MR. ALIBEK. EVEN THE G-8 GOVERNMENTS PAYING US HUSH MONEY FOR THE HORRORS WE FIND ADMIT THAT.
ULTIMATELY, WE HAVE TO RESCUE OURSELVES FROM THE THINGS VISITED UPON US. AND WE CAN'T ALWAYS BE NICE ABOUT IT.

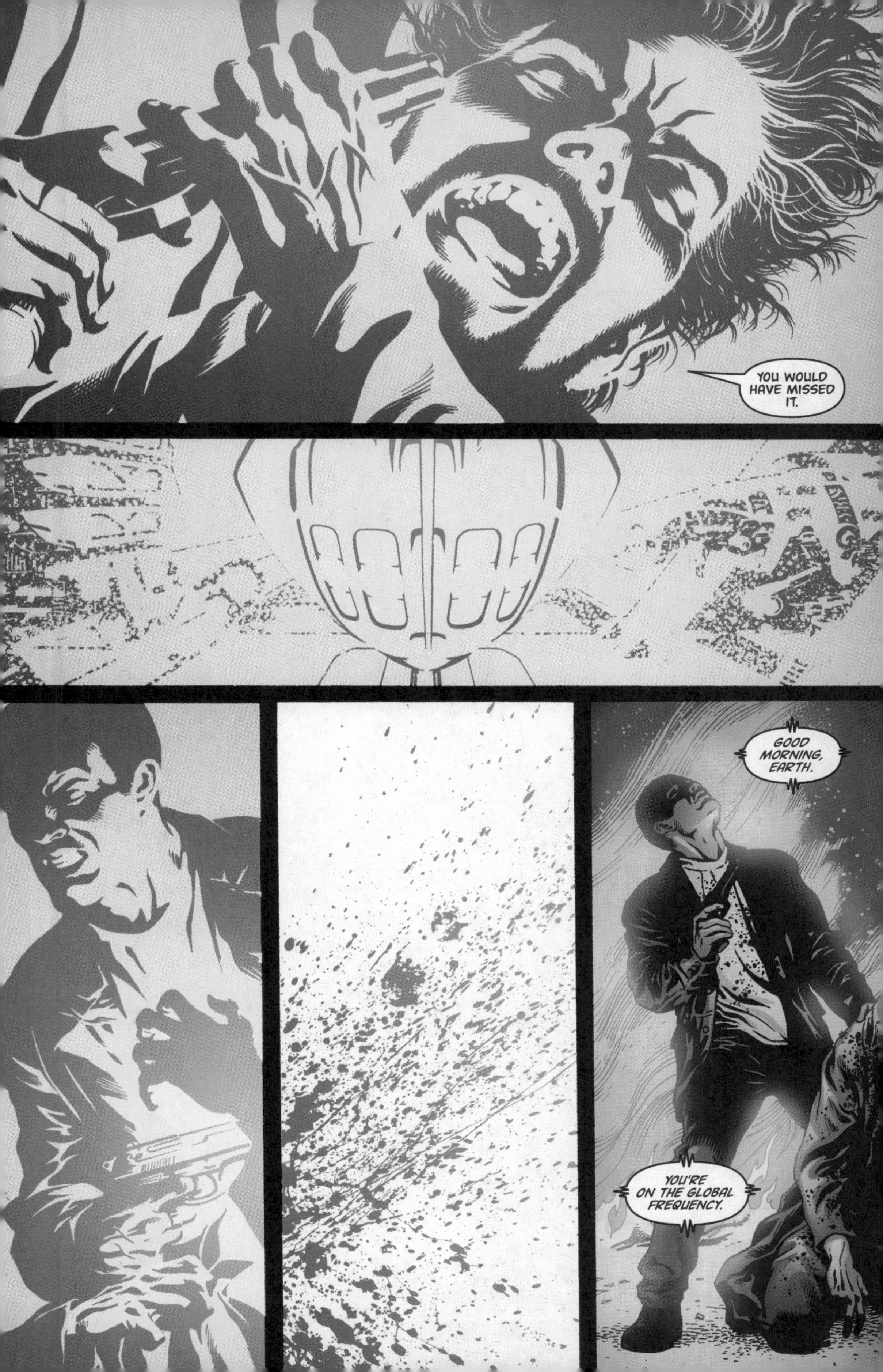
YOU WOULD HAVE MISSED IT.
GOOD MORNING, EARTH.
YOU'RE ON THE GLOBAL FREQUENCY.

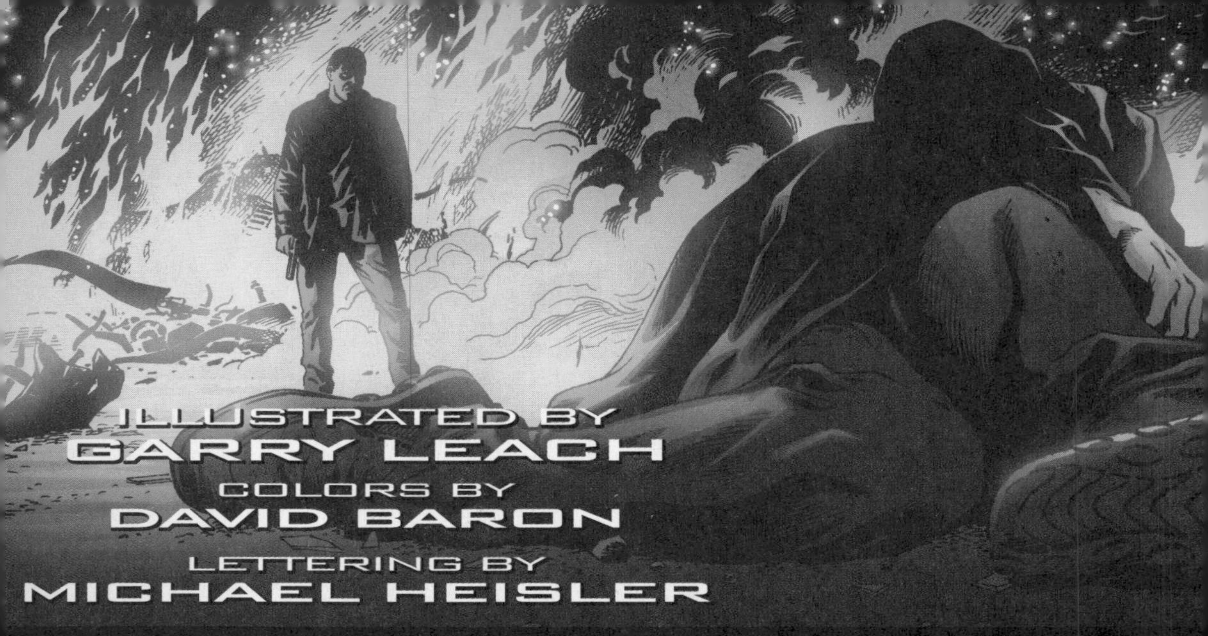
ILLUSTRATED BY
GARRY LEACH
COLORS BY
DAVID BARON
LETTERING BY
MICHAEL HEISLER

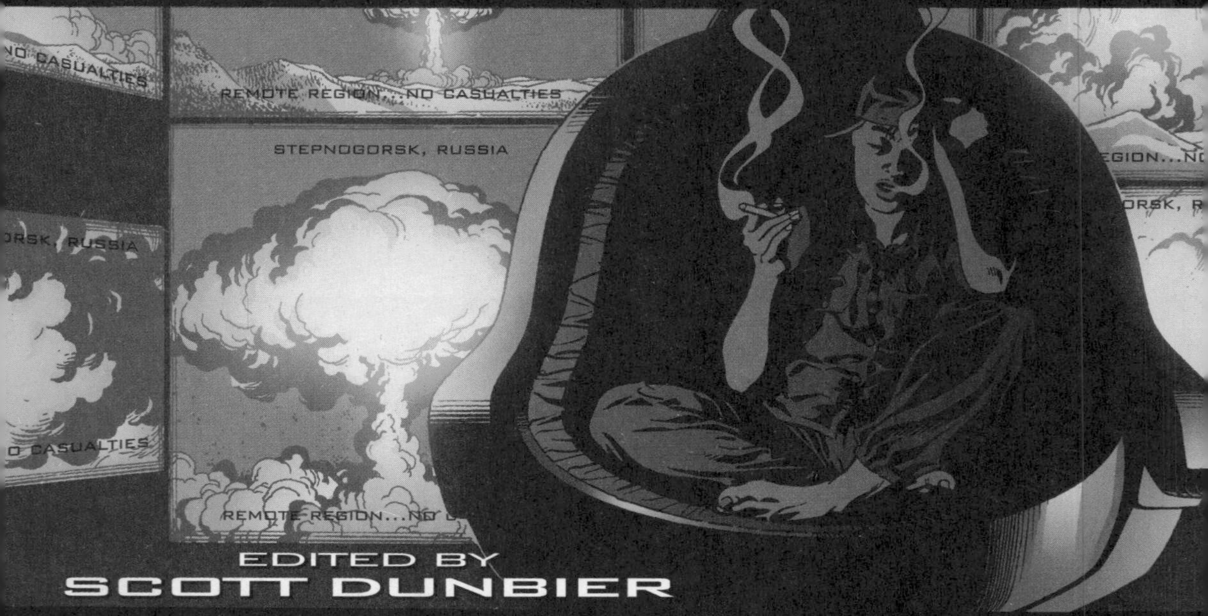
NO CASUALTIES
REMOTE REGION...NO CASUALTIES
STEPNOGORSK, RUSSIA
ORSK, RUSSIA
O CASUALTIES
EGION...NO
ORSK, R
EDITED BY
SCOTT DUNBIER

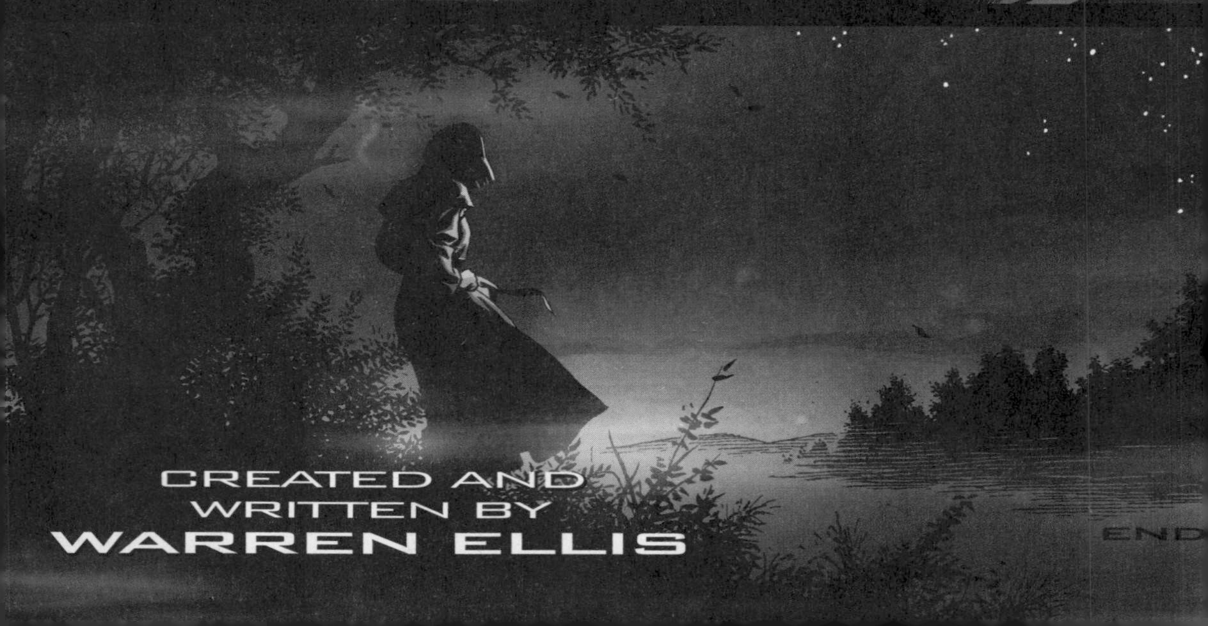
CREATED AND
WRITTEN BY
WARREN ELLIS
END

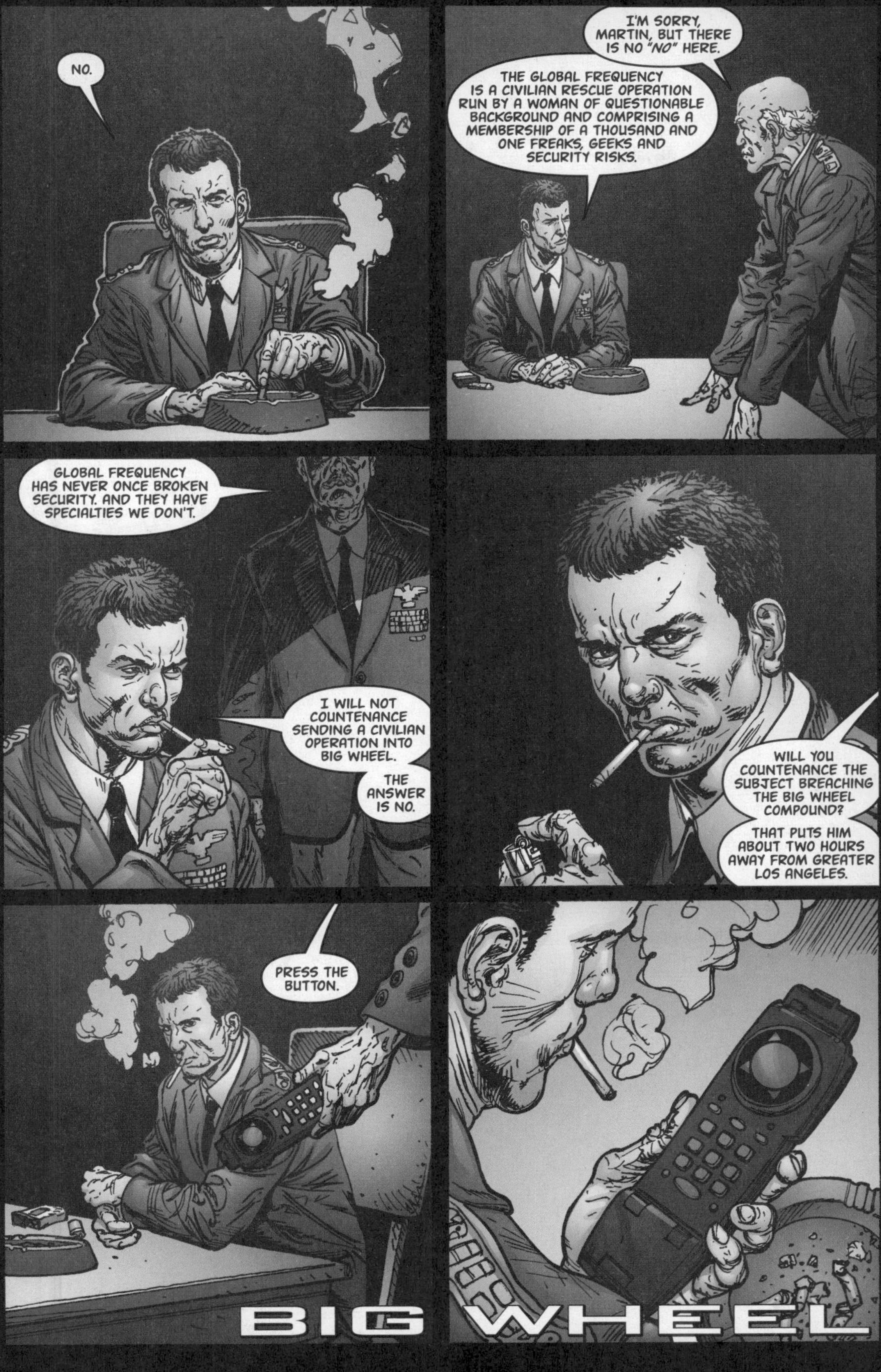
NO.
I'M SORRY, MARTIN, BUT THERE IS NO "NO" HERE.
THE GLOBAL FREQUENCY IS A CIVILIAN RESCUE OPERATION RUN BY A WOMAN OF QUESTIONABLE BACKGROUND AND COMPRISING A MEMBERSHIP OF A THOUSAND AND ONE FREAKS, GEEKS AND SECURITY RISKS.
GLOBAL FREQUENCY HAS NEVER ONCE BROKEN SECURITY. AND THEY HAVE SPECIALTIES WE DON'T.
I WILL NOT COUNTENANCE SENDING A CIVILIAN OPERATION INTO BIG WHEEL.
THE ANSWER IS NO.
WILL YOU COUNTENANCE THE SUBJECT BREACHING THE BIG WHEEL COMPOUND?
THAT PUTS HIM ABOUT TWO HOURS AWAY FROM GREATER LOS ANGELES.
PRESS THE BUTTON.
BIG WHEEL

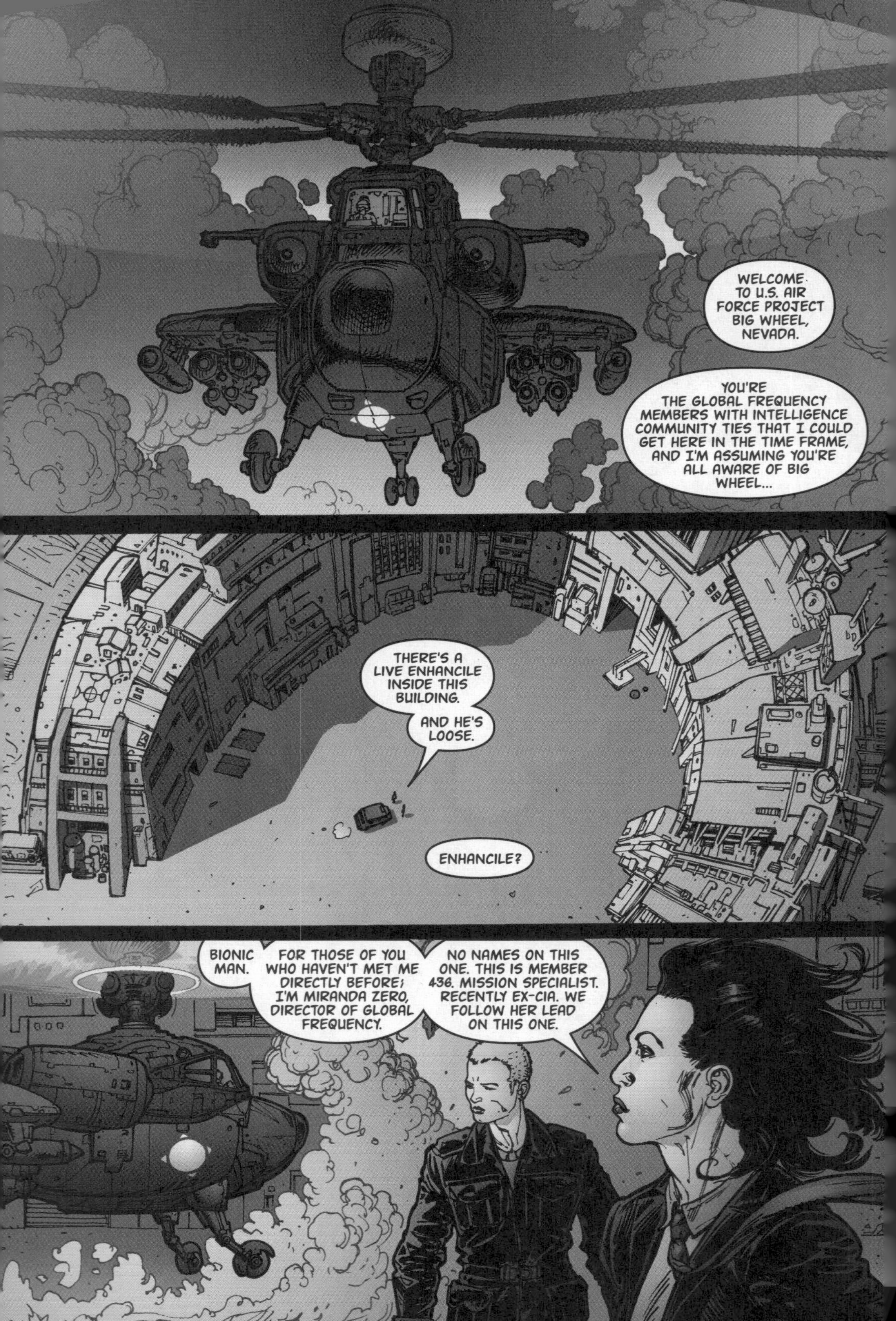
WELCOME TO U.S. AIR FORCE PROJECT BIG WHEEL, NEVADA.
YOU'RE THE GLOBAL FREQUENCY MEMBERS WITH INTELLIGENCE COMMUNITY TIES THAT I COULD GET HERE IN THE TIME FRAME, AND I'M ASSUMING YOU'RE ALL AWARE OF BIG WHEEL...
THERE'S A LIVE ENHANCILE INSIDE THIS BUILDING.
AND HE'S LOOSE.
ENHANCILE?
BIONIC MAN.
FOR THOSE OF YOU WHO HAVEN'T MET ME DIRECTLY BEFORE; I'M MIRANDA ZERO, DIRECTOR OF GLOBAL FREQUENCY.
NO NAMES ON THIS ONE. THIS IS MEMBER 436. MISSION SPECIALIST. RECENTLY EX-CIA. WE FOLLOW HER LEAD ON THIS ONE.

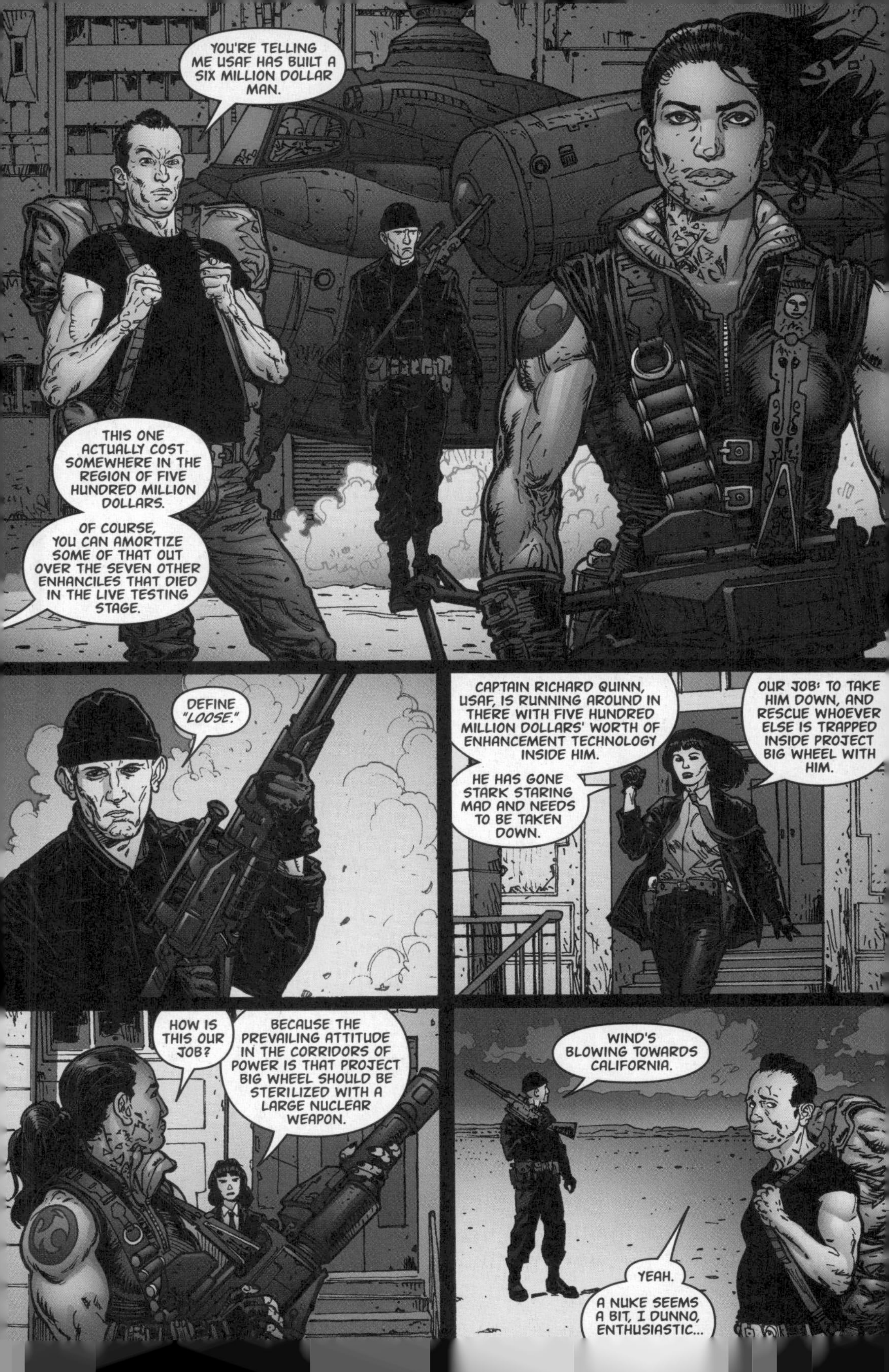
YOU'RE TELLING ME USAF HAS BUILT A SIX MILLION DOLLAR MAN.
THIS ONE ACTUALLY COST SOMEWHERE IN THE REGION OF FIVE HUNDRED MILLION DOLLARS.
OF COURSE, YOU CAN AMORTIZE SOME OF THAT OUT OVER THE SEVEN OTHER ENHANCILES THAT DIED IN THE LIVE TESTING STAGE.
DEFINE "LOOSE."
CAPTAIN RICHARD QUINN, USAF, IS RUNNING AROUND IN THERE WITH FIVE HUNDRED MILLION DOLLARS' WORTH OF ENHANCEMENT TECHNOLOGY INSIDE HIM.
HE HAS GONE STARK STARING MAD AND NEEDS TO BE TAKEN DOWN.
OUR JOB: TO TAKE HIM DOWN, AND RESCUE WHOEVER ELSE IS TRAPPED INSIDE PROJECT BIG WHEEL WITH HIM.
HOW IS THIS OUR JOB?
BECAUSE THE PREVAILING ATTITUDE IN THE CORRIDORS OF POWER IS THAT PROJECT BIG WHEEL SHOULD BE STERILIZED WITH A LARGE NUCLEAR WEAPON.
WIND'S BLOWING TOWARDS CALIFORNIA.
YEAH.
A NUKE SEEMS A BIT, I DUNNO, ENTHUSIASTIC...

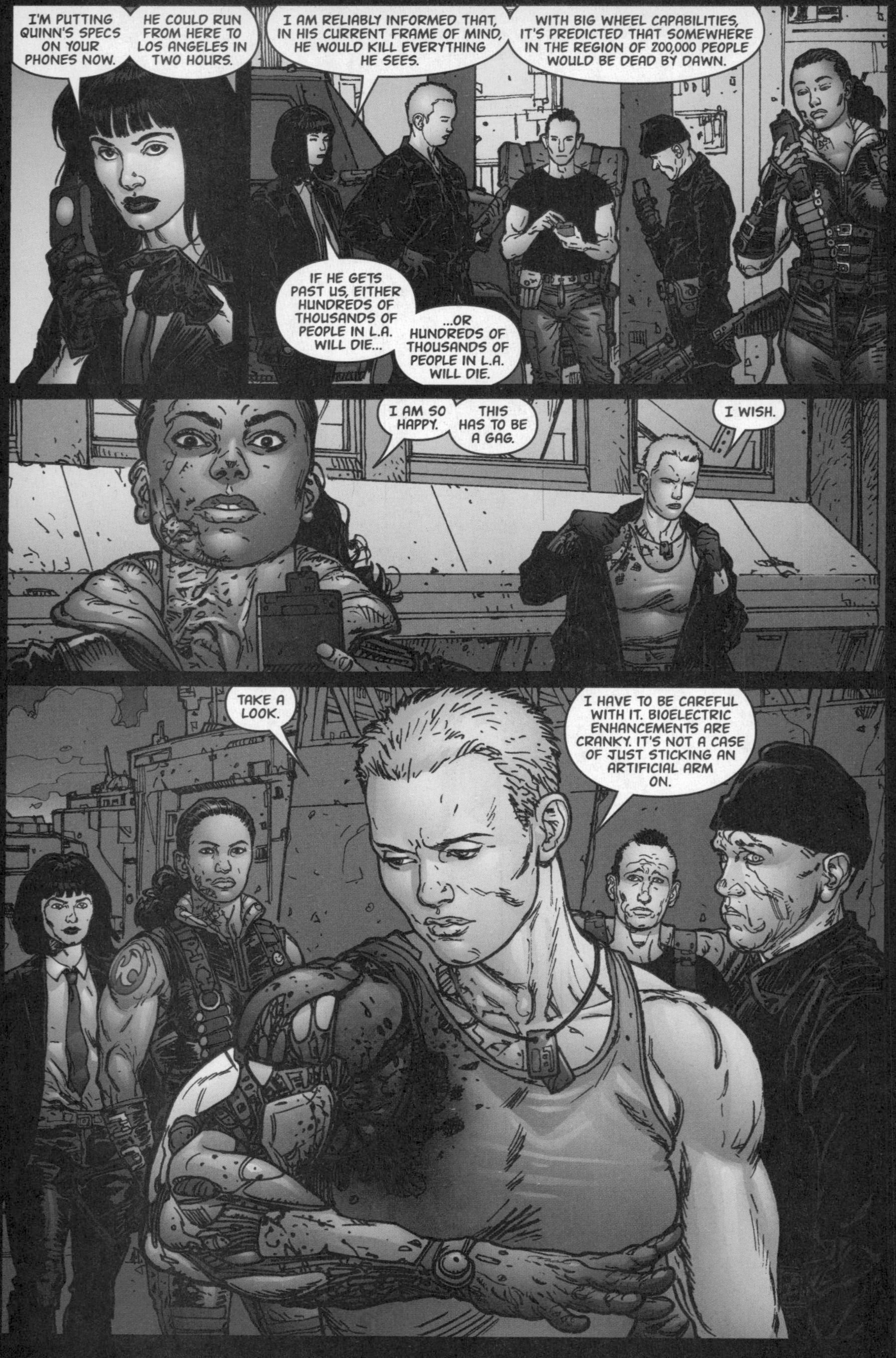
I'M PUTTING QUINN'S SPECS ON YOUR PHONES NOW.
HE COULD RUN FROM HERE TO LOS ANGELES IN TWO HOURS.
I AM RELIABLY INFORMED THAT, IN HIS CURRENT FRAME OF MIND, HE WOULD KILL EVERYTHING HE SEES.
WITH BIG WHEEL CAPABILITIES, IT'S PREDICTED THAT SOMEWHERE IN THE REGION OF 200,000 PEOPLE WOULD BE DEAD BY DAWN.
IF HE GETS PAST US, EITHER HUNDREDS OF THOUSANDS OF PEOPLE IN L.A. WILL DIE...
...OR HUNDREDS OF THOUSANDS OF PEOPLE IN L.A. WILL DIE.
I AM SO HAPPY.
THIS HAS TO BE A GAG.
I WISH.
TAKE A LOOK.
I HAVE TO BE CAREFUL WITH IT. BIOELECTRIC ENHANCEMENTS ARE CRANKY. IT'S NOT A CASE OF JUST STICKING AN ARTIFICIAL ARM ON.

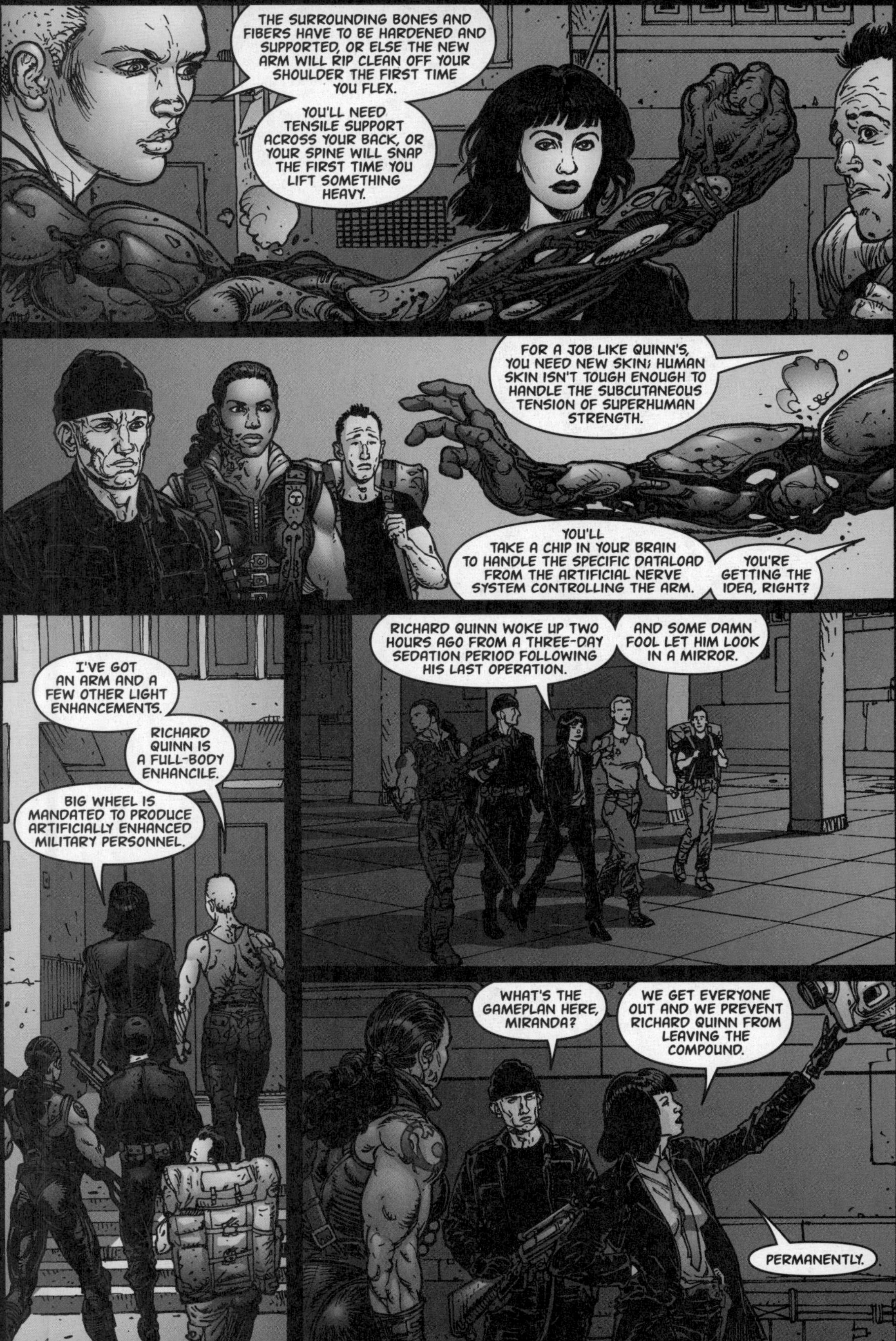
THE SURROUNDING BONES AND FIBERS HAVE TO BE HARDENED AND SUPPORTED, OR ELSE THE NEW ARM WILL RIP CLEAN OFF YOUR SHOULDER THE FIRST TIME YOU FLEX.
YOU'LL NEED TENSILE SUPPORT ACROSS YOUR BACK, OR YOUR SPINE WILL SNAP THE FIRST TIME YOU LIFT SOMETHING HEAVY.
FOR A JOB LIKE QUINN'S, YOU NEED NEW SKIN; HUMAN SKIN ISN'T TOUGH ENOUGH TO HANDLE THE SUBCUTANEOUS TENSION OF SUPERHUMAN STRENGTH.
YOU'LL TAKE A CHIP IN YOUR BRAIN TO HANDLE THE SPECIFIC DATALOAD FROM THE ARTIFICIAL NERVE SYSTEM CONTROLLING THE ARM.
YOU'RE GETTING THE IDEA, RIGHT?
I'VE GOT AN ARM AND A FEW OTHER LIGHT ENHANCEMENTS.
RICHARD QUINN IS A FULL-BODY ENHANCILE.
BIG WHEEL IS MANDATED TO PRODUCE ARTIFICIALLY ENHANCED MILITARY PERSONNEL.
RICHARD QUINN WOKE UP TWO HOURS AGO FROM A THREE-DAY SEDATION PERIOD FOLLOWING HIS LAST OPERATION.
AND SOME DAMN FOOL LET HIM LOOK IN A MIRROR.
WHAT'S THE GAMEPLAN HERE, MIRANDA?
WE GET EVERYONE OUT AND WE PREVENT RICHARD QUINN FROM LEAVING THE COMPOUND.
PERMANENTLY.

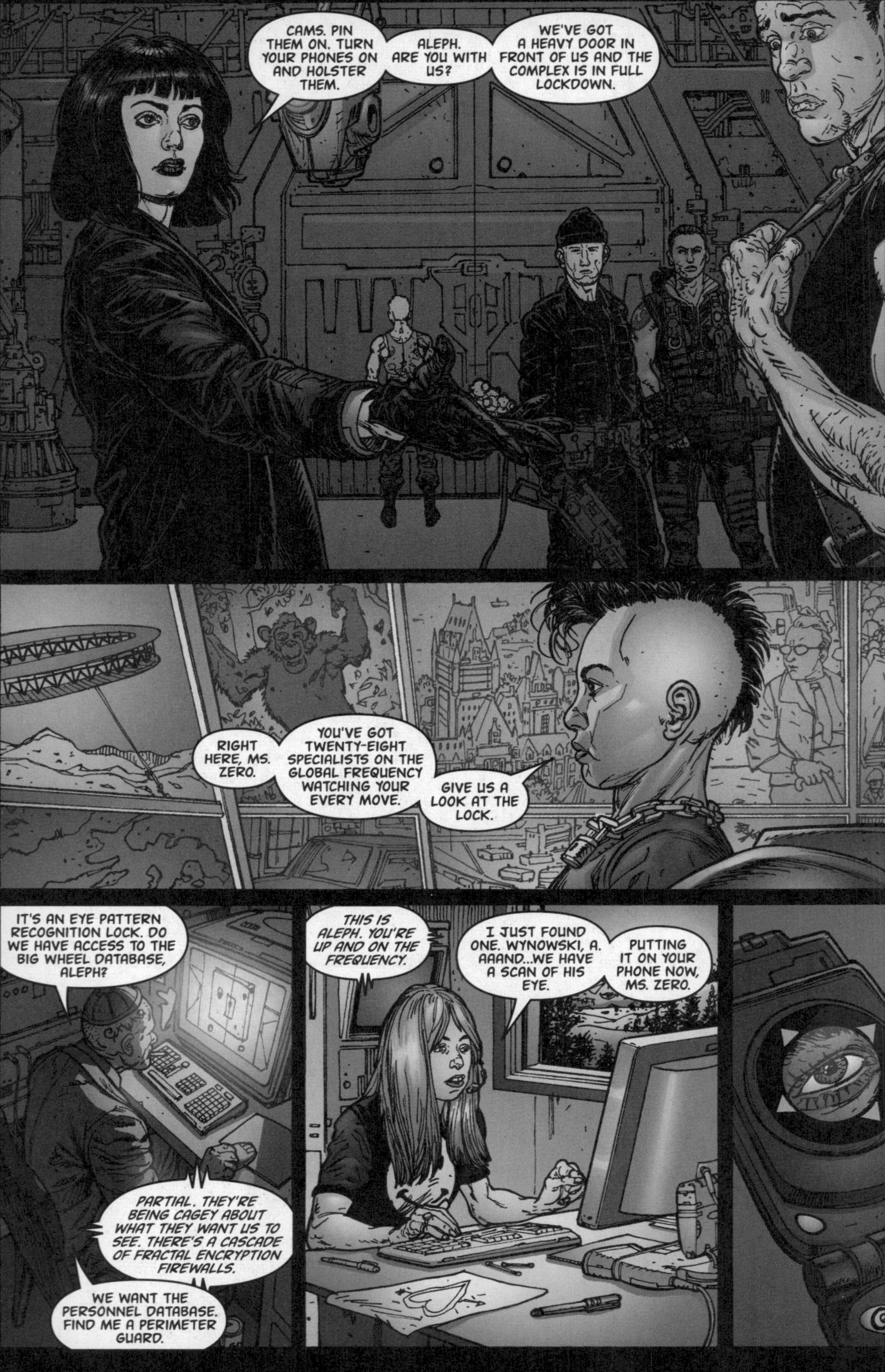
CAMS. PIN THEM ON. TURN YOUR PHONES ON AND HOLSTER THEM.
ALEPH. ARE YOU WITH US?
WE'VE GOT A HEAVY DOOR IN FRONT OF US AND THE COMPLEX IS IN FULL LOCKDOWN.
RIGHT HERE, MS. ZERO.
YOU'VE GOT TWENTY-EIGHT SPECIALISTS ON THE GLOBAL FREQUENCY WATCHING YOUR EVERY MOVE.
GIVE US A LOOK AT THE LOCK.
IT'S AN EYE PATTERN RECOGNITION LOCK. DO WE HAVE ACCESS TO THE BIG WHEEL DATABASE, ALEPH?
PARTIAL. THEY'RE BEING CAGEY ABOUT WHAT THEY WANT US TO SEE. THERE'S A CASCADE OF FRACTAL ENCRYPTION FIREWALLS.
WE WANT THE PERSONNEL DATABASE. FIND ME A PERIMETER GUARD.
THIS IS ALEPH. YOU'RE UP AND ON THE FREQUENCY.
I JUST FOUND ONE. WYNOWSKI, A. AAAND...WE HAVE A SCAN OF HIS EYE.
PUTTING IT ON YOUR PHONE NOW, MS. ZERO.

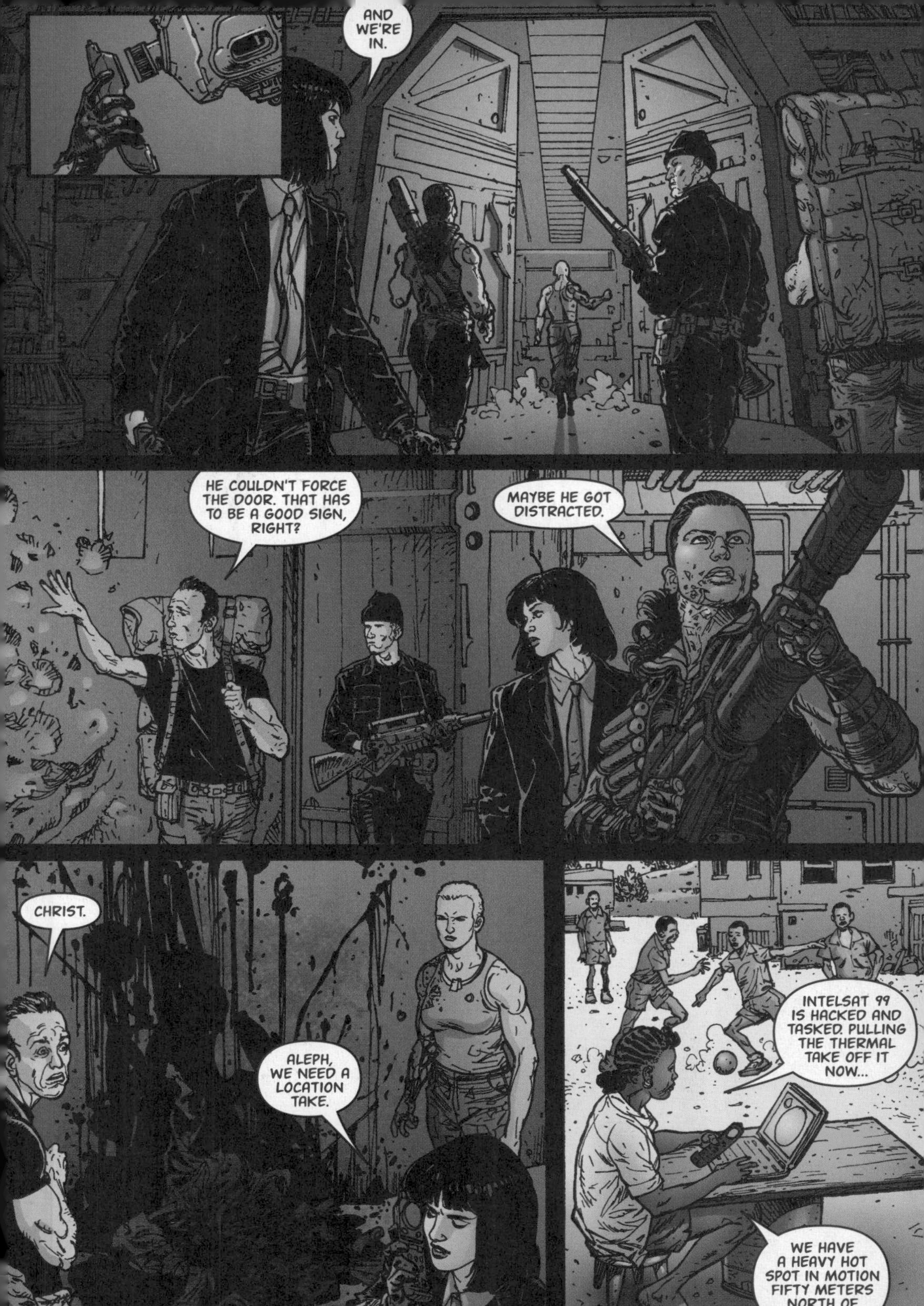
AND WE'RE IN.
HE COULDN'T FORCE THE DOOR. THAT HAS TO BE A GOOD SIGN, RIGHT?
MAYBE HE GOT DISTRACTED.
CHRIST.
ALEPH, WE NEED A LOCATION TAKE.
INTELSAT 99 IS HACKED AND TASKED, PULLING THE THERMAL TAKE OFF IT NOW...
WE HAVE A HEAVY HOT SPOT IN MOTION FIFTY METERS NORTH OF THE TEAM.
IT'S NOT HUMAN. TOO HOT.

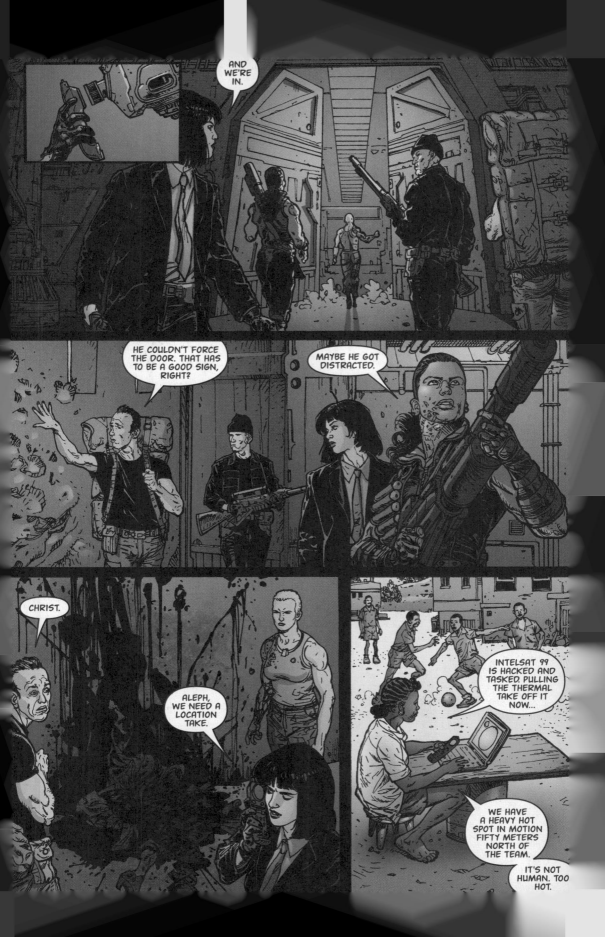

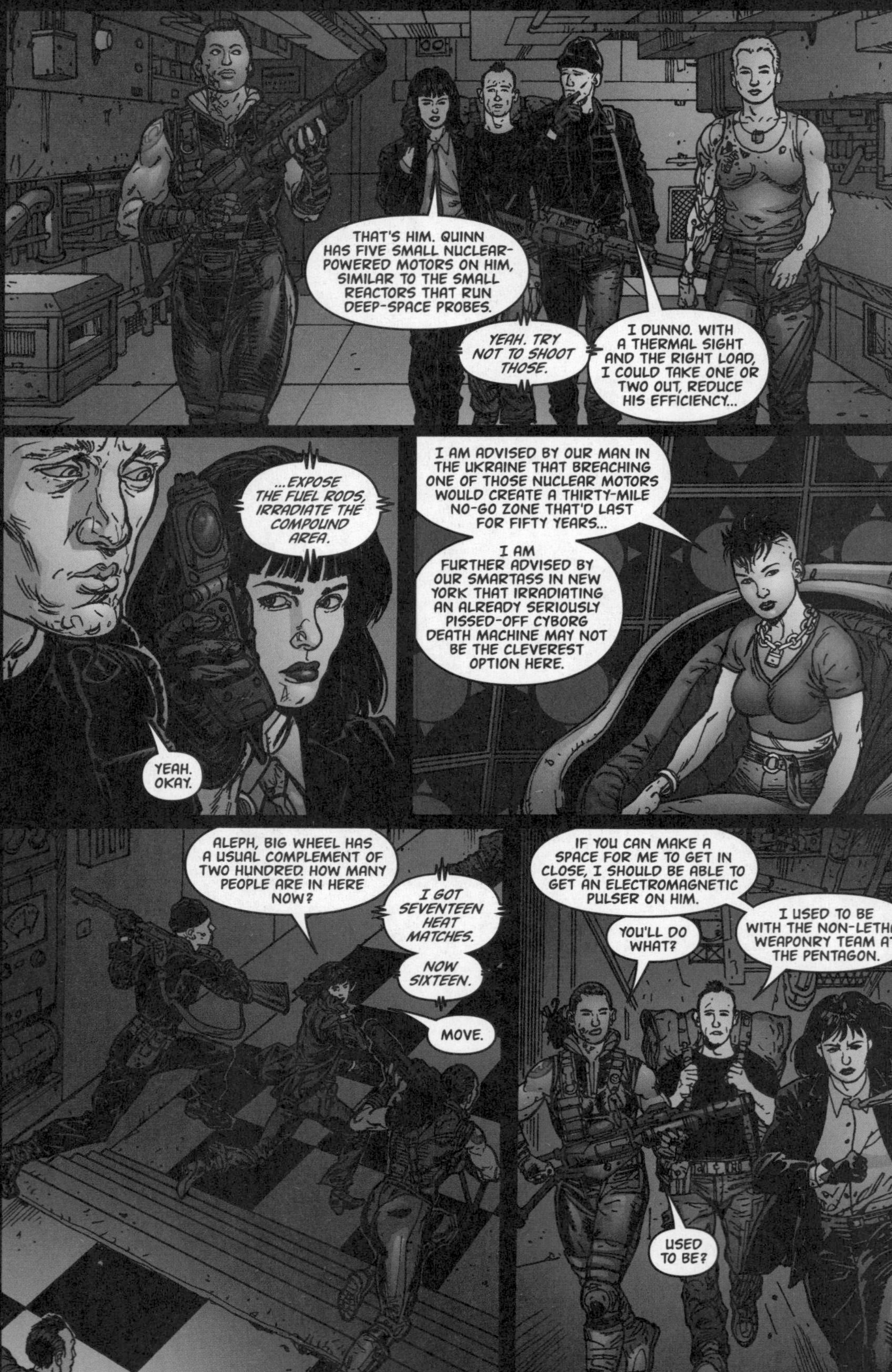
THAT'S HIM. QUINN HAS FIVE SMALL NUCLEAR-POWERED MOTORS ON HIM, SIMILAR TO THE SMALL REACTORS THAT RUN DEEP-SPACE PROBES.
YEAH. TRY NOT TO SHOOT THOSE.
I DUNNO. WITH A THERMAL SIGHT AND THE RIGHT LOAD, I COULD TAKE ONE OR TWO OUT, REDUCE HIS EFFICIENCY...
...EXPOSE THE FUEL RODS, IRRADIATE THE COMPOUND AREA.
YEAH. OKAY.
I AM ADVISED BY OUR MAN IN THE UKRAINE THAT BREACHING ONE OF THOSE NUCLEAR MOTORS WOULD CREATE A THIRTY-MILE NO-GO ZONE THAT'D LAST FOR FIFTY YEARS...
I AM FURTHER ADVISED BY OUR SMARTASS IN NEW YORK THAT IRRADIATING AN ALREADY SERIOUSLY PISSED-OFF CYBORG DEATH MACHINE MAY NOT BE THE CLEVEREST OPTION HERE.
ALEPH, BIG WHEEL HAS A USUAL COMPLEMENT OF TWO HUNDRED. HOW MANY PEOPLE ARE IN HERE NOW?
I GOT SEVENTEEN HEAT MATCHES.
NOW SIXTEEN.
MOVE.
IF YOU CAN MAKE A SPACE FOR ME TO GET IN CLOSE, I SHOULD BE ABLE TO GET AN ELECTROMAGNETIC PULSER ON HIM.
YOU'LL DO WHAT?
I USED TO BE WITH THE NON-LETHAL WEAPONRY TEAM AT THE PENTAGON.
USED TO BE?

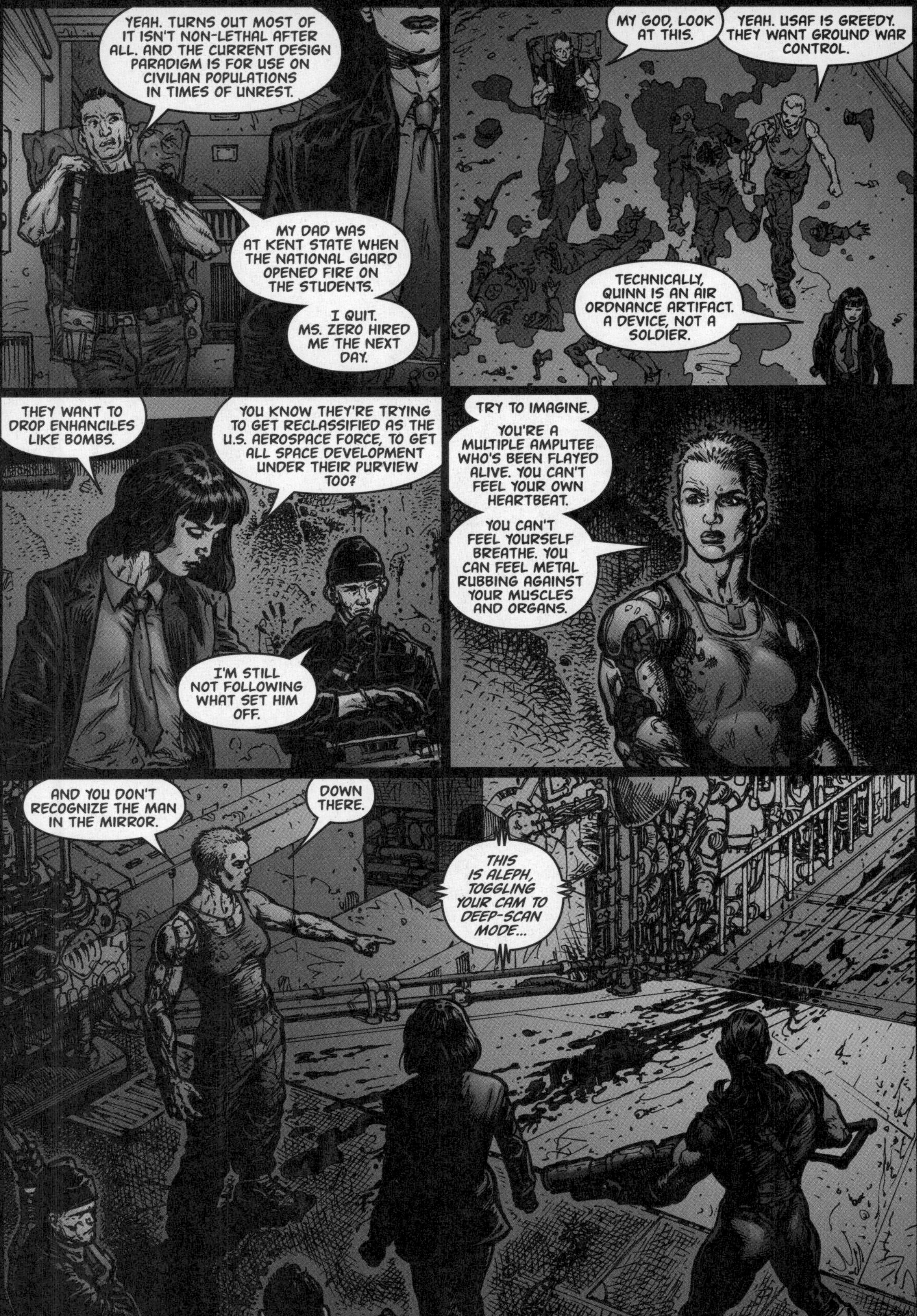
YEAH. TURNS OUT MOST OF IT ISN'T NON-LETHAL AFTER ALL. AND THE CURRENT DESIGN PARADIGM IS FOR USE ON CIVILIAN POPULATIONS IN TIMES OF UNREST.
MY DAD WAS AT KENT STATE WHEN THE NATIONAL GUARD OPENED FIRE ON THE STUDENTS.
I QUIT. MS. ZERO HIRED ME THE NEXT DAY.
MY GOD, LOOK AT THIS.
YEAH. USAF IS GREEDY. THEY WANT GROUND WAR CONTROL.
TECHNICALLY, QUINN IS AN AIR ORDNANCE ARTIFACT. A DEVICE, NOT A SOLDIER.
THEY WANT TO DROP ENHANCILES LIKE BOMBS.
YOU KNOW THEY'RE TRYING TO GET RECLASSIFIED AS THE U.S. AEROSPACE FORCE, TO GET ALL SPACE DEVELOPMENT UNDER THEIR PURVIEW TOO?
I'M STILL NOT FOLLOWING WHAT SET HIM OFF.
TRY TO IMAGINE.
YOU'RE A MULTIPLE AMPUTEE WHO'S BEEN FLAYED ALIVE. YOU CAN'T FEEL YOUR OWN HEARTBEAT.
YOU CAN'T FEEL YOURSELF BREATHE. YOU CAN FEEL METAL RUBBING AGAINST YOUR MUSCLES AND ORGANS.
AND YOU DON'T RECOGNIZE THE MAN IN THE MIRROR.
DOWN THERE.
THIS IS ALEPH, TOGGLING YOUR CAM TO DEEP-SCAN MODE...

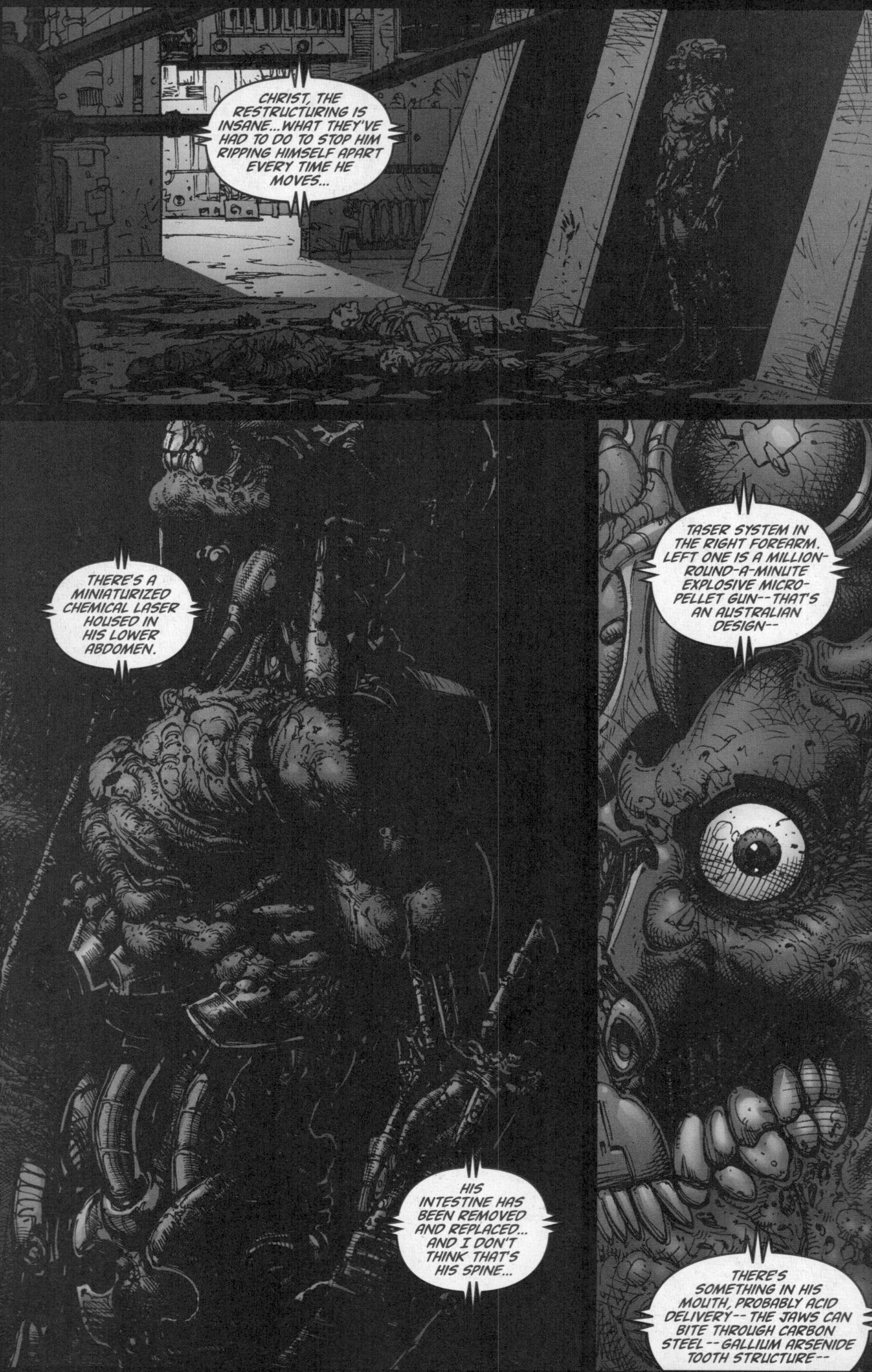
CHRIST, THE RESTRUCTURING IS INSANE...WHAT THEY'VE HAD TO DO TO STOP HIM RIPPING HIMSELF APART EVERY TIME HE MOVES...
THERE'S A MINIATURIZED CHEMICAL LASER HOUSED IN HIS LOWER ABDOMEN.
TASER SYSTEM IN THE RIGHT FOREARM. LEFT ONE IS A MILLION-ROUND-A-MINUTE EXPLOSIVE MICRO-PELLET GUN--THAT'S AN AUSTRALIAN DESIGN--
HIS INTESTINE HAS BEEN REMOVED AND REPLACED... AND I DON'T THINK THAT'S HIS SPINE...
THERE'S SOMETHING IN HIS MOUTH, PROBABLY ACID DELIVERY-- THE JAWS CAN BITE THROUGH CARBON STEEL--GALLIUM ARSENIDE TOOTH STRUCTURE--

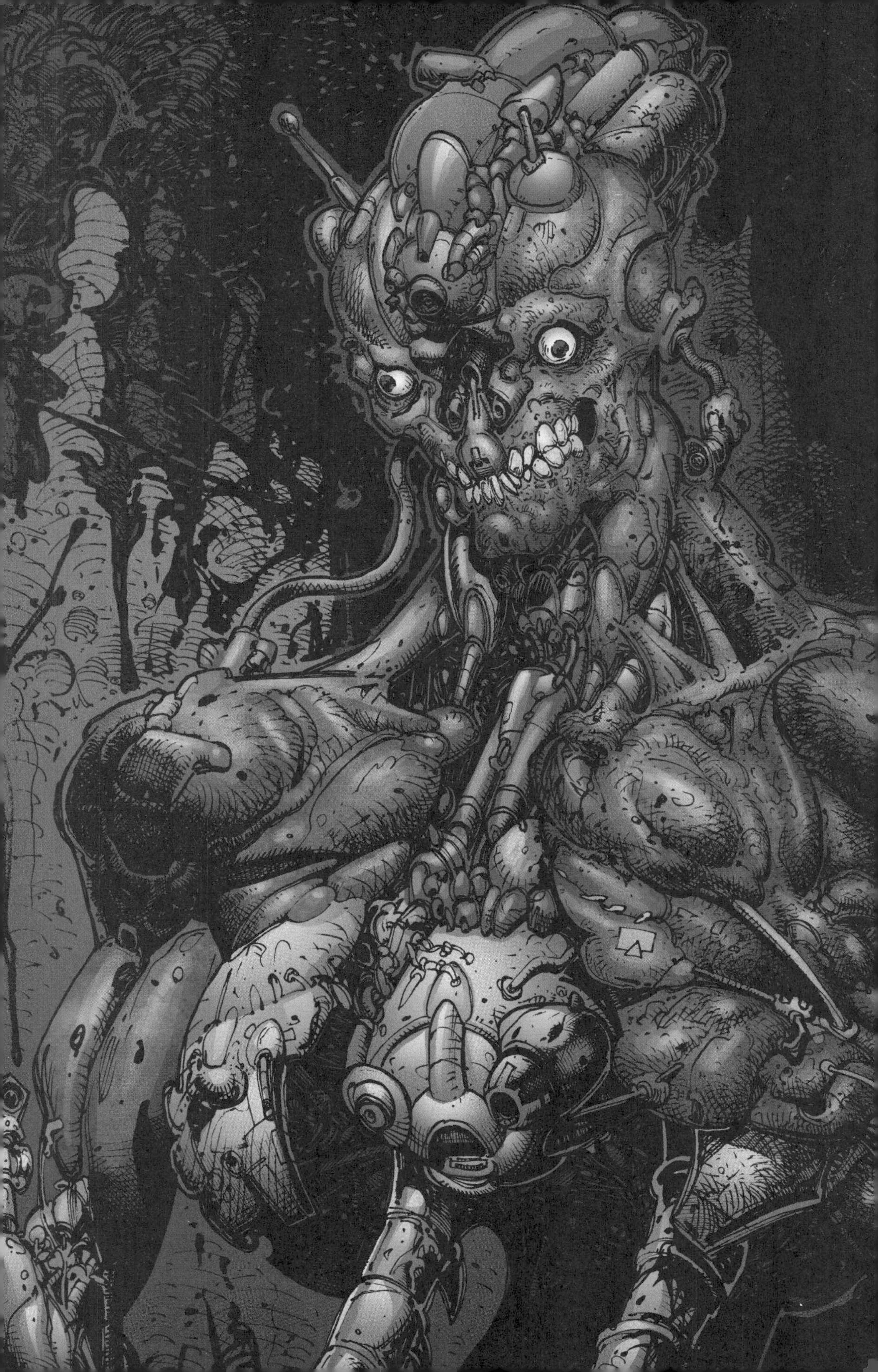

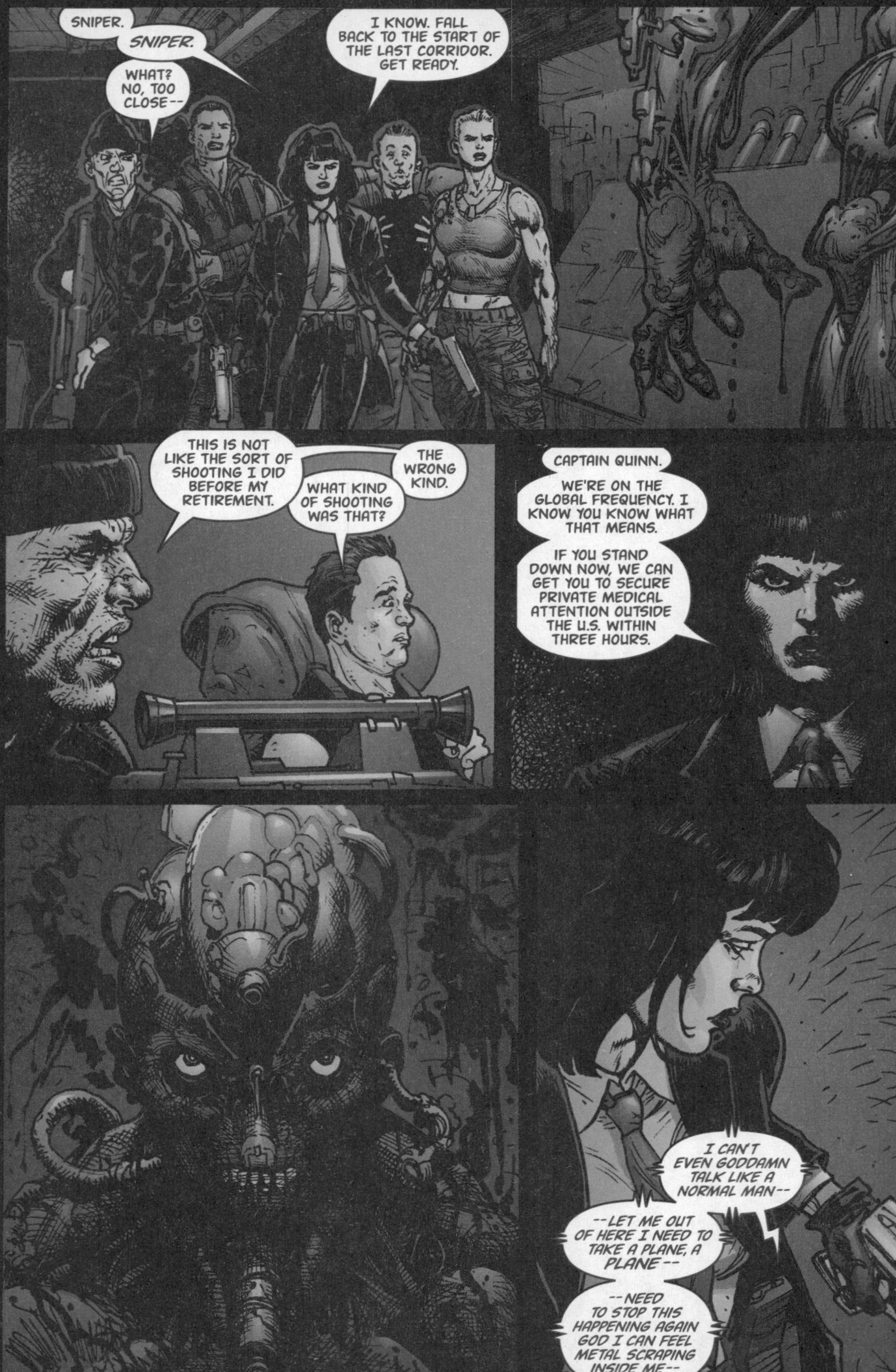
SNIPER.
SNIPER.
WHAT? NO, TOO CLOSE--
I KNOW. FALL BACK TO THE START OF THE LAST CORRIDOR. GET READY.
THIS IS NOT LIKE THE SORT OF SHOOTING I DID BEFORE MY RETIREMENT.
WHAT KIND OF SHOOTING WAS THAT?
THE WRONG KIND.
CAPTAIN QUINN.
WE'RE ON THE GLOBAL FREQUENCY. I KNOW YOU KNOW WHAT THAT MEANS.
IF YOU STAND DOWN NOW, WE CAN GET YOU TO SECURE PRIVATE MEDICAL ATTENTION OUTSIDE THE U.S. WITHIN THREE HOURS.
I CAN'T EVEN GODDAMN TALK LIKE A NORMAL MAN--
--LET ME OUT OF HERE I NEED TO TAKE A PLANE, A PLANE--
--NEED TO STOP THIS HAPPENING AGAIN GOD I CAN FEEL METAL SCRAPING INSIDE ME--

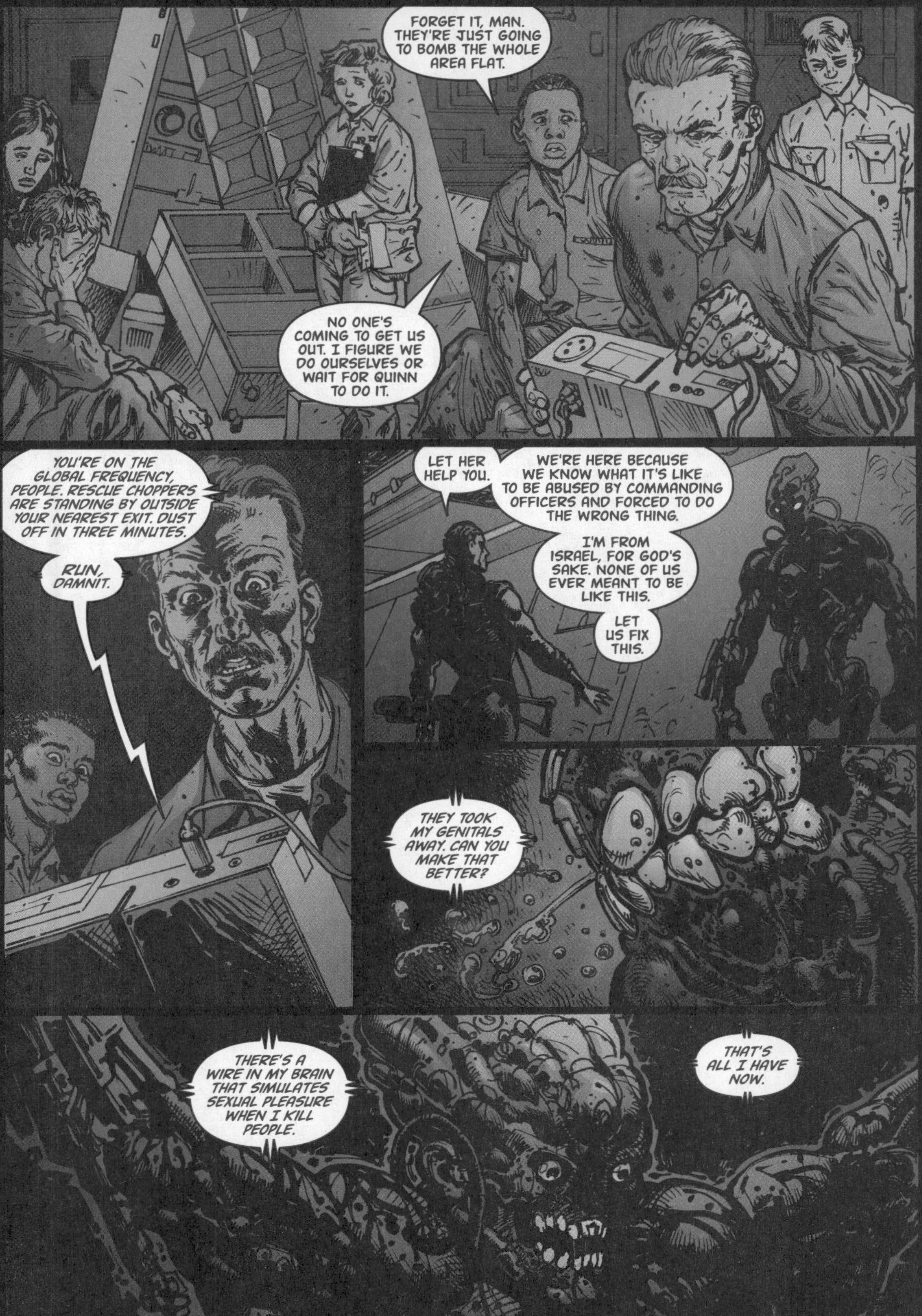
FORGET IT, MAN. THEY'RE JUST GOING TO BOMB THE WHOLE AREA FLAT.
NO ONE'S COMING TO GET US OUT. I FIGURE WE DO OURSELVES OR WAIT FOR QUINN TO DO IT.
YOU'RE ON THE GLOBAL FREQUENCY, PEOPLE. RESCUE CHOPPERS ARE STANDING BY OUTSIDE YOUR NEAREST EXIT. DUST OFF IN THREE MINUTES.
RUN, DAMNIT.
LET HER HELP YOU.
WE'RE HERE BECAUSE WE KNOW WHAT IT'S LIKE TO BE ABUSED BY COMMANDING OFFICERS AND FORCED TO DO THE WRONG THING.
I'M FROM ISRAEL, FOR GOD'S SAKE. NONE OF US EVER MEANT TO BE LIKE THIS.
LET US FIX THIS.
THEY TOOK MY GENITALS AWAY. CAN YOU MAKE THAT BETTER?
THERE'S A WIRE IN MY BRAIN THAT SIMULATES SEXUAL PLEASURE WHEN I KILL PEOPLE.
THAT'S ALL I HAVE NOW.

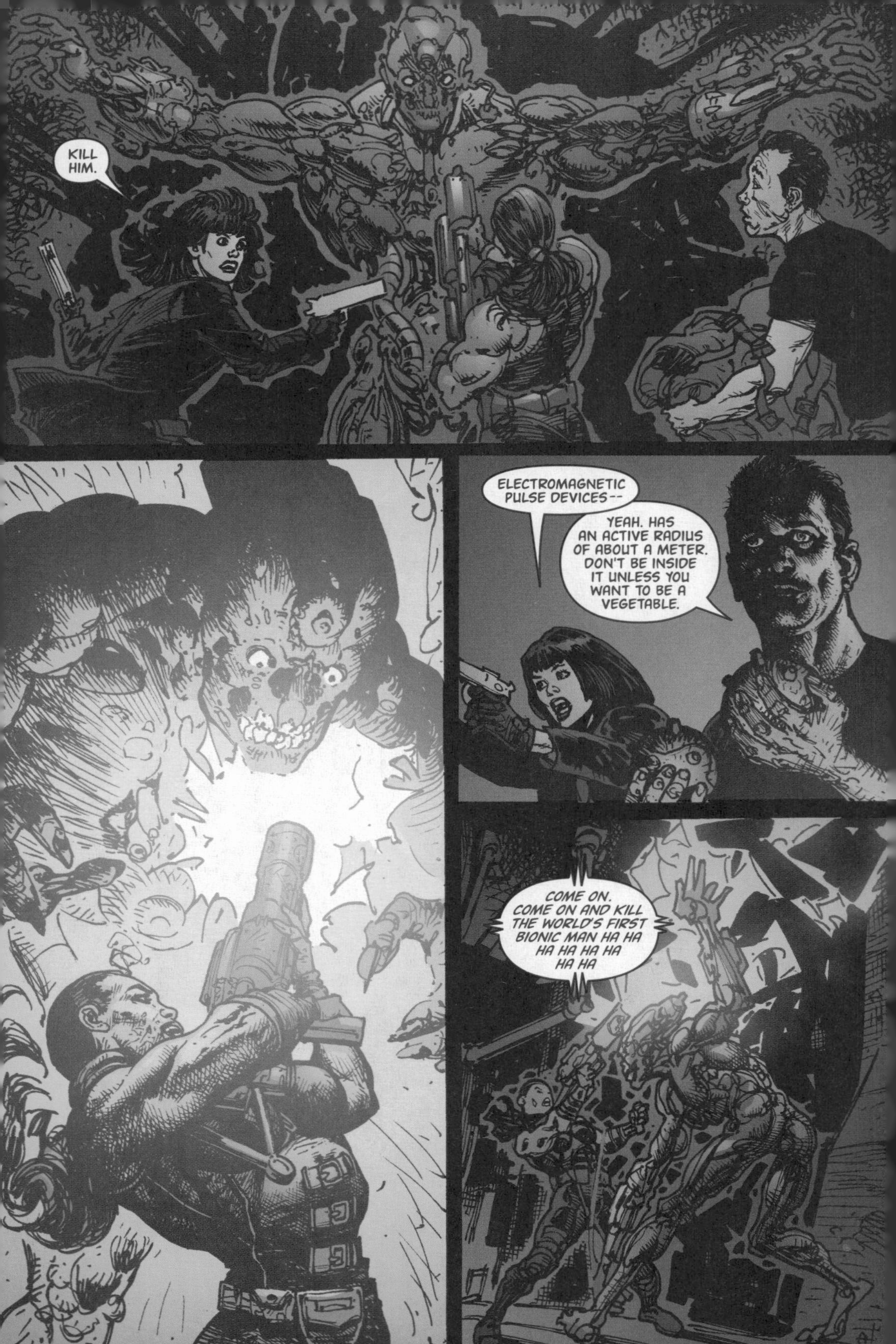
KILL HIM.
ELECTROMAGNETIC PULSE DEVICES--
YEAH. HAS AN ACTIVE RADIUS OF ABOUT A METER. DON'T BE INSIDE IT UNLESS YOU WANT TO BE A VEGETABLE.
COME ON. COME ON AND KILL THE WORLD'S FIRST BIONIC MAN HA HA HA HA HA HA HA HA

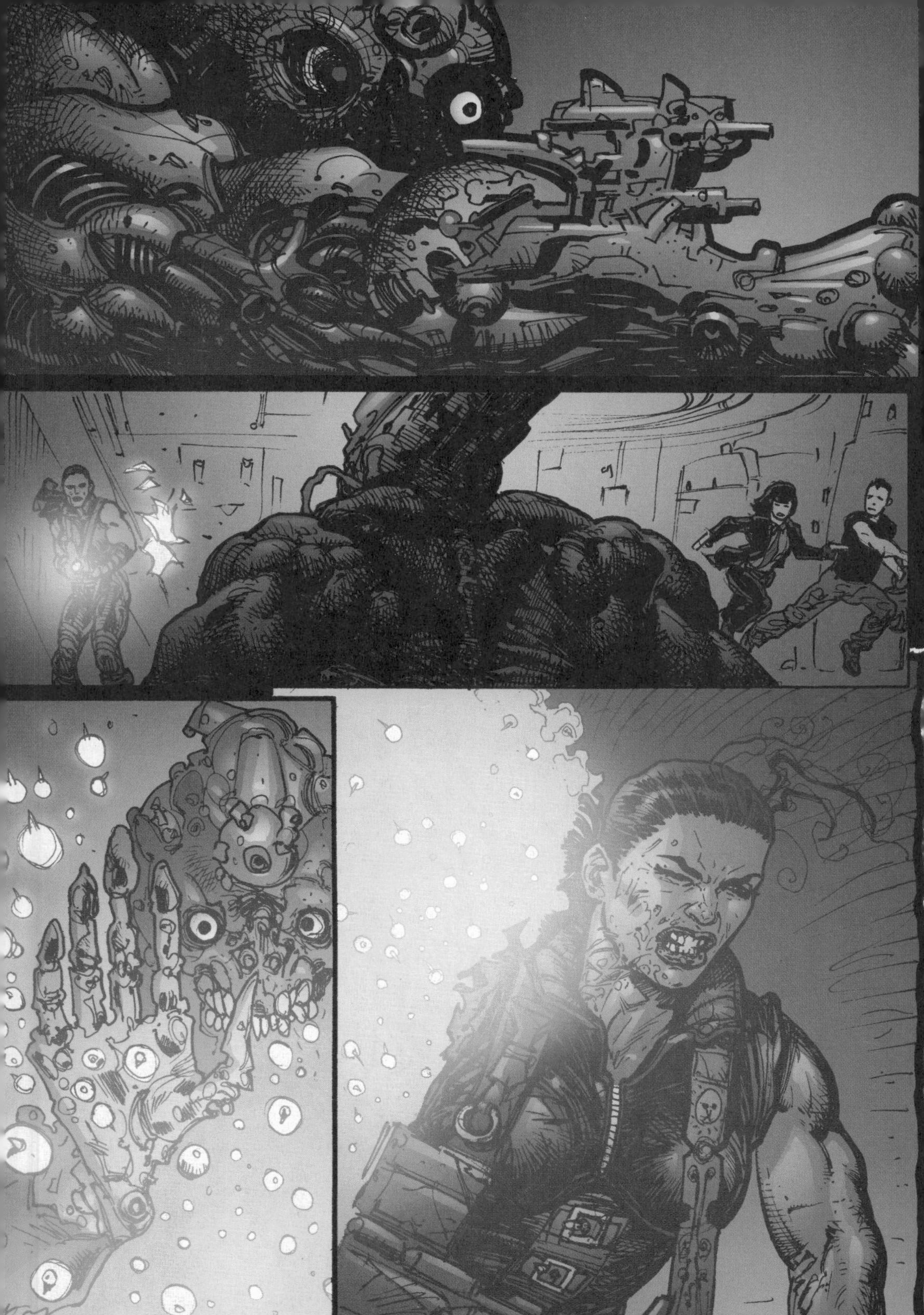

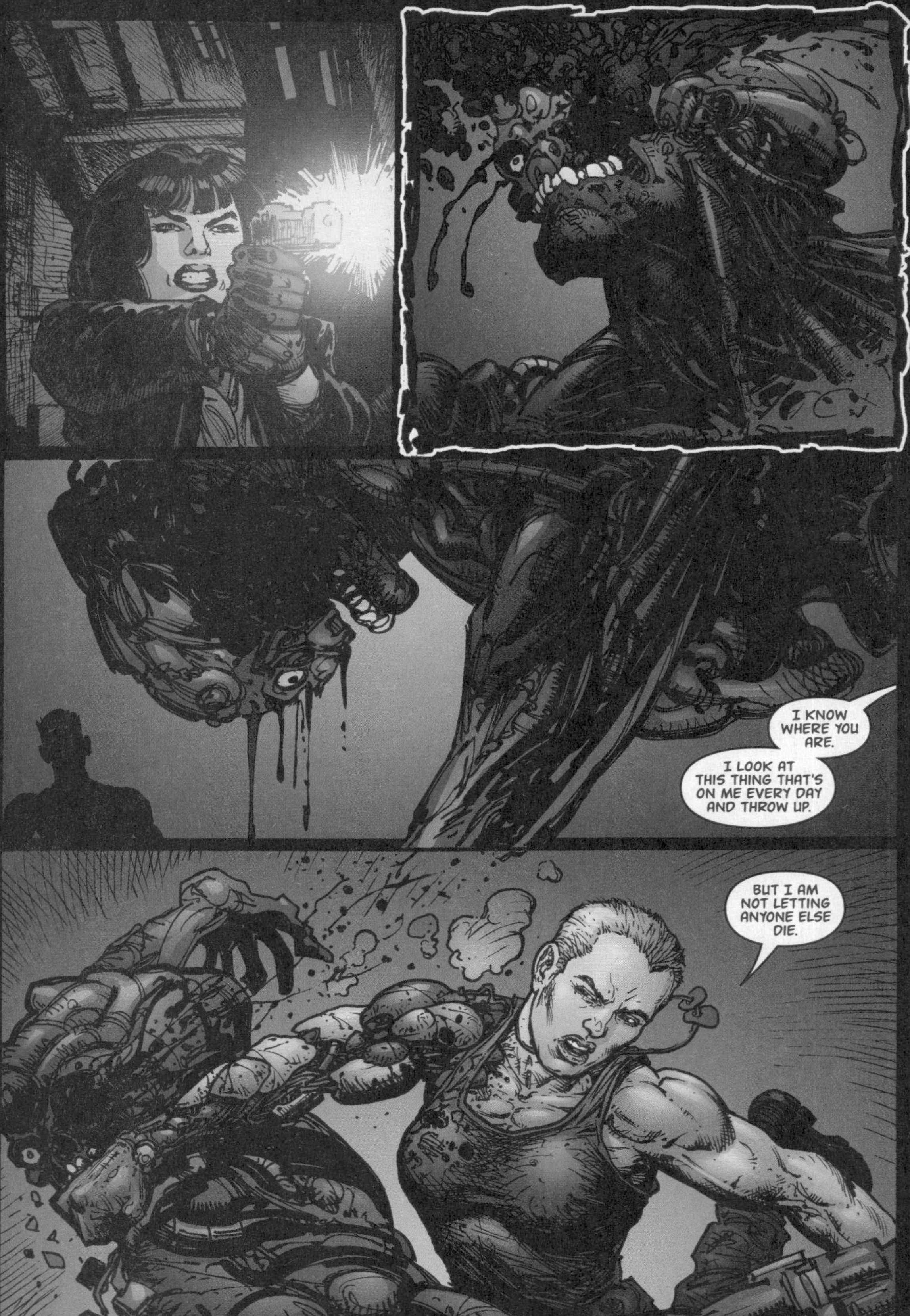
I KNOW WHERE YOU ARE.
I LOOK AT THIS THING THAT'S ON ME EVERY DAY AND THROW UP.
BUT I AM NOT LETTING ANYONE ELSE DIE.

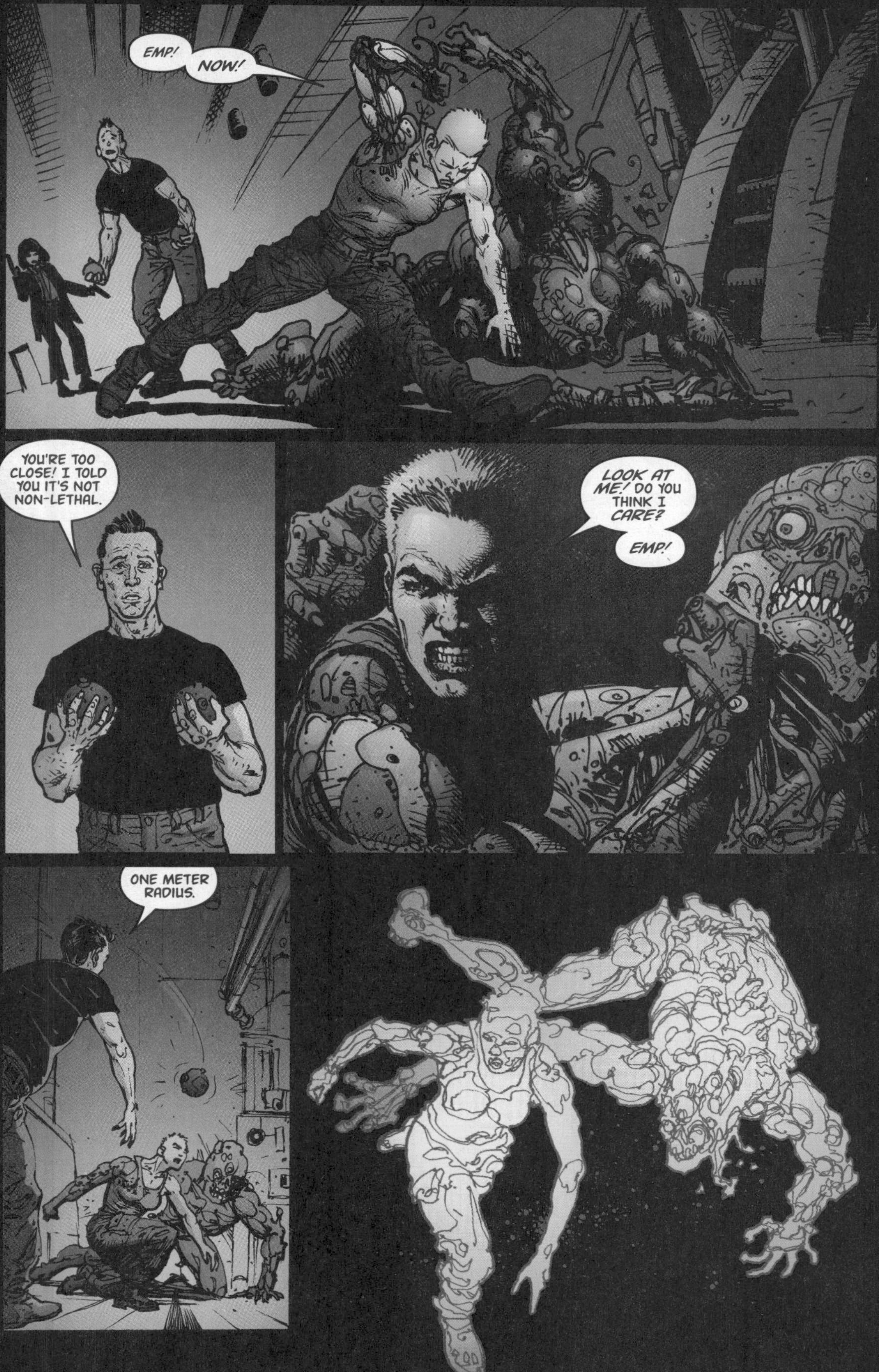
EMP!
NOW!
YOU'RE TOO CLOSE! I TOLD YOU IT'S NOT NON-LETHAL.
LOOK AT ME! DO YOU THINK I CARE?
EMP!
ONE METER RADIUS.

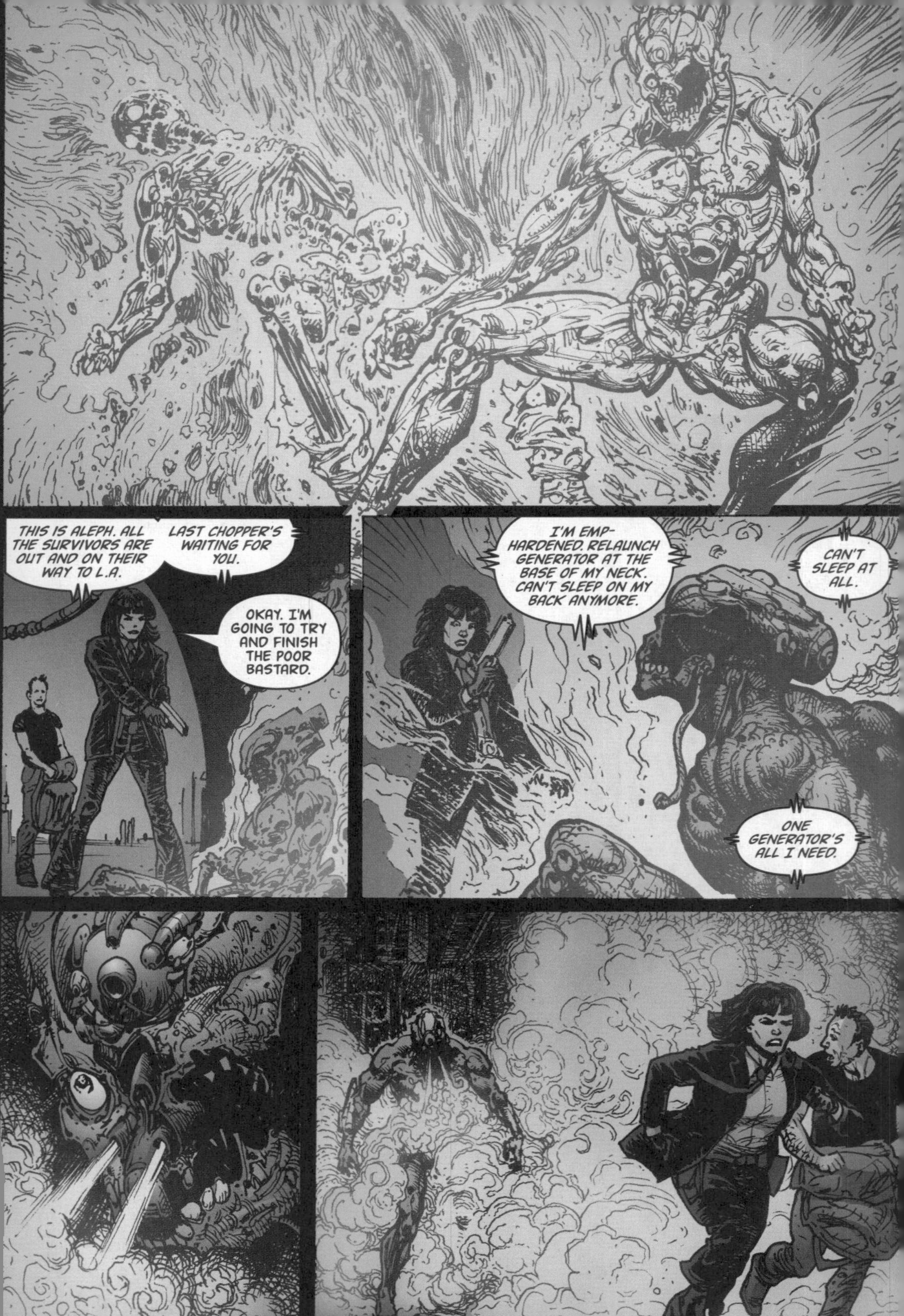
THIS IS ALEPH. ALL THE SURVIVORS ARE OUT AND ON THEIR WAY TO L.A.
LAST CHOPPER'S WAITING FOR YOU.
OKAY. I'M GOING TO TRY AND FINISH THE POOR BASTARD.
I'M EMP-HARDENED. RELAUNCH GENERATOR AT THE BASE OF MY NECK. CAN'T SLEEP ON MY BACK ANYMORE.
CAN'T SLEEP AT ALL.
ONE GENERATOR'S ALL I NEED.

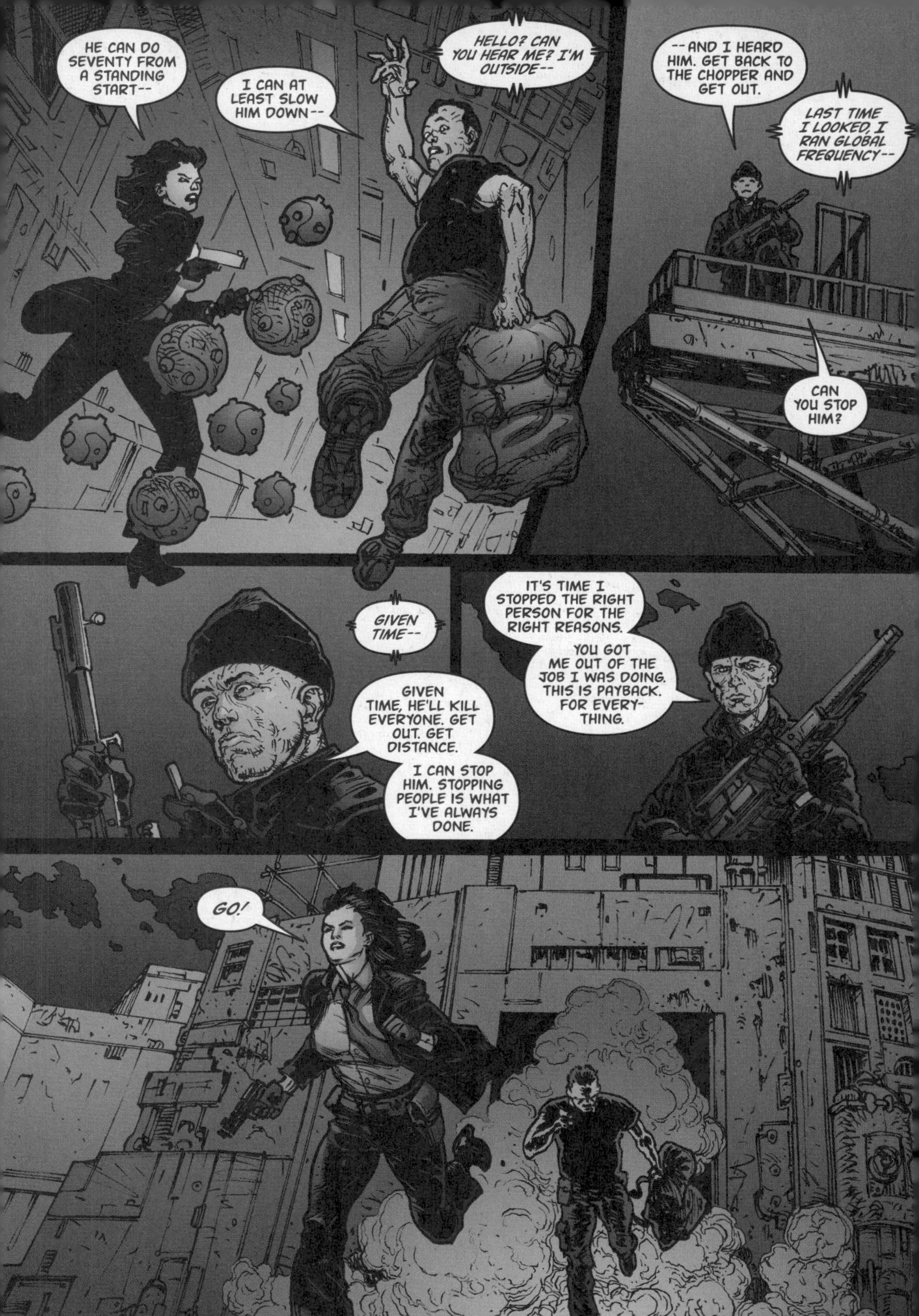
HE CAN DO SEVENTY FROM A STANDING START--
I CAN AT LEAST SLOW HIM DOWN--
HELLO? CAN YOU HEAR ME? I'M OUTSIDE--
--AND I HEARD HIM. GET BACK TO THE CHOPPER AND GET OUT.
LAST TIME I LOOKED, I RAN GLOBAL FREQUENCY--
CAN YOU STOP HIM?
GIVEN TIME--
GIVEN TIME, HE'LL KILL EVERYONE. GET OUT. GET DISTANCE.
I CAN STOP HIM. STOPPING PEOPLE IS WHAT I'VE ALWAYS DONE.
IT'S TIME I STOPPED THE RIGHT PERSON FOR THE RIGHT REASONS.
YOU GOT ME OUT OF THE JOB I WAS DOING. THIS IS PAYBACK. FOR EVERY-THING.
GO!

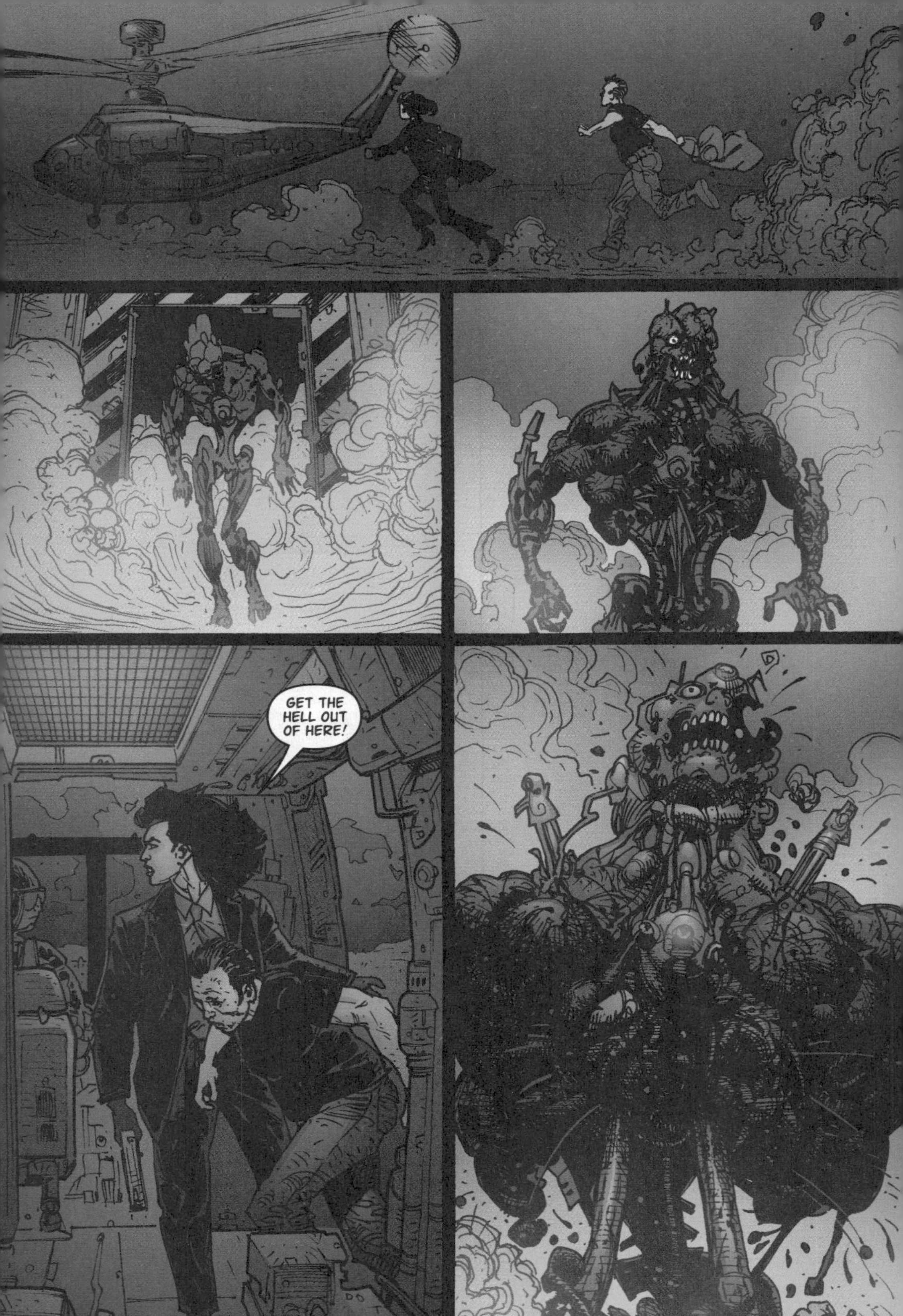
GET THE HELL OUT OF HERE!

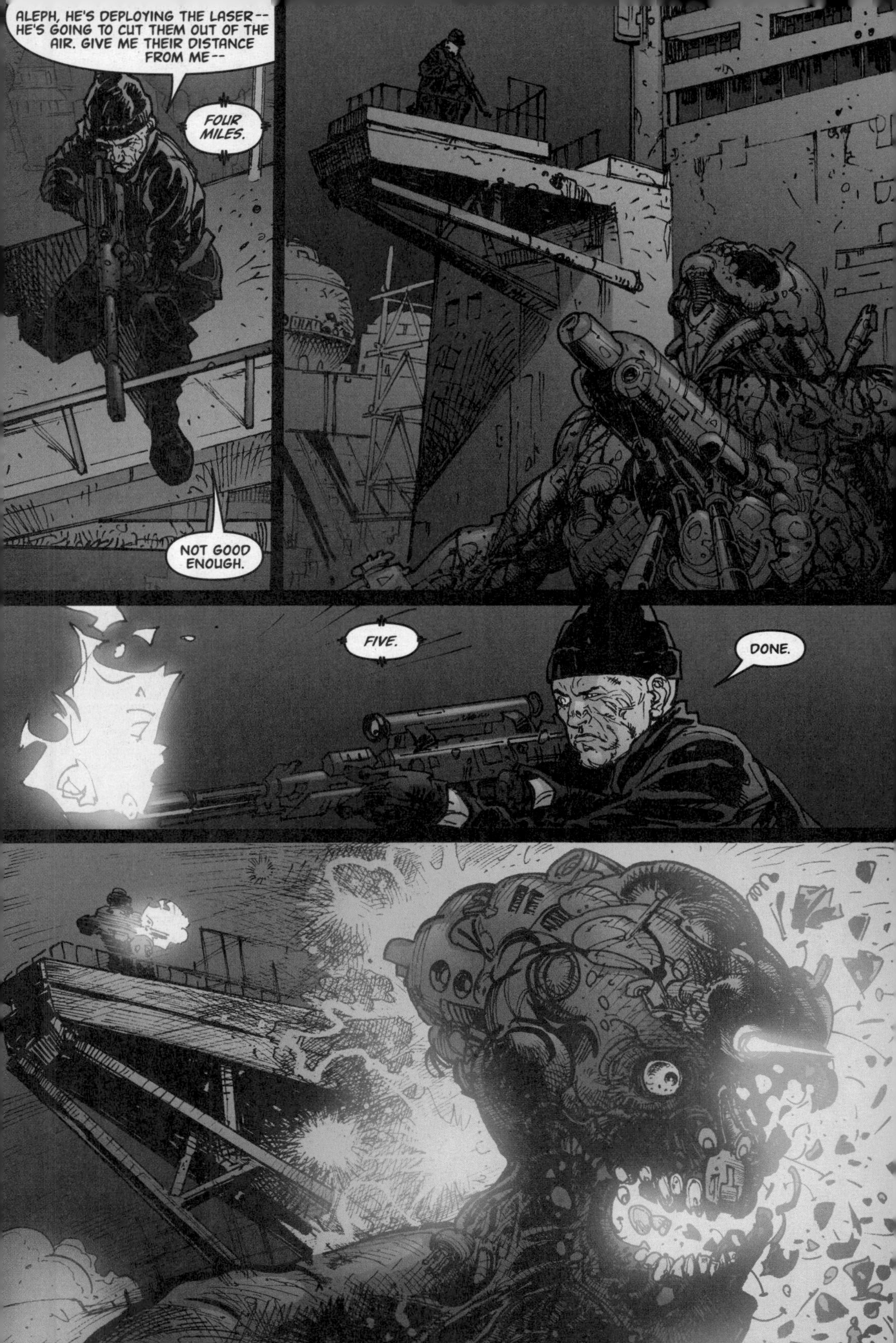
ALEPH, HE'S DEPLOYING THE LASER--
HE'S GOING TO CUT THEM OUT OF THE AIR. GIVE ME THEIR DISTANCE FROM ME--
FOUR MILES.
NOT GOOD ENOUGH.
FIVE.
DONE.

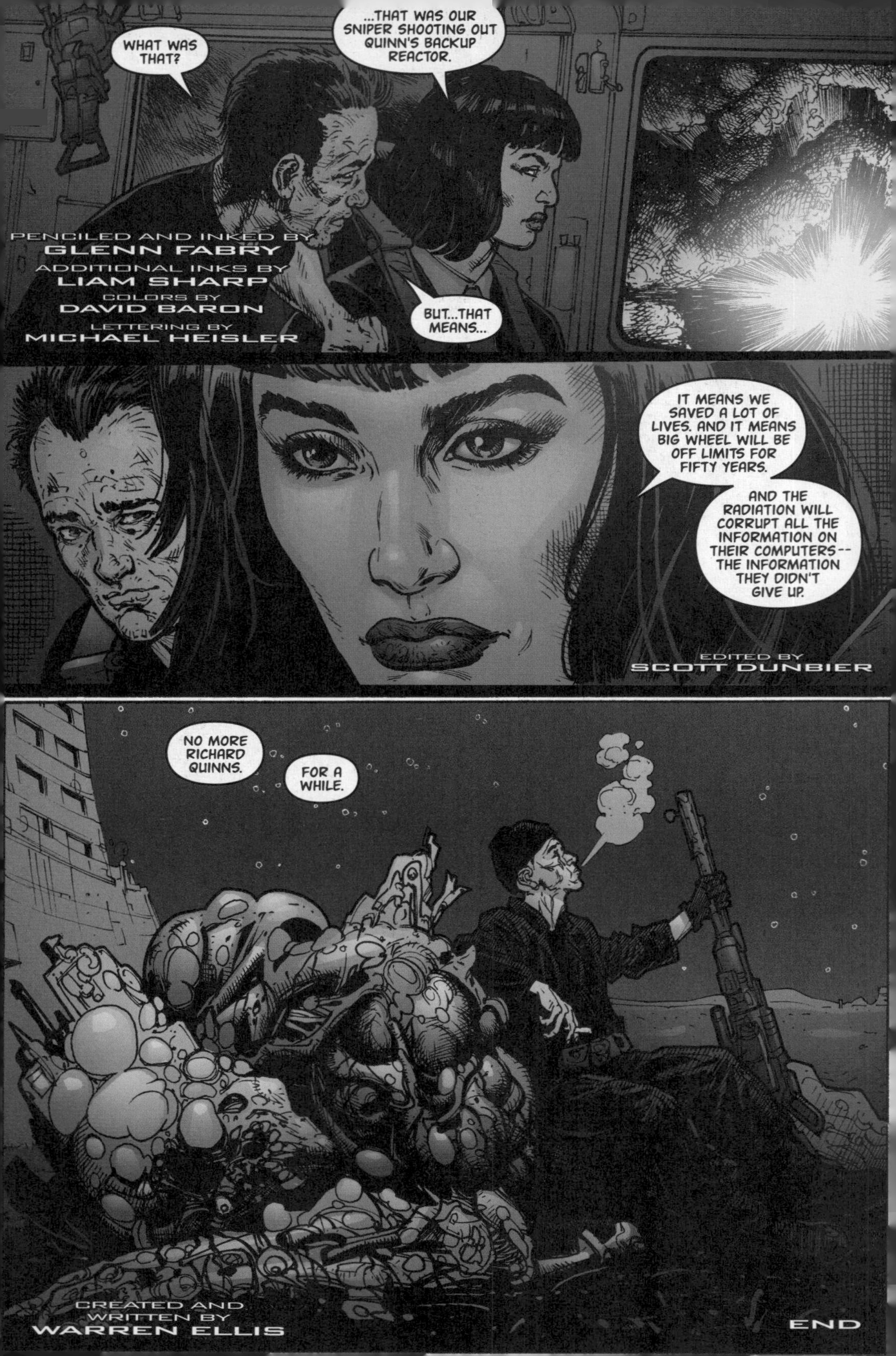

WHAT WAS THAT?
...THAT WAS OUR SNIPER SHOOTING OUT QUINN'S BACKUP REACTOR.
PENCILED AND INKED BY GLENN FABRY
ADDITIONAL INKS BY LIAM SHARP
COLORS BY DAVID BARON
LETTERING BY MICHAEL HEISLER
BUT...THAT MEANS...
IT MEANS WE SAVED A LOT OF LIVES. AND IT MEANS BIG WHEEL WILL BE OFF LIMITS FOR FIFTY YEARS.
AND THE RADIATION WILL CORRUPT ALL THE INFORMATION ON THEIR COMPUTERS-- THE INFORMATION THEY DIDN'T GIVE UP.
EDITED BY SCOTT DUNBIER
NO MORE RICHARD QUINNS.
FOR A WHILE.
CREATED AND WRITTEN BY WARREN ELLIS
END

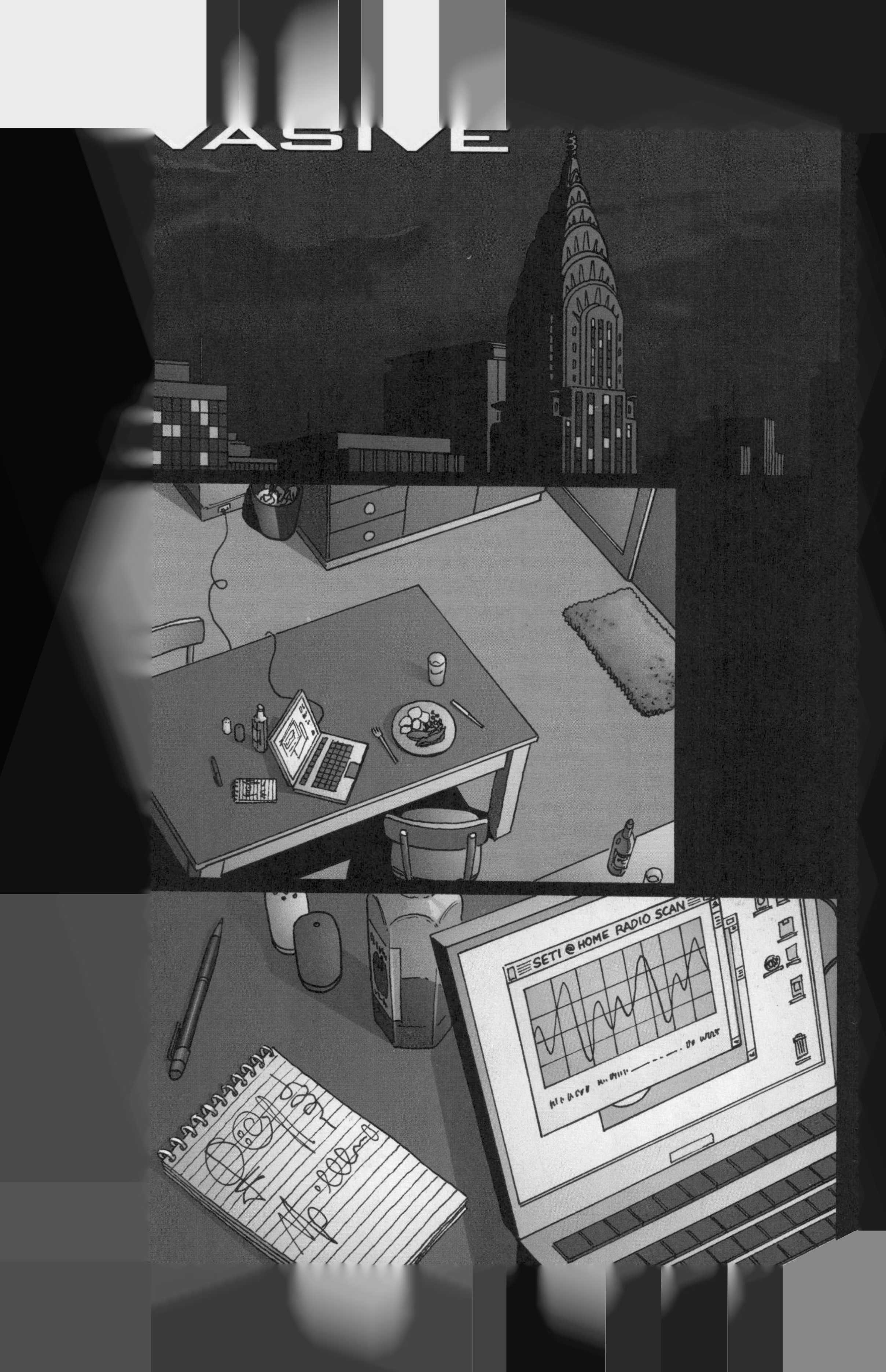

VASIVE
SETI @ HOME RADIO SCAN

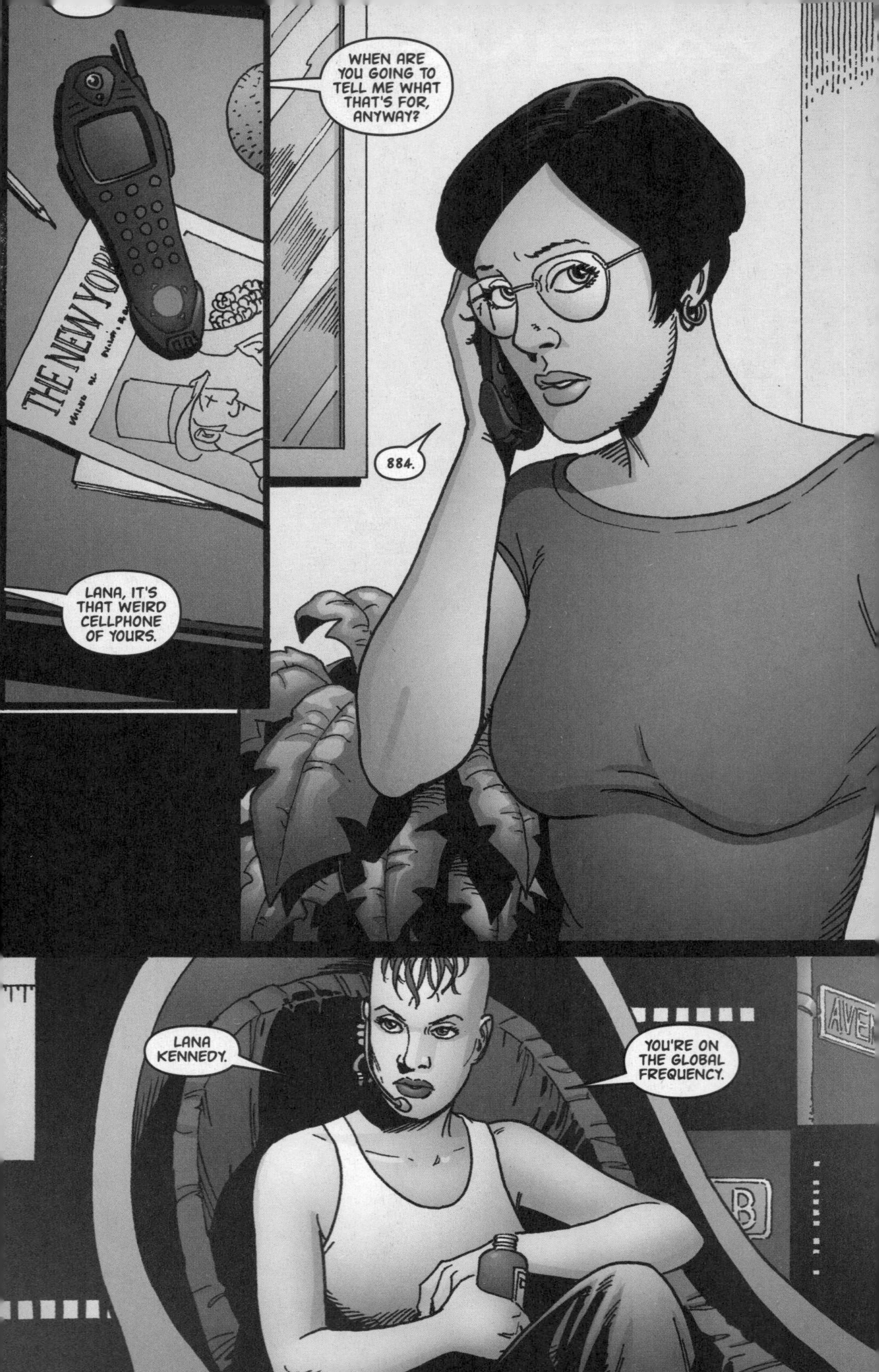
THE NEW YORK
LANA, IT'S THAT WEIRD CELLPHONE OF YOURS.
884.
WHEN ARE YOU GOING TO TELL ME WHAT THAT'S FOR, ANYWAY?
LANA KENNEDY.
YOU'RE ON THE GLOBAL FREQUENCY.

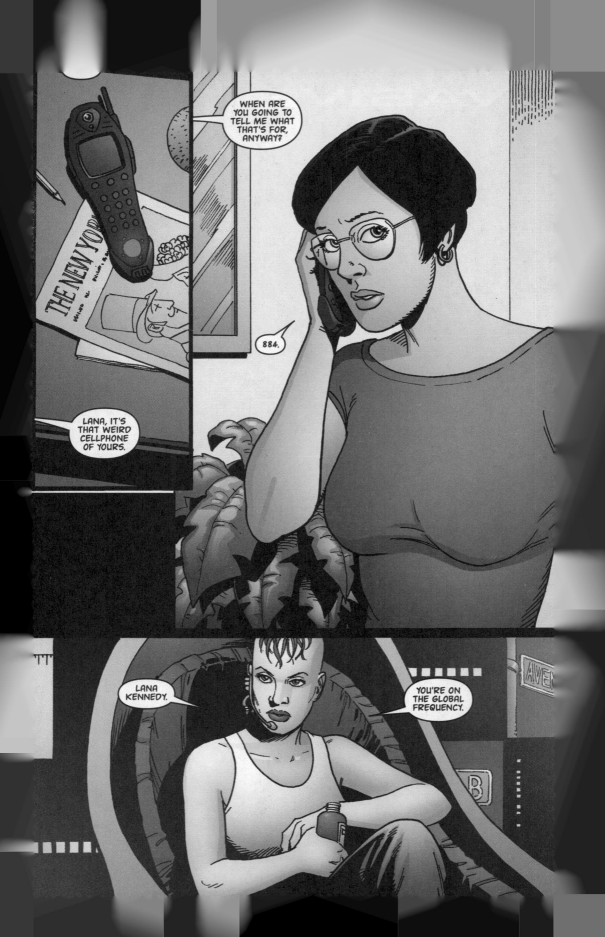

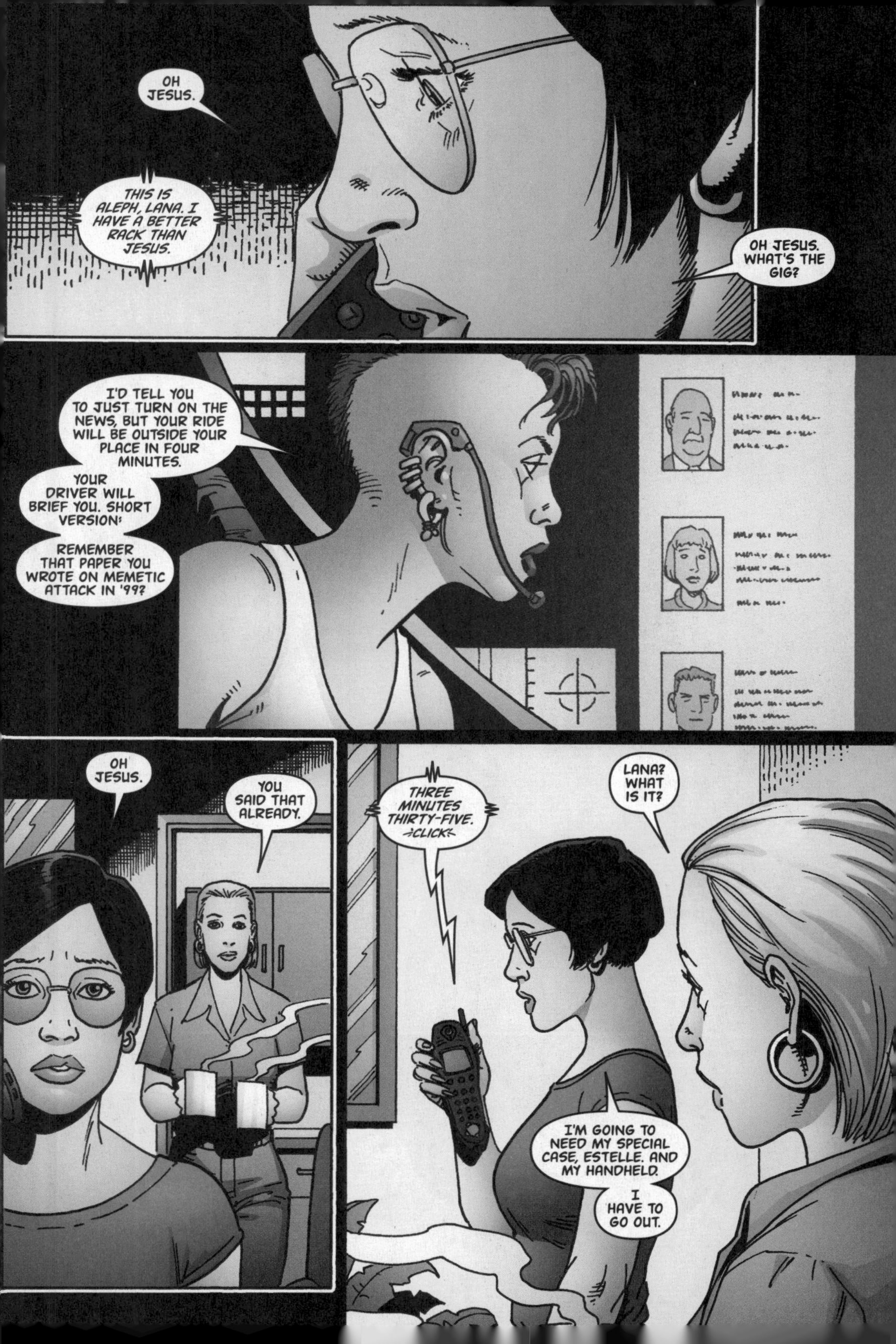

OH JESUS.
THIS IS ALEPH, LANA. I HAVE A BETTER RACK THAN JESUS.
OH JESUS. WHAT'S THE GIG?
I'D TELL YOU TO JUST TURN ON THE NEWS, BUT YOUR RIDE WILL BE OUTSIDE YOUR PLACE IN FOUR MINUTES.
YOUR DRIVER WILL BRIEF YOU. SHORT VERSION:
REMEMBER THAT PAPER YOU WROTE ON MEMETIC ATTACK IN '99?
OH JESUS.
YOU SAID THAT ALREADY.
THREE MINUTES THIRTY-FIVE.
CLICK
LANA? WHAT IS IT?
I'M GOING TO NEED MY SPECIAL CASE, ESTELLE. AND MY HANDHELD.
I HAVE TO GO OUT.

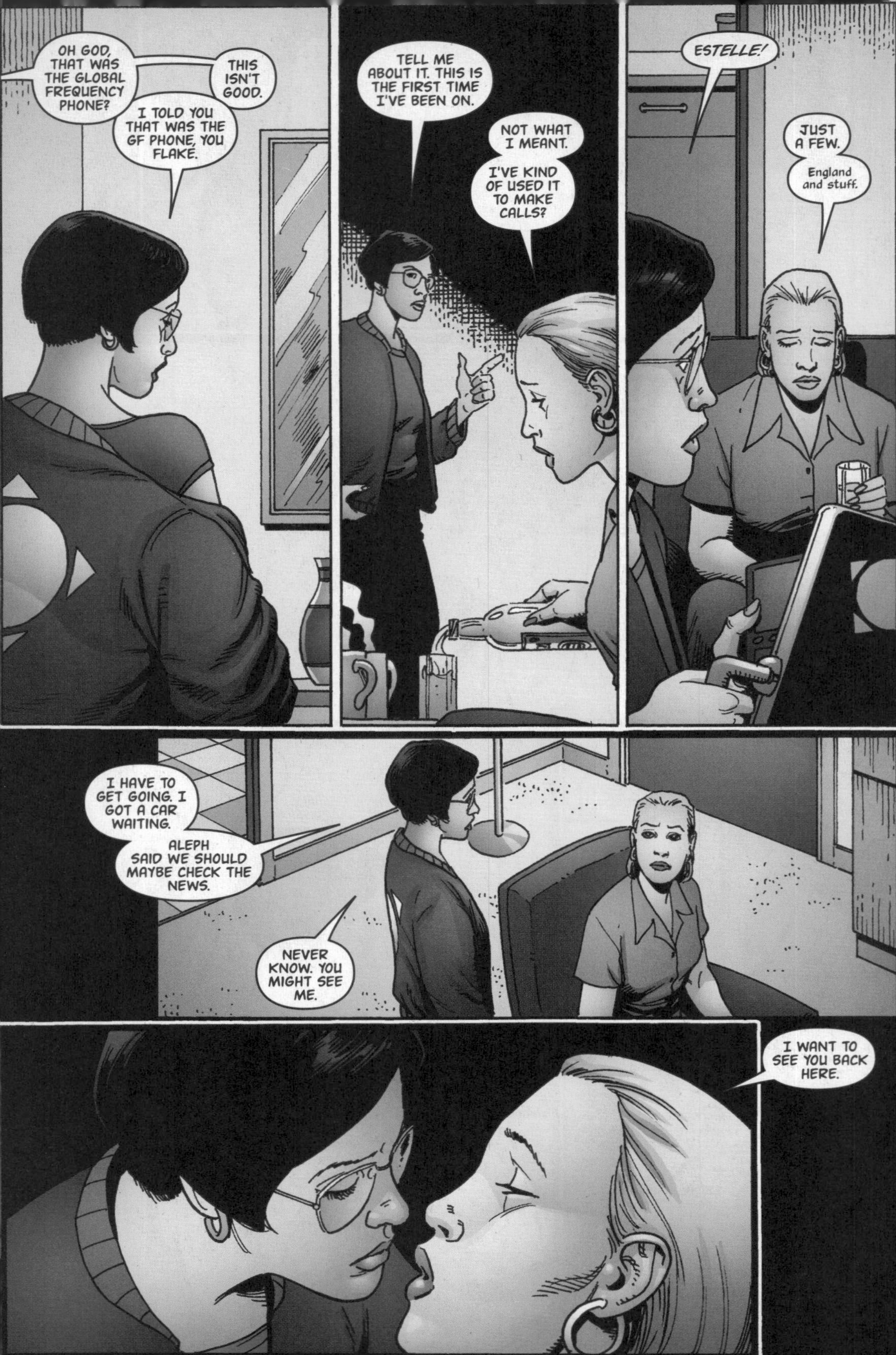
OH GOD, THAT WAS THE GLOBAL FREQUENCY PHONE?
THIS ISN'T GOOD.
I TOLD YOU THAT WAS THE GF PHONE, YOU FLAKE.
TELL ME ABOUT IT. THIS IS THE FIRST TIME I'VE BEEN ON.
NOT WHAT I MEANT.
I'VE KIND OF USED IT TO MAKE CALLS?
ESTELLE!
JUST A FEW.
England and stuff.
I HAVE TO GET GOING. I GOT A CAR WAITING.
ALEPH SAID WE SHOULD MAYBE CHECK THE NEWS.
NEVER KNOW. YOU MIGHT SEE ME.
I WANT TO SEE YOU BACK HERE.

I'M NICK CHO, ON THE FREQUENCY.

LET'S RIDE.

ALEPH, I GOT LANA KENNEDY AND WE'RE EN ROUTE.

WE'RE GOING TO SEE IF WE CAN GET YOU THERE A LITTLE FASTER. MS. ZERO IS ALREADY ON THE SCENE.

MIRANDA ZERO? REALLY? EXTREMELY COOL! ONLY MET HER ONCE. YOU?

JUST THE ONCE. LISTEN, SHOULD YOU HAVE YOUR FOOT DOWN IN--

HA! CHECK THIS OUT!

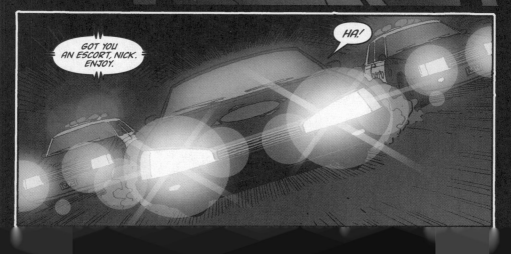

GOT YOU AN ESCORT, NICK. ENJOY.

HA!

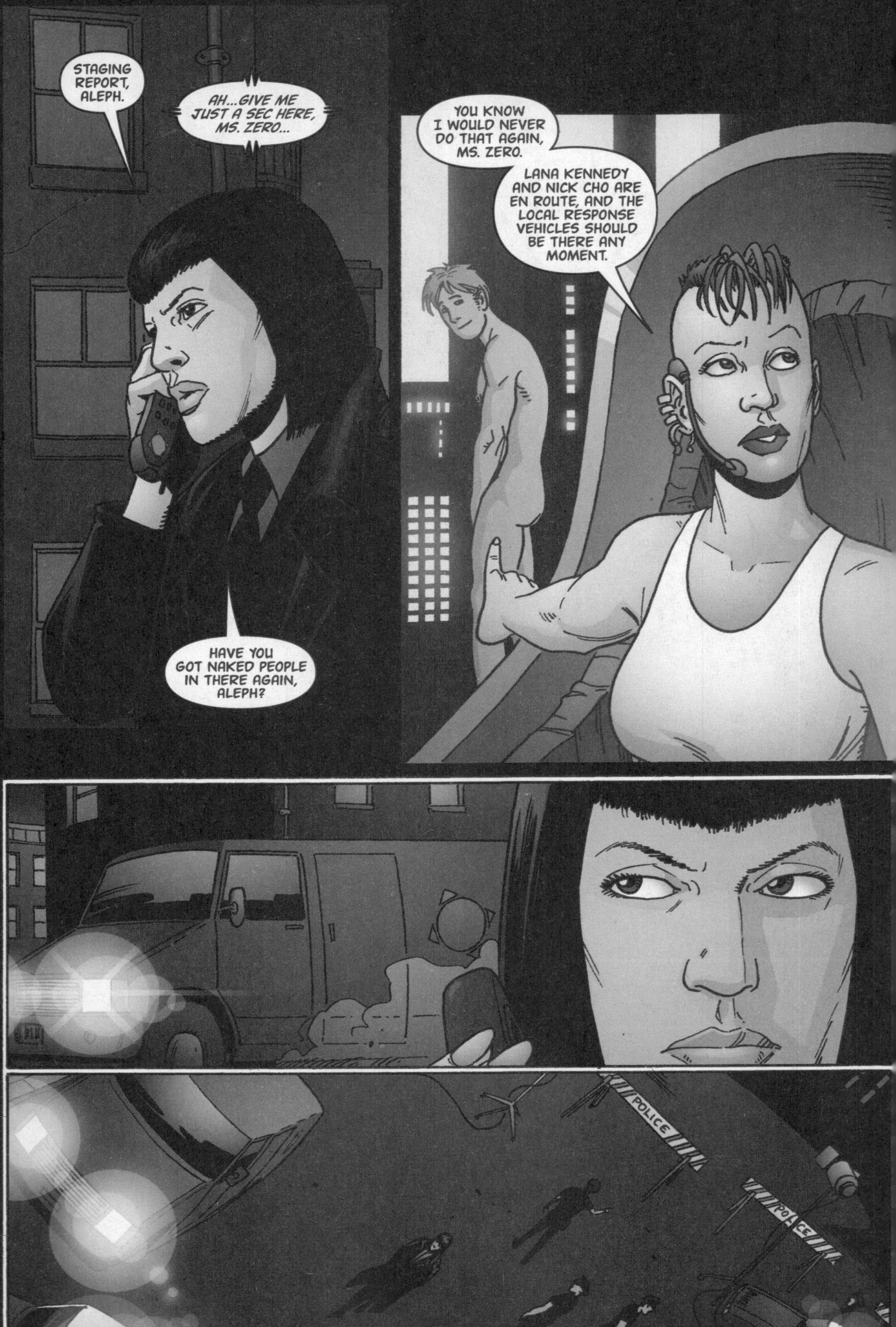
STAGING REPORT, ALEPH.
AH...GIVE ME JUST A SEC HERE, MS. ZERO...
HAVE YOU GOT NAKED PEOPLE IN THERE AGAIN, ALEPH?
YOU KNOW I WOULD NEVER DO THAT AGAIN, MS. ZERO.
LANA KENNEDY AND NICK CHO ARE EN ROUTE, AND THE LOCAL RESPONSE VEHICLES SHOULD BE THERE ANY MOMENT.
POLICE
POLICE

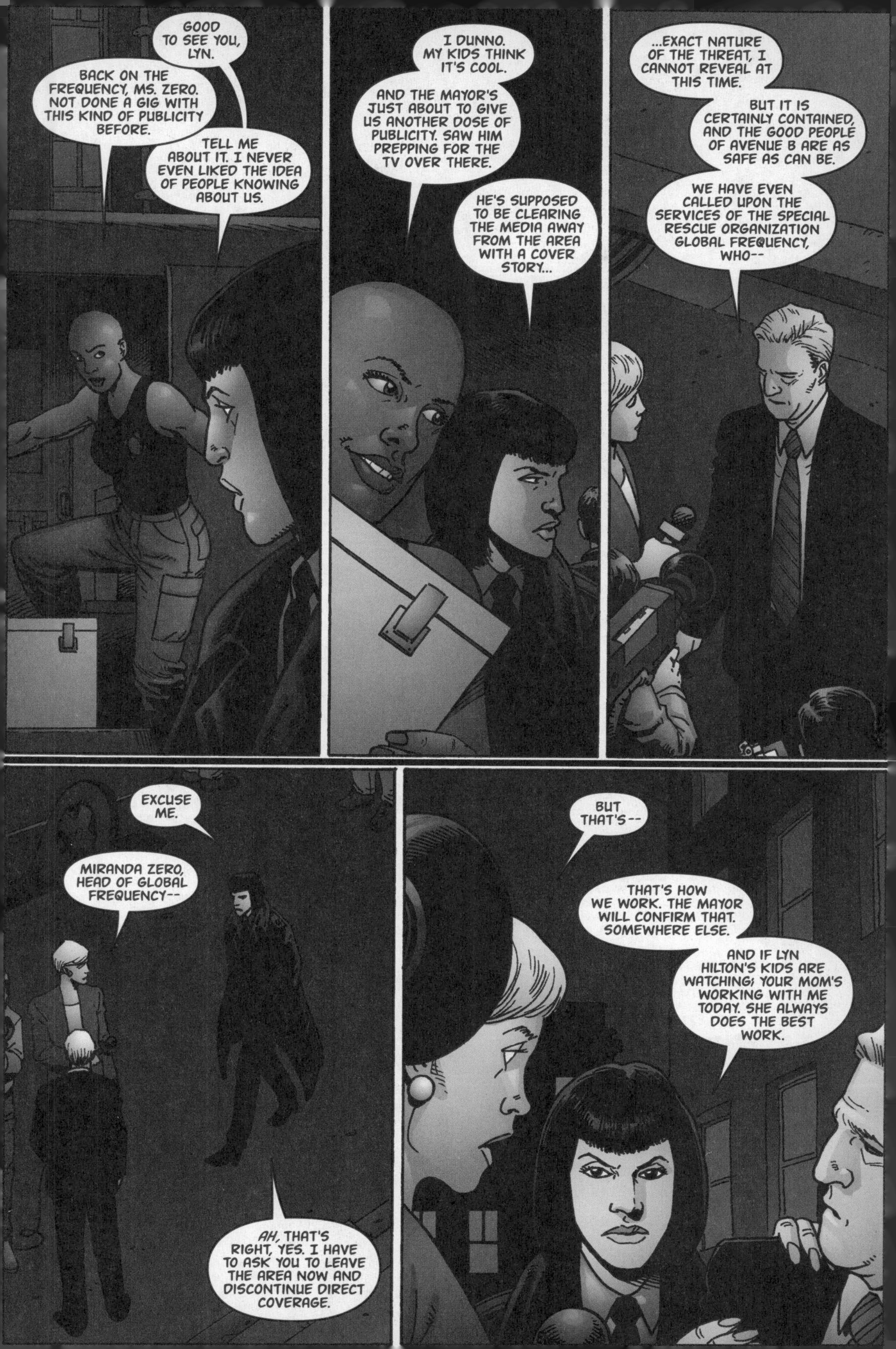
GOOD TO SEE YOU, LYN.
BACK ON THE FREQUENCY, MS. ZERO. NOT DONE A GIG WITH THIS KIND OF PUBLICITY BEFORE.
TELL ME ABOUT IT. I NEVER EVEN LIKED THE IDEA OF PEOPLE KNOWING ABOUT US.
I DUNNO. MY KIDS THINK IT'S COOL.
AND THE MAYOR'S JUST ABOUT TO GIVE US ANOTHER DOSE OF PUBLICITY. SAW HIM PREPPING FOR THE TV OVER THERE.
HE'S SUPPOSED TO BE CLEARING THE MEDIA AWAY FROM THE AREA WITH A COVER STORY...
...EXACT NATURE OF THE THREAT, I CANNOT REVEAL AT THIS TIME.
BUT IT IS CERTAINLY CONTAINED, AND THE GOOD PEOPLE OF AVENUE B ARE AS SAFE AS CAN BE.
WE HAVE EVEN CALLED UPON THE SERVICES OF THE SPECIAL RESCUE ORGANIZATION GLOBAL FREQUENCY, WHO--
EXCUSE ME.
MIRANDA ZERO, HEAD OF GLOBAL FREQUENCY--
AH, THAT'S RIGHT, YES. I HAVE TO ASK YOU TO LEAVE THE AREA NOW AND DISCONTINUE DIRECT COVERAGE.
BUT THAT'S--
THAT'S HOW WE WORK. THE MAYOR WILL CONFIRM THAT. SOMEWHERE ELSE.
AND IF LYN HILTON'S KIDS ARE WATCHING; YOUR MOM'S WORKING WITH ME TODAY. SHE ALWAYS DOES THE BEST WORK.

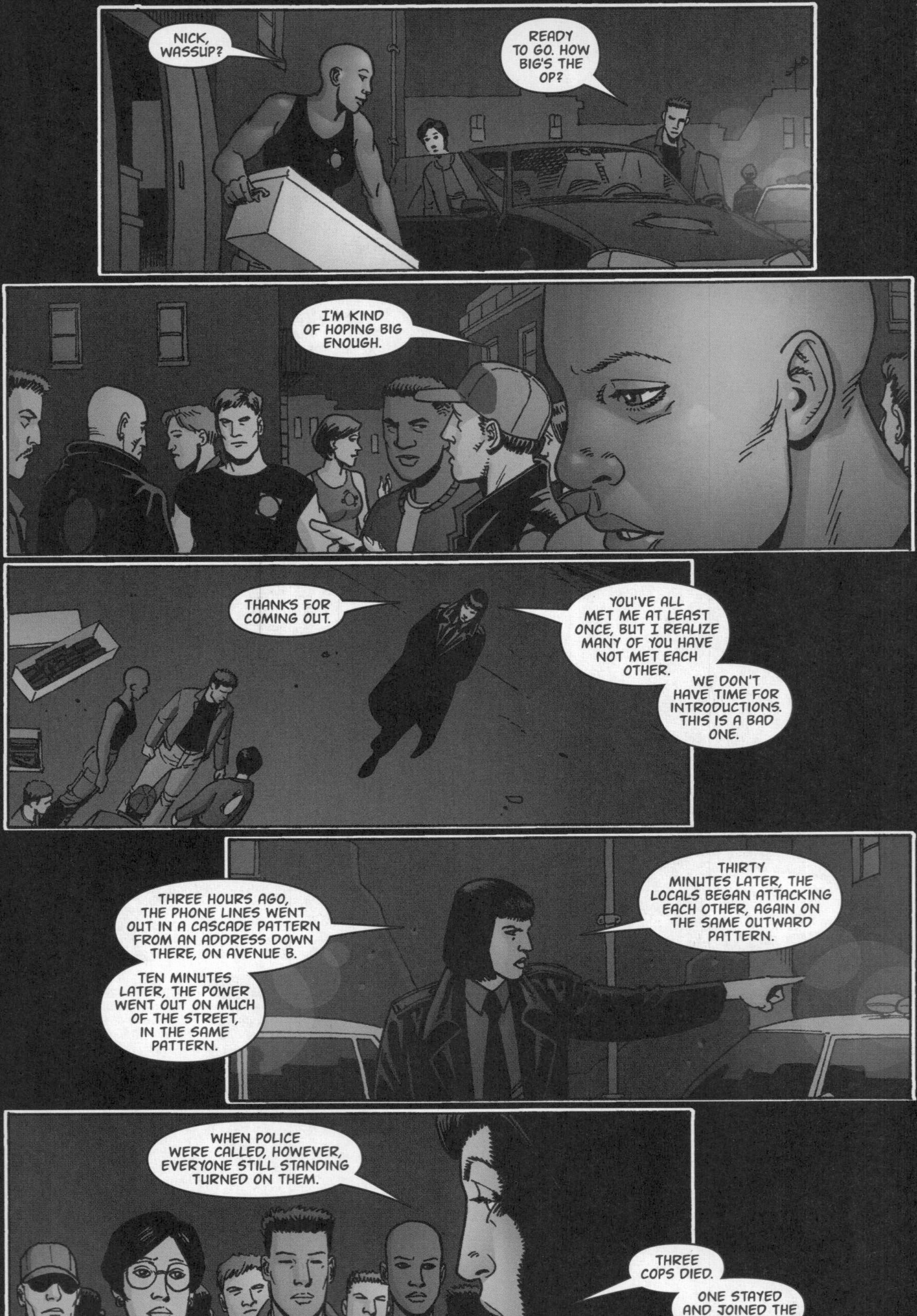
NICK, WASSUP?
READY TO GO. HOW BIG'S THE OP?
I'M KIND OF HOPING BIG ENOUGH.
THANKS FOR COMING OUT.
YOU'VE ALL MET ME AT LEAST ONCE, BUT I REALIZE MANY OF YOU HAVE NOT MET EACH OTHER.
WE DON'T HAVE TIME FOR INTRODUCTIONS. THIS IS A BAD ONE.
THREE HOURS AGO, THE PHONE LINES WENT OUT IN A CASCADE PATTERN FROM AN ADDRESS DOWN THERE, ON AVENUE B.
TEN MINUTES LATER, THE POWER WENT OUT ON MUCH OF THE STREET, IN THE SAME PATTERN.
THIRTY MINUTES LATER, THE LOCALS BEGAN ATTACKING EACH OTHER, AGAIN ON THE SAME OUTWARD PATTERN.
WHEN POLICE WERE CALLED, HOWEVER, EVERYONE STILL STANDING TURNED ON THEM.
THREE COPS DIED.
ONE STAYED AND JOINED THE PACK.

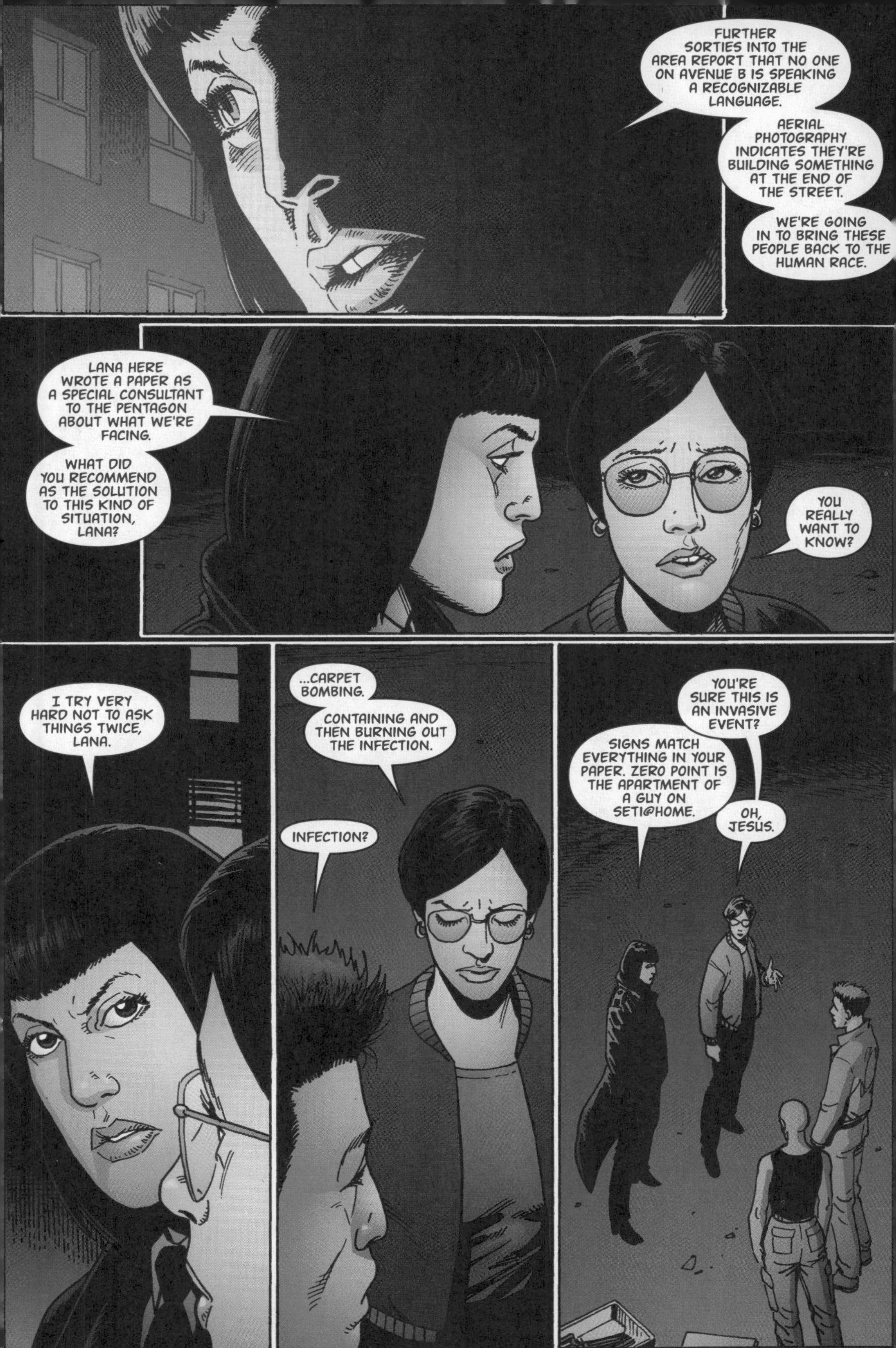
FURTHER SORTIES INTO THE AREA REPORT THAT NO ONE ON AVENUE B IS SPEAKING A RECOGNIZABLE LANGUAGE.
AERIAL PHOTOGRAPHY INDICATES THEY'RE BUILDING SOMETHING AT THE END OF THE STREET.
WE'RE GOING IN TO BRING THESE PEOPLE BACK TO THE HUMAN RACE.
LANA HERE WROTE A PAPER AS A SPECIAL CONSULTANT TO THE PENTAGON ABOUT WHAT WE'RE FACING.
WHAT DID YOU RECOMMEND AS THE SOLUTION TO THIS KIND OF SITUATION, LANA?
YOU REALLY WANT TO KNOW?
I TRY VERY HARD NOT TO ASK THINGS TWICE, LANA.
...CARPET BOMBING.
CONTAINING AND THEN BURNING OUT THE INFECTION.
INFECTION?
YOU'RE SURE THIS IS AN INVASIVE EVENT?
SIGNS MATCH EVERYTHING IN YOUR PAPER. ZERO POINT IS THE APARTMENT OF A GUY ON SETI@HOME.
OH, JESUS.

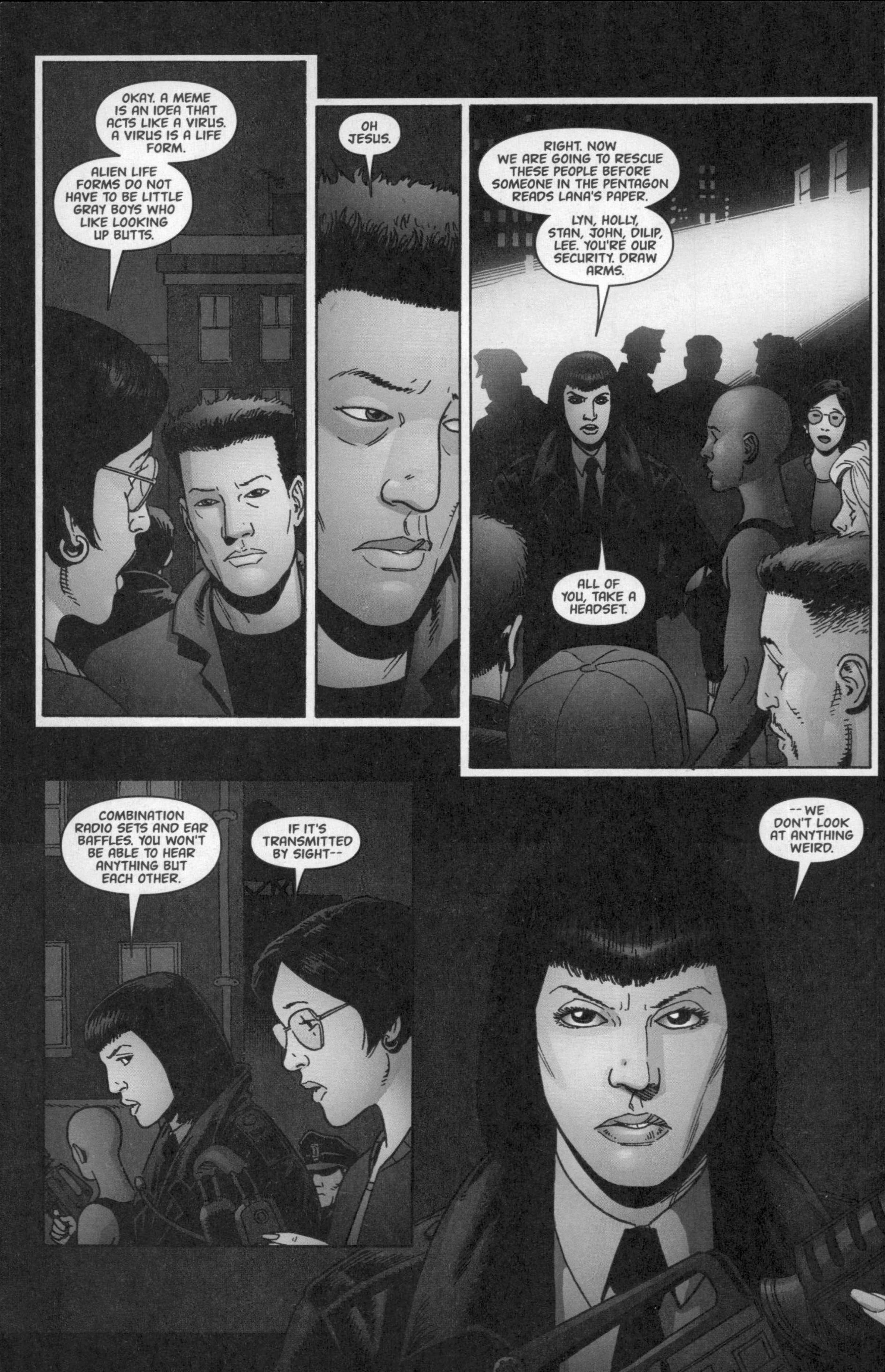
OKAY. A MEME IS AN IDEA THAT ACTS LIKE A VIRUS. A VIRUS IS A LIFE FORM.
ALIEN LIFE FORMS DO NOT HAVE TO BE LITTLE GRAY BOYS WHO LIKE LOOKING UP BUTTS.
OH JESUS.
RIGHT. NOW WE ARE GOING TO RESCUE THESE PEOPLE BEFORE SOMEONE IN THE PENTAGON READS LANA'S PAPER.
LYN, HOLLY, STAN, JOHN, DILIP, LEE. YOU'RE OUR SECURITY. DRAW ARMS.
ALL OF YOU, TAKE A HEADSET.
COMBINATION RADIO SETS AND EAR BAFFLES. YOU WON'T BE ABLE TO HEAR ANYTHING BUT EACH OTHER.
IF IT'S TRANSMITTED BY SIGHT--
--WE DON'T LOOK AT ANYTHING WEIRD.

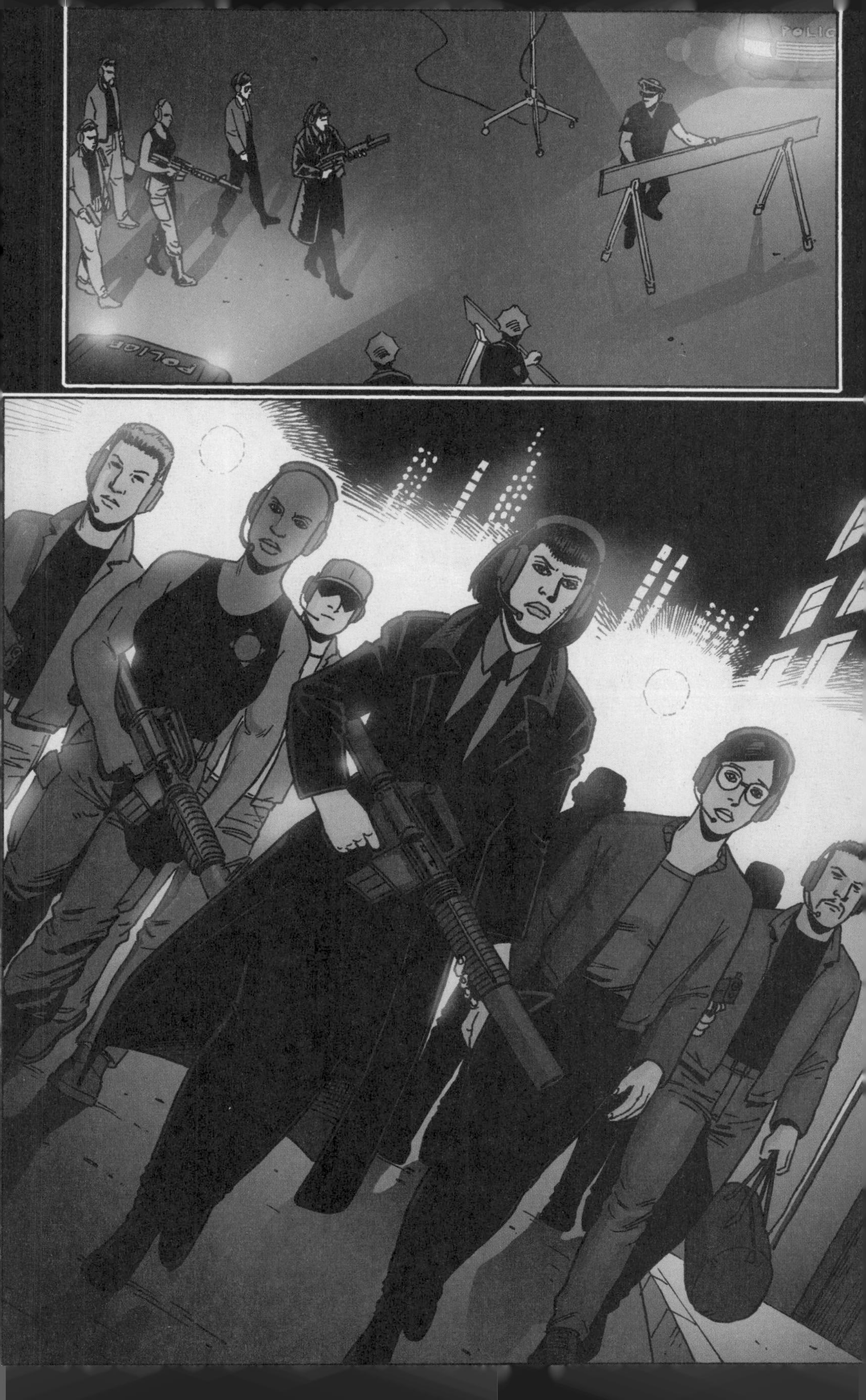
POLIC

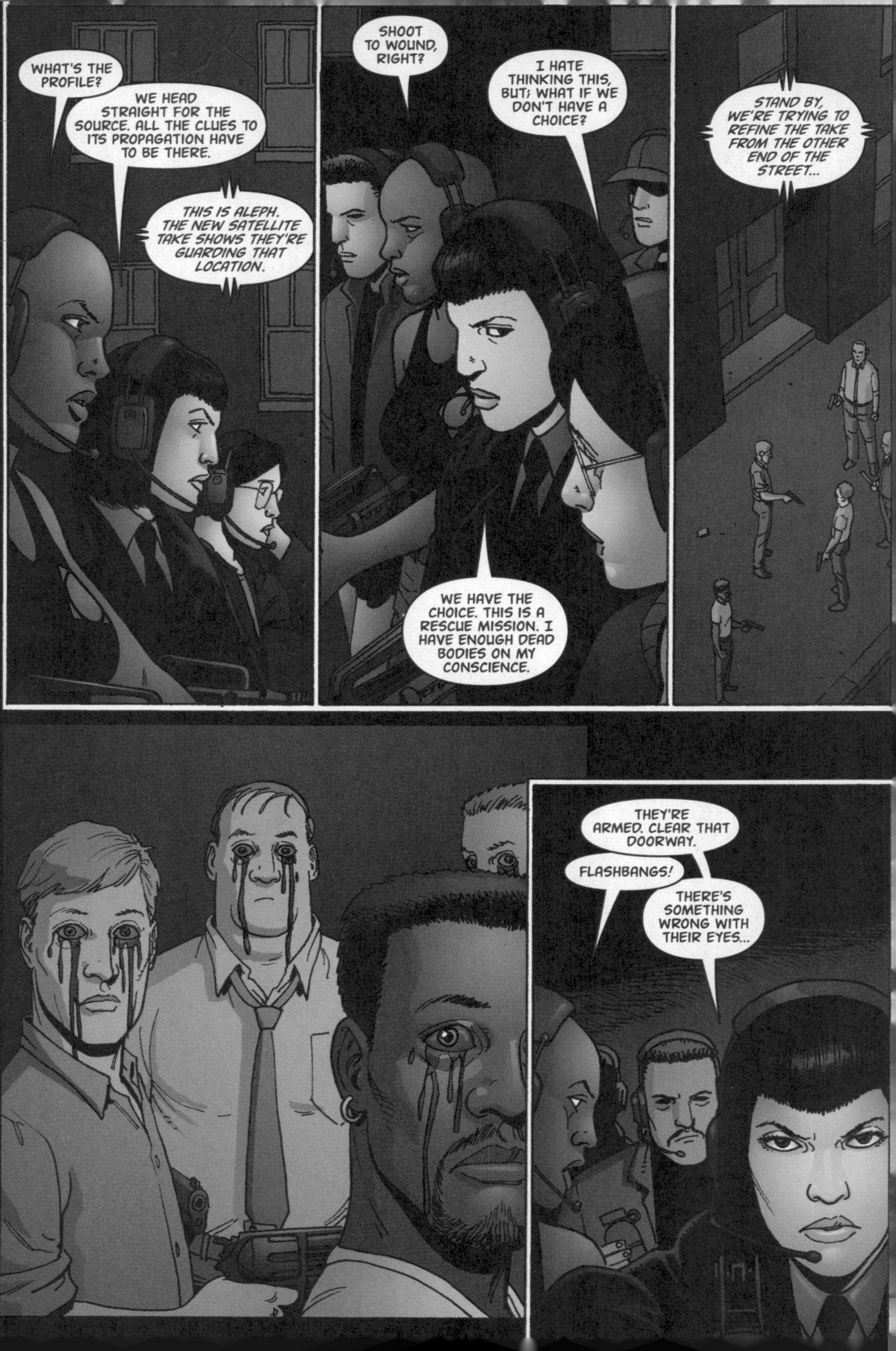
WHAT'S THE PROFILE?
WE HEAD STRAIGHT FOR THE SOURCE. ALL THE CLUES TO ITS PROPAGATION HAVE TO BE THERE.
THIS IS ALEPH. THE NEW SATELLITE TAKE SHOWS THEY'RE GUARDING THAT LOCATION.
SHOOT TO WOUND, RIGHT?
I HATE THINKING THIS, BUT; WHAT IF WE DON'T HAVE A CHOICE?
WE HAVE THE CHOICE. THIS IS A RESCUE MISSION. I HAVE ENOUGH DEAD BODIES ON MY CONSCIENCE.
STAND BY, WE'RE TRYING TO REFINE THE TAKE FROM THE OTHER END OF THE STREET...
THEY'RE ARMED. CLEAR THAT DOORWAY.
FLASHBANGS!
THERE'S SOMETHING WRONG WITH THEIR EYES...

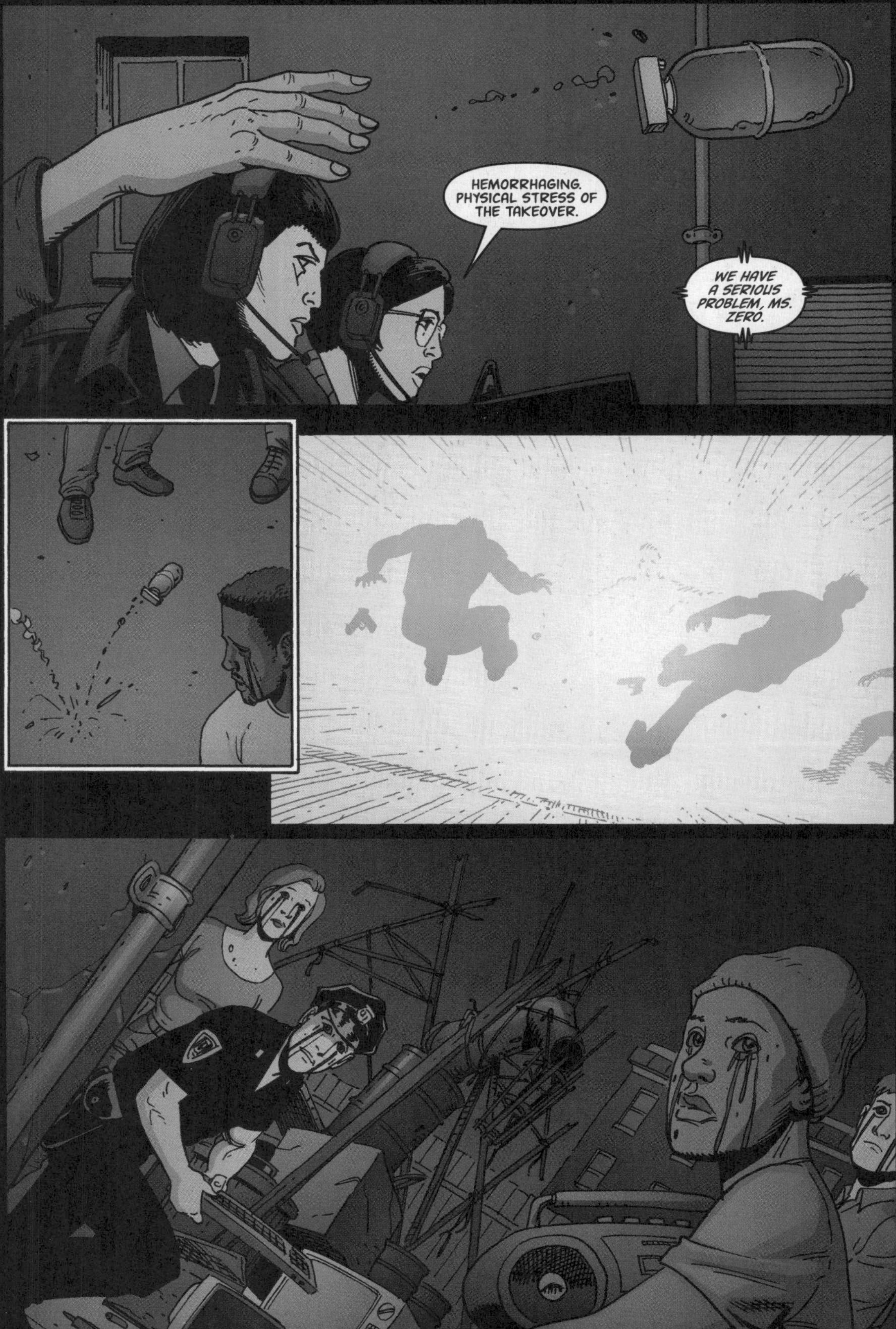
HEMORRHAGING. PHYSICAL STRESS OF THE TAKEOVER.
WE HAVE A SERIOUS PROBLEM, MS. ZERO.

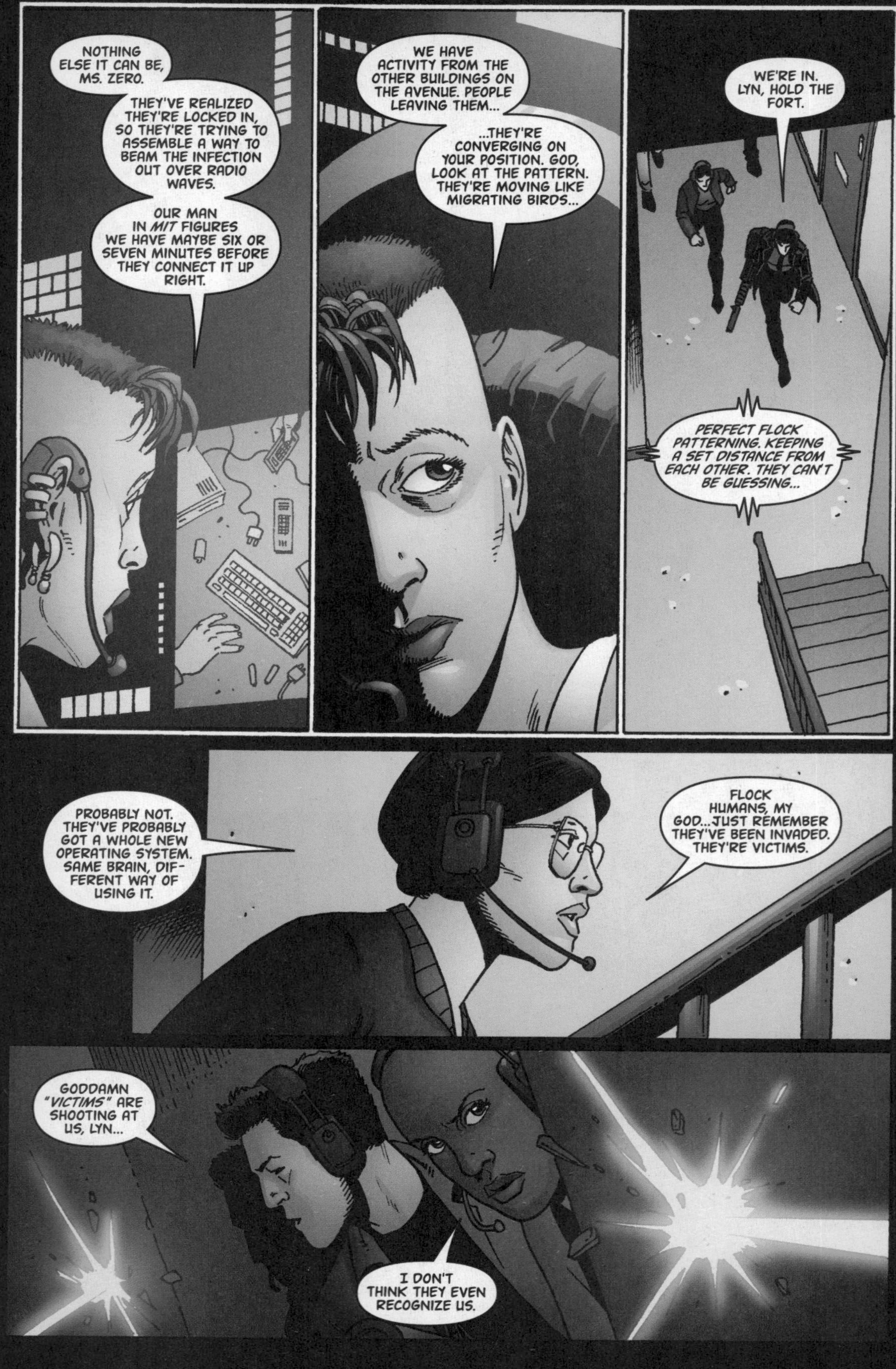
NOTHING ELSE IT CAN BE, MS. ZERO.
THEY'VE REALIZED THEY'RE LOCKED IN, SO THEY'RE TRYING TO ASSEMBLE A WAY TO BEAM THE INFECTION OUT OVER RADIO WAVES.
OUR MAN IN *MIT* FIGURES WE HAVE MAYBE SIX OR SEVEN MINUTES BEFORE THEY CONNECT IT UP RIGHT.
WE HAVE ACTIVITY FROM THE OTHER BUILDINGS ON THE AVENUE. PEOPLE LEAVING THEM...
...THEY'RE CONVERGING ON YOUR POSITION. GOD, LOOK AT THE PATTERN. THEY'RE MOVING LIKE MIGRATING BIRDS...
WE'RE IN. LYN, HOLD THE FORT.
PERFECT FLOCK PATTERNING. KEEPING A SET DISTANCE FROM EACH OTHER. THEY CAN'T BE GUESSING...
PROBABLY NOT. THEY'VE PROBABLY GOT A WHOLE NEW OPERATING SYSTEM. SAME BRAIN, DIFFERENT WAY OF USING IT.
FLOCK HUMANS, MY GOD...JUST REMEMBER THEY'VE BEEN INVADED. THEY'RE VICTIMS.
GODDAMN *"VICTIMS"* ARE SHOOTING AT US, LYN...
I DON'T THINK THEY EVEN RECOGNIZE US.

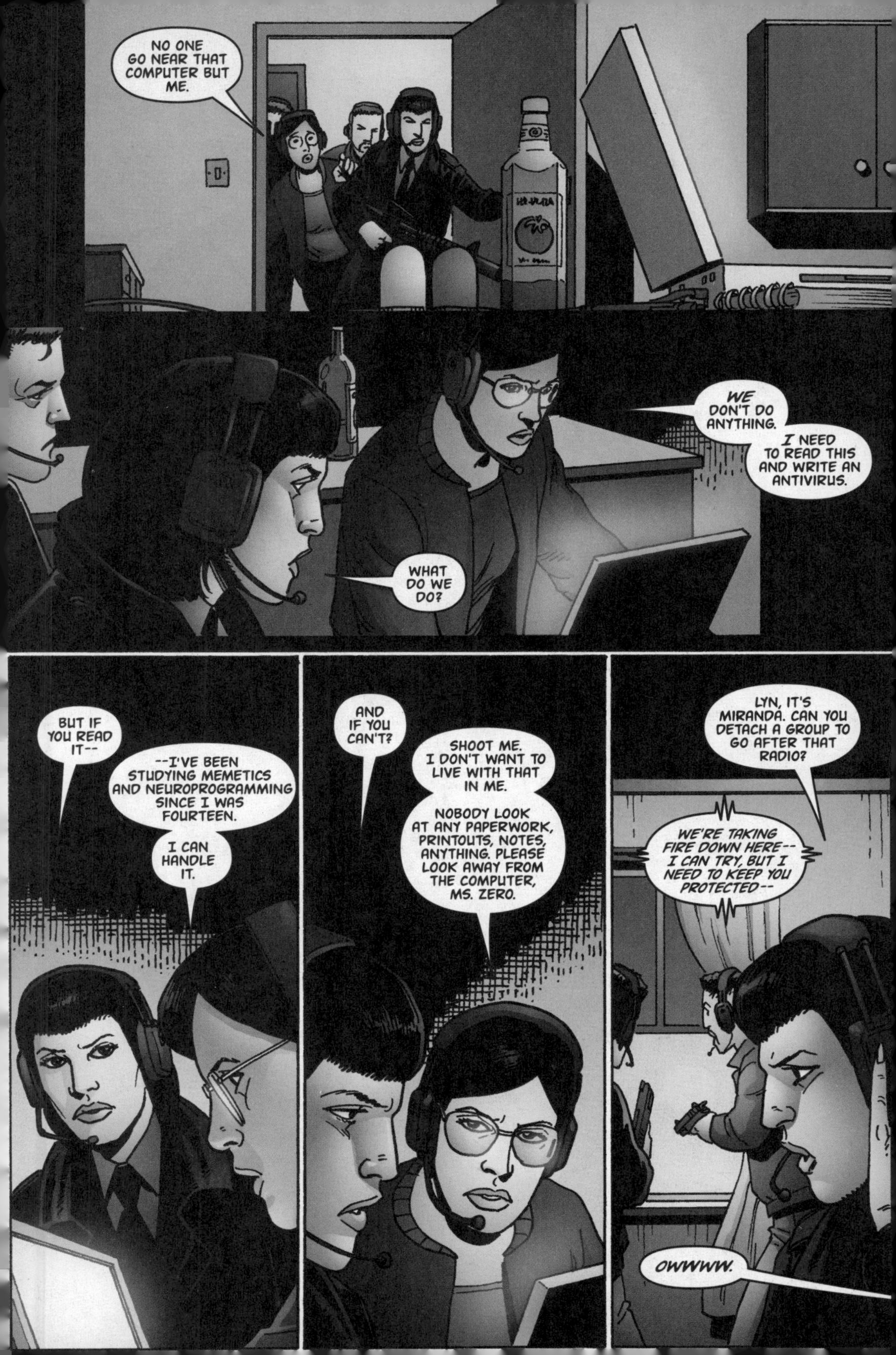
NO ONE GO NEAR THAT COMPUTER BUT ME.
WE DON'T DO ANYTHING.
I NEED TO READ THIS AND WRITE AN ANTIVIRUS.
WHAT DO WE DO?
BUT IF YOU READ IT--
--I'VE BEEN STUDYING MEMETICS AND NEUROPROGRAMMING SINCE I WAS FOURTEEN.
I CAN HANDLE IT.
AND IF YOU CAN'T?
SHOOT ME. I DON'T WANT TO LIVE WITH THAT IN ME.
NOBODY LOOK AT ANY PAPERWORK, PRINTOUTS, NOTES, ANYTHING. PLEASE LOOK AWAY FROM THE COMPUTER, MS. ZERO.
LYN, IT'S MIRANDA. CAN YOU DETACH A GROUP TO GO AFTER THAT RADIO?
WE'RE TAKING FIRE DOWN HERE-- I CAN TRY, BUT I NEED TO KEEP YOU PROTECTED--
OWWWW.

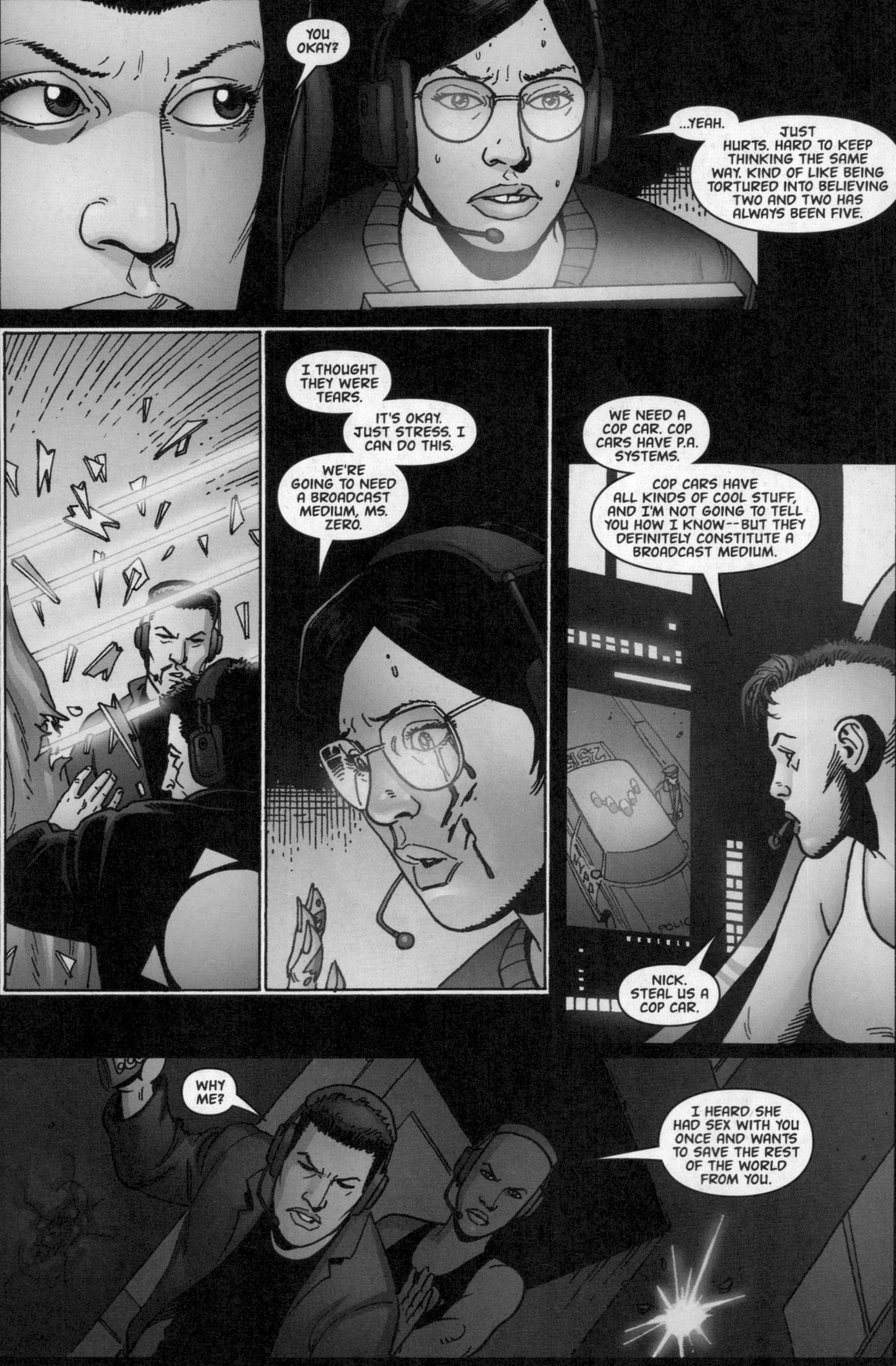
YOU OKAY?
...YEAH.
JUST HURTS. HARD TO KEEP THINKING THE SAME WAY. KIND OF LIKE BEING TORTURED INTO BELIEVING TWO AND TWO HAS ALWAYS BEEN FIVE.
I THOUGHT THEY WERE TEARS.
IT'S OKAY. JUST STRESS. I CAN DO THIS.
WE'RE GOING TO NEED A BROADCAST MEDIUM, MS. ZERO.
WE NEED A COP CAR. COP CARS HAVE P.A. SYSTEMS.
COP CARS HAVE ALL KINDS OF COOL STUFF, AND I'M NOT GOING TO TELL YOU HOW I KNOW--BUT THEY DEFINITELY CONSTITUTE A BROADCAST MEDIUM.
NICK. STEAL US A COP CAR.
WHY ME?
I HEARD SHE HAD SEX WITH YOU ONCE AND WANTS TO SAVE THE REST OF THE WORLD FROM YOU.

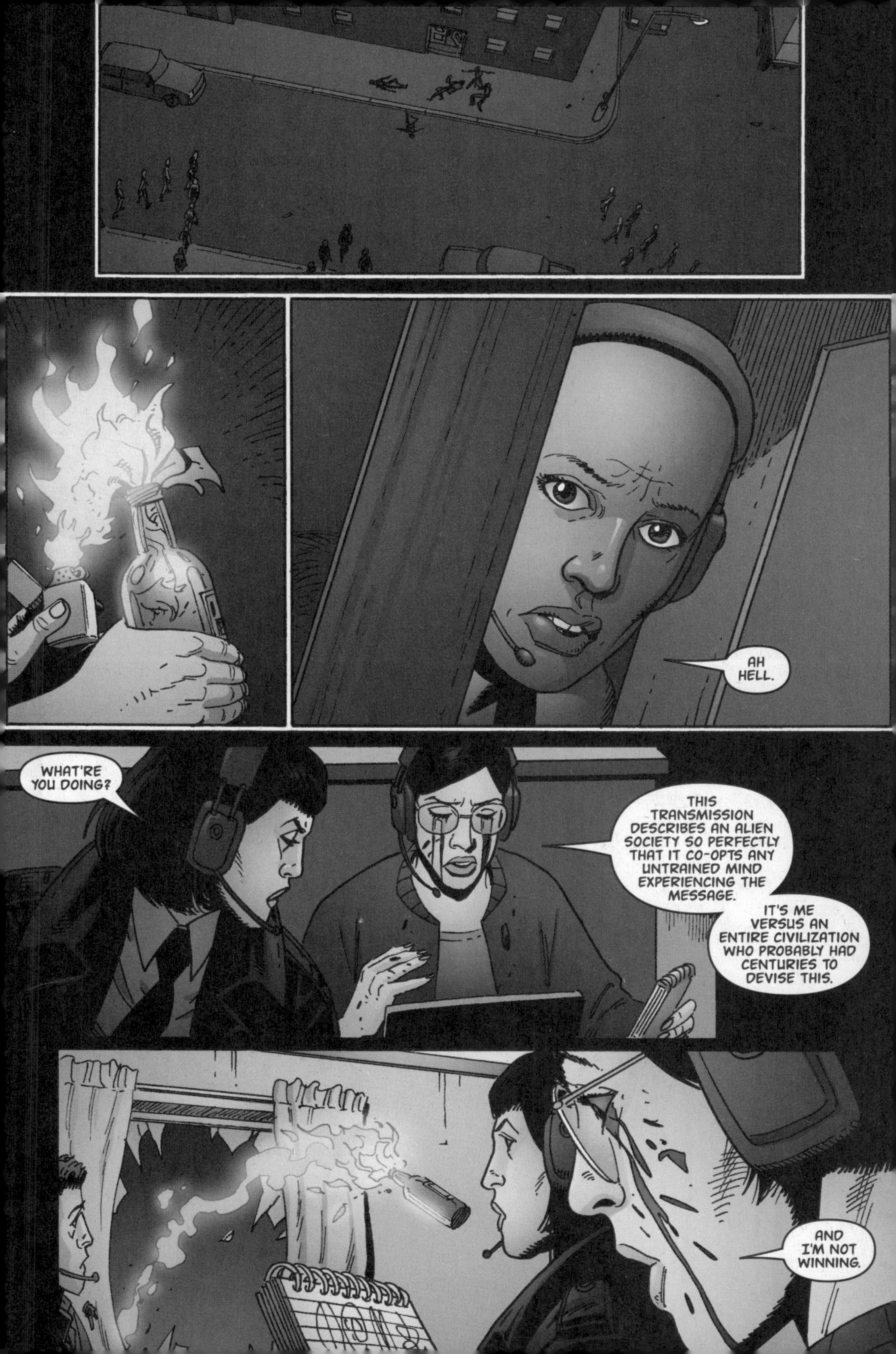
AH HELL.
WHAT'RE YOU DOING?
THIS TRANSMISSION DESCRIBES AN ALIEN SOCIETY SO PERFECTLY THAT IT CO-OPTS ANY UNTRAINED MIND EXPERIENCING THE MESSAGE.
IT'S ME VERSUS AN ENTIRE CIVILIZATION WHO PROBABLY HAD CENTURIES TO DEVISE THIS.
AND I'M NOT WINNING.

WHAT'S THE KEY, WHAT'S THE KEY...WHAT'S MISSING...

CAN WE TRANSFER THIS OUT OF HERE? WORK ON IT SOMEWHERE ELSE?

IT'S HERE AND NOW OR NOT AT ALL.

GREAT. WE'VE GOT TWO MINUTES BEFORE WE ALL DIE.

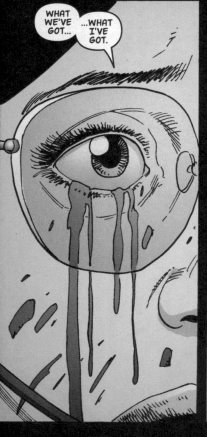

WHAT WE'VE GOT...   ...WHAT I'VE GOT.

WHAT DEFINES THE HUMAN RACE?

RIGHT NOW? ITS ABILITY TO PISS ME OFF.

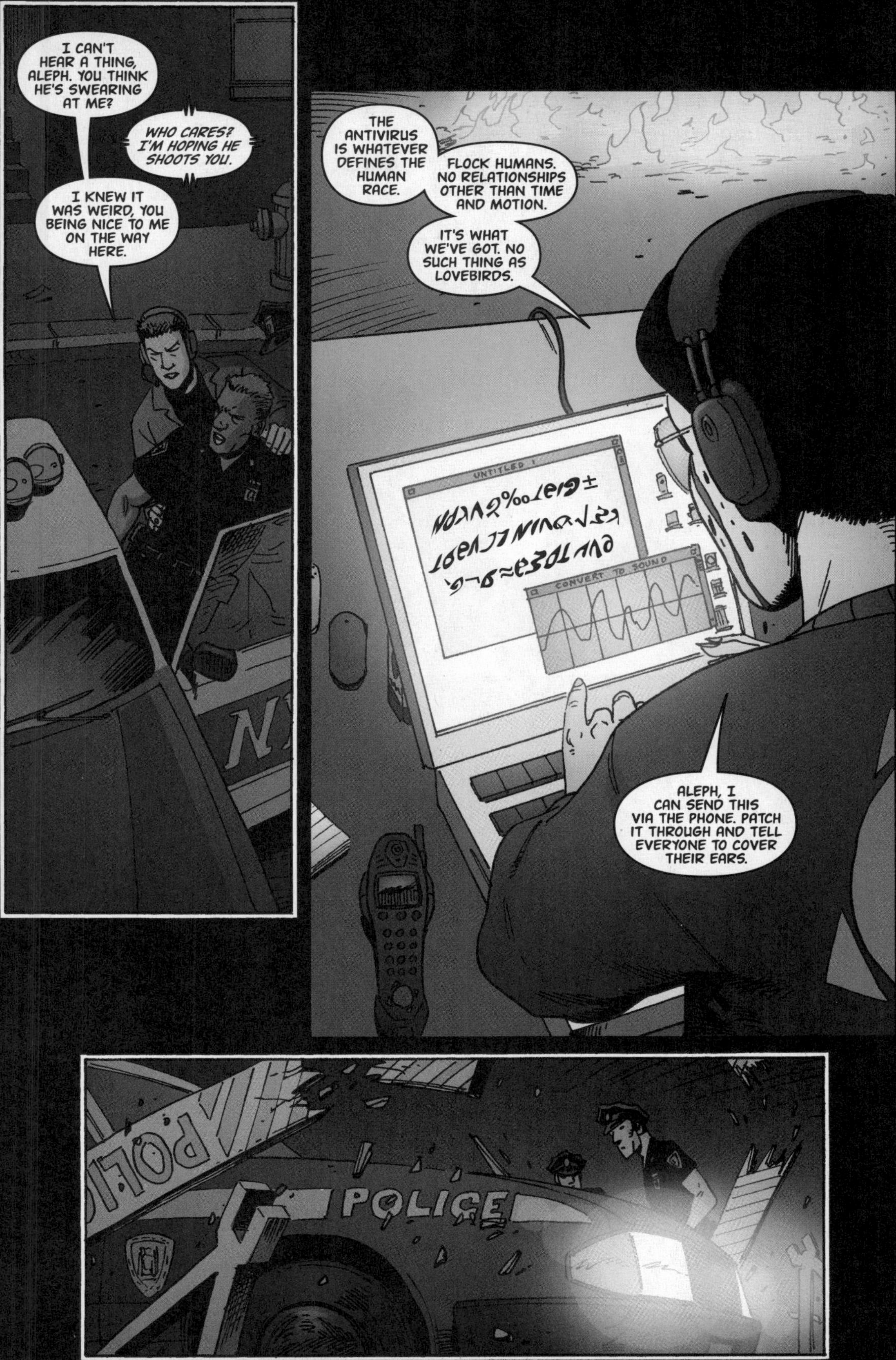

I CAN'T HEAR A THING, ALEPH. YOU THINK HE'S SWEARING AT ME?
WHO CARES? I'M HOPING HE SHOOTS YOU.
I KNEW IT WAS WEIRD, YOU BEING NICE TO ME ON THE WAY HERE.
THE ANTIVIRUS IS WHATEVER DEFINES THE HUMAN RACE.
FLOCK HUMANS. NO RELATIONSHIPS OTHER THAN TIME AND MOTION.
IT'S WHAT WE'VE GOT. NO SUCH THING AS LOVEBIRDS.
UNTITLED 1
CONVERT TO SOUND
ALEPH, I CAN SEND THIS VIA THE PHONE. PATCH IT THROUGH AND TELL EVERYONE TO COVER THEIR EARS.
POLICE

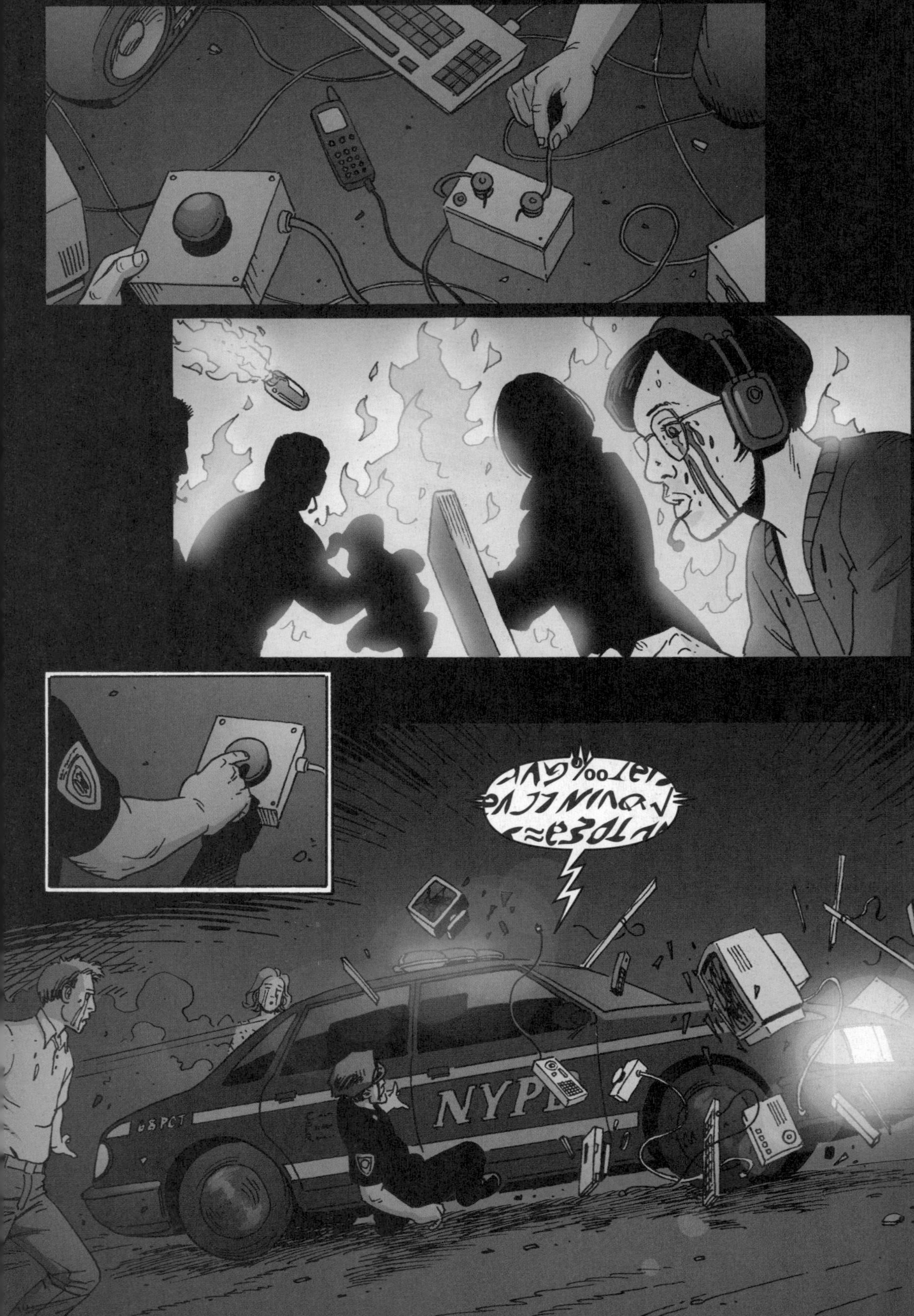

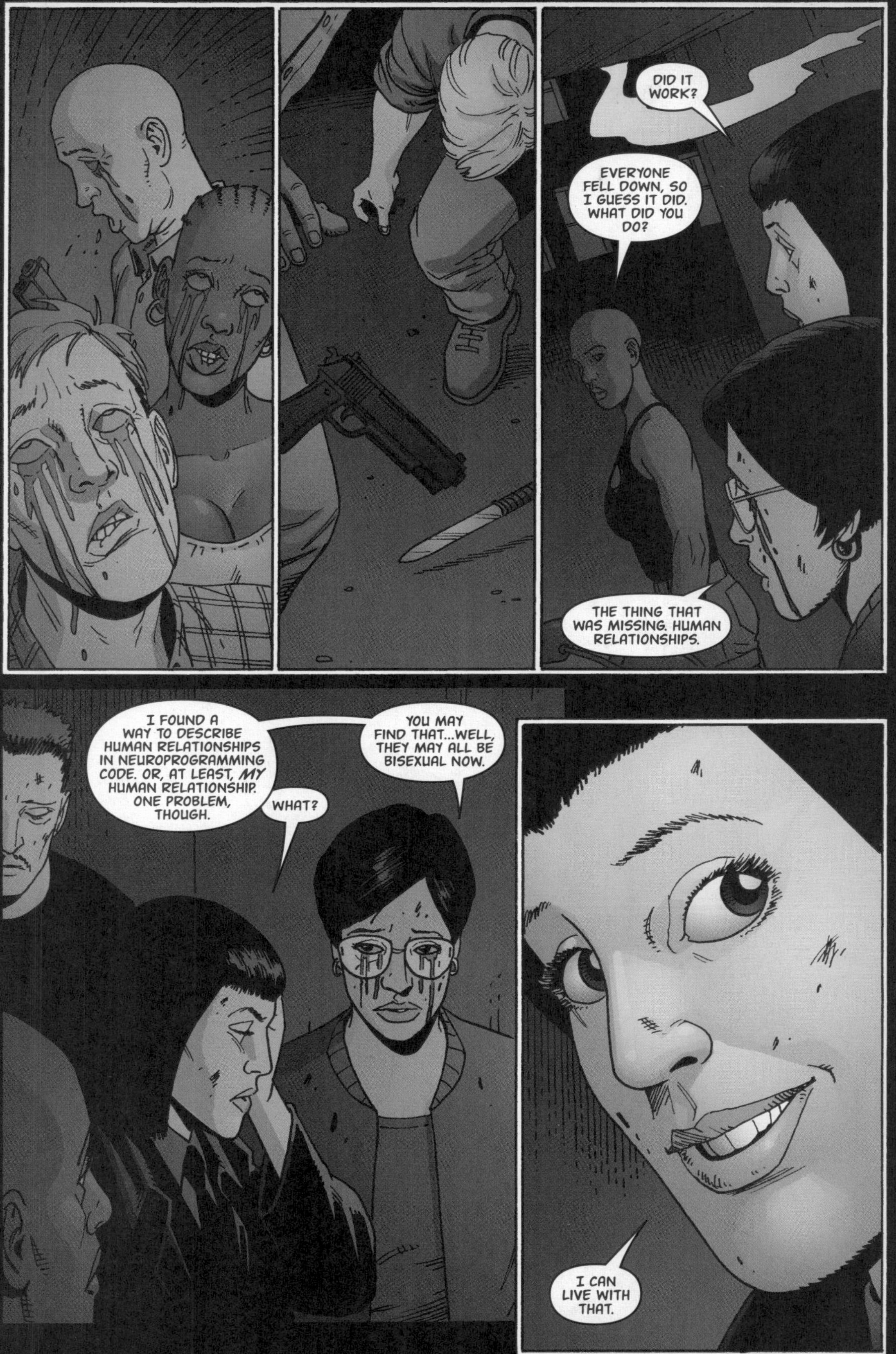
DID IT WORK?
EVERYONE FELL DOWN, SO I GUESS IT DID. WHAT DID YOU DO?
THE THING THAT WAS MISSING. HUMAN RELATIONSHIPS.
I FOUND A WAY TO DESCRIBE HUMAN RELATIONSHIPS IN NEUROPROGRAMMING CODE. OR, AT LEAST, *MY* HUMAN RELATIONSHIP. ONE PROBLEM, THOUGH.
WHAT?
YOU MAY FIND THAT...WELL, THEY MAY ALL BE BISEXUAL NOW.
I CAN LIVE WITH THAT.

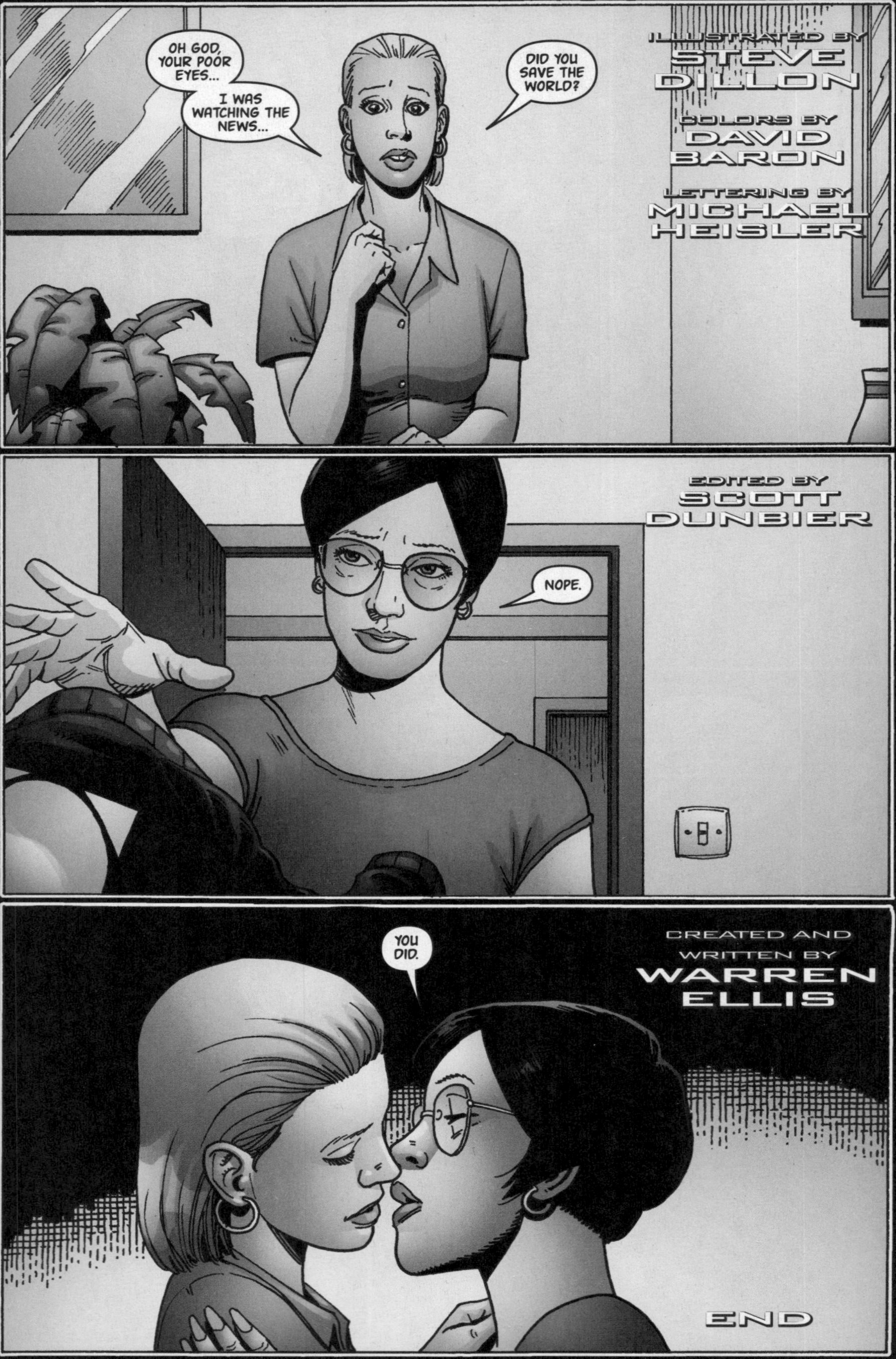
ILLUSTRATED BY
STEVE DILLON
COLORS BY
DAVID BARON
LETTERING BY
MICHAEL HEISLER
OH GOD, YOUR POOR EYES...
I WAS WATCHING THE NEWS...
DID YOU SAVE THE WORLD?
EDITED BY
SCOTT DUNBIER
NOPE.
CREATED AND WRITTEN BY
WARREN ELLIS
YOU DID.
END

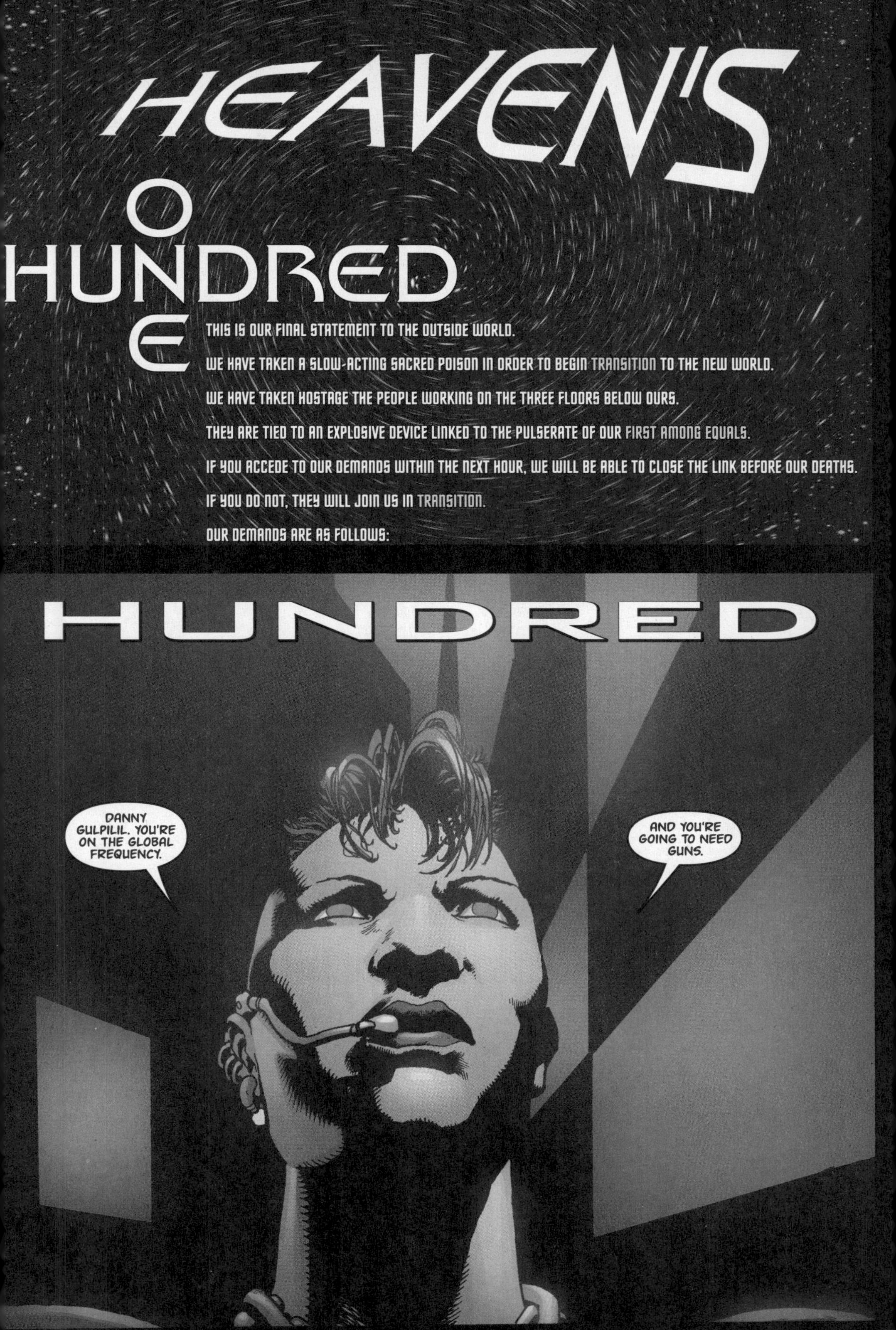
HEAVEN'S
ONE
HUNDRED
THIS IS OUR FINAL STATEMENT TO THE OUTSIDE WORLD.
WE HAVE TAKEN A SLOW-ACTING SACRED POISON IN ORDER TO BEGIN TRANSITION TO THE NEW WORLD.
WE HAVE TAKEN HOSTAGE THE PEOPLE WORKING ON THE THREE FLOORS BELOW OURS.
THEY ARE TIED TO AN EXPLOSIVE DEVICE LINKED TO THE PULSERATE OF OUR FIRST AMONG EQUALS.
IF YOU ACCEDE TO OUR DEMANDS WITHIN THE NEXT HOUR, WE WILL BE ABLE TO CLOSE THE LINK BEFORE OUR DEATHS.
IF YOU DO NOT, THEY WILL JOIN US IN TRANSITION.
OUR DEMANDS ARE AS FOLLOWS:
HUNDRED
DANNY GULPILIL. YOU'RE ON THE GLOBAL FREQUENCY.
AND YOU'RE GOING TO NEED GUNS.

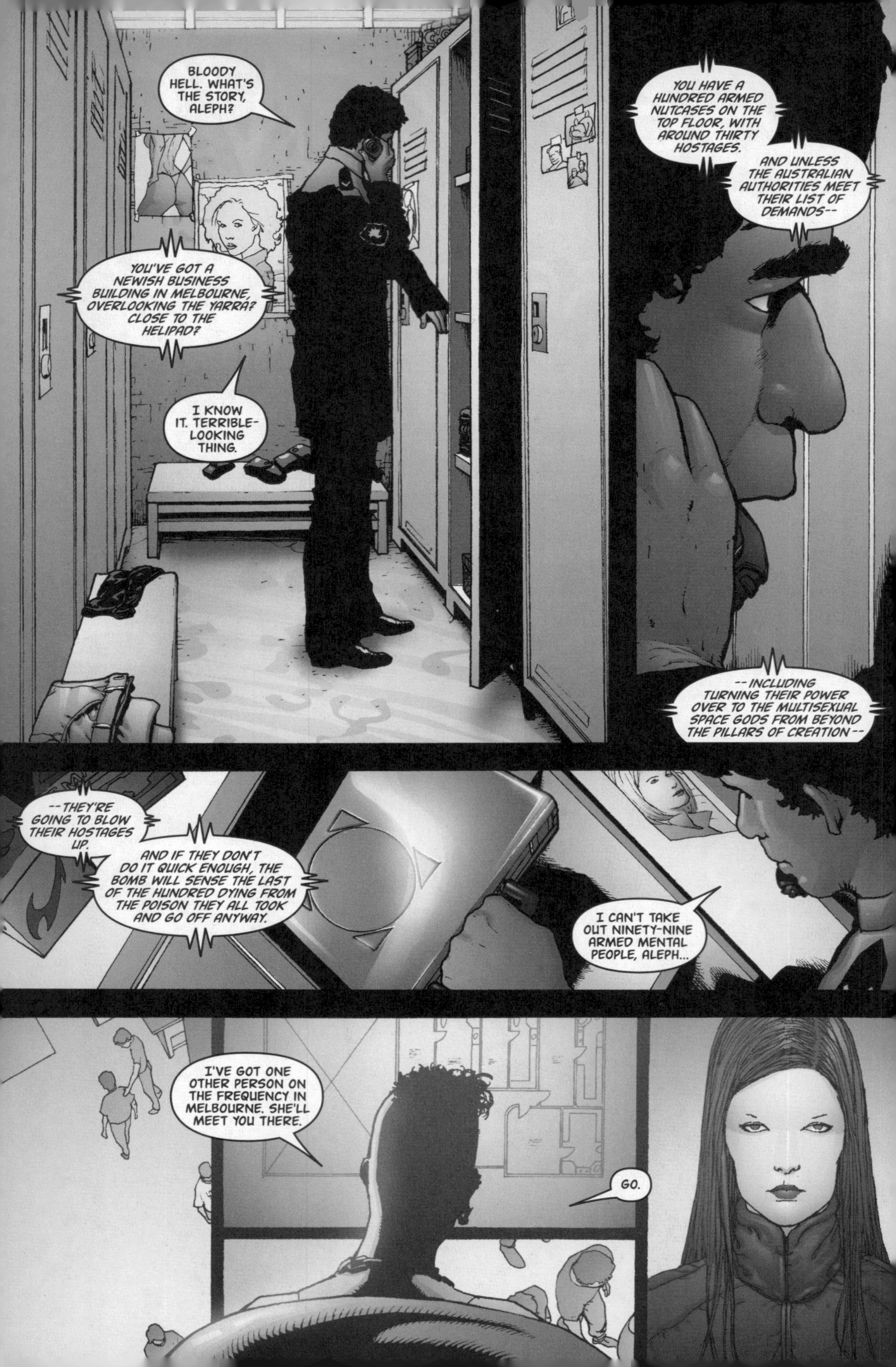
BLOODY HELL. WHAT'S THE STORY, ALEPH?
YOU'VE GOT A NEWISH BUSINESS BUILDING IN MELBOURNE, OVERLOOKING THE YARRA? CLOSE TO THE HELIPAD?
I KNOW IT. TERRIBLE-LOOKING THING.
YOU HAVE A HUNDRED ARMED NUTCASES ON THE TOP FLOOR, WITH AROUND THIRTY HOSTAGES.
AND UNLESS THE AUSTRALIAN AUTHORITIES MEET THEIR LIST OF DEMANDS--
--INCLUDING TURNING THEIR POWER OVER TO THE MULTISEXUAL SPACE GODS FROM BEYOND THE PILLARS OF CREATION--
--THEY'RE GOING TO BLOW THEIR HOSTAGES UP.
AND IF THEY DON'T DO IT QUICK ENOUGH, THE BOMB WILL SENSE THE LAST OF THE HUNDRED DYING FROM THE POISON THEY ALL TOOK AND GO OFF ANYWAY.
I CAN'T TAKE OUT NINETY-NINE ARMED MENTAL PEOPLE, ALEPH...
I'VE GOT ONE OTHER PERSON ON THE FREQUENCY IN MELBOURNE. SHE'LL MEET YOU THERE.
GO.

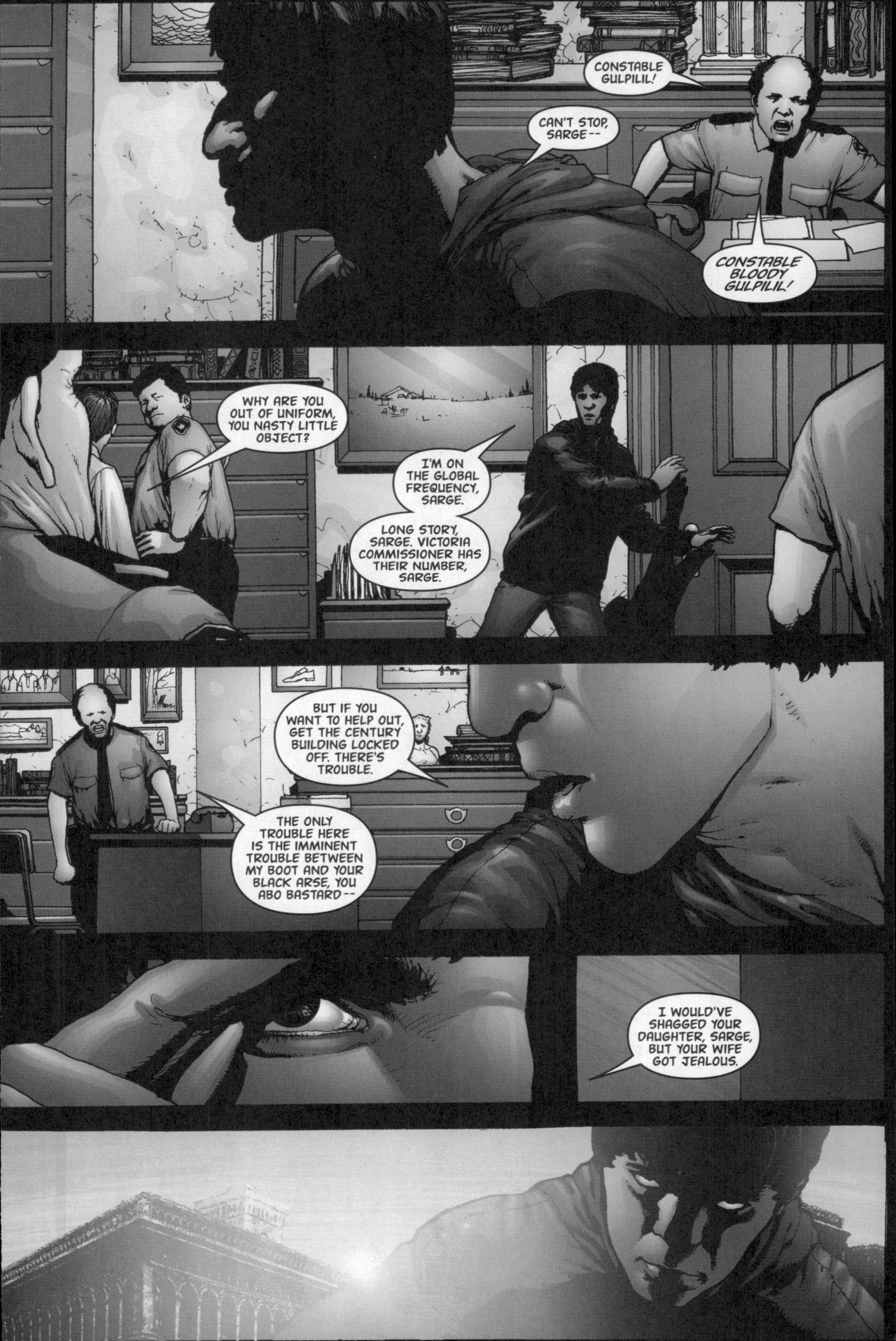
CONSTABLE GULPILIL!
CAN'T STOP, SARGE--
CONSTABLE BLOODY GULPILIL!
WHY ARE YOU OUT OF UNIFORM, YOU NASTY LITTLE OBJECT?
I'M ON THE GLOBAL FREQUENCY, SARGE.
LONG STORY, SARGE. VICTORIA COMMISSIONER HAS THEIR NUMBER, SARGE.
BUT IF YOU WANT TO HELP OUT, GET THE CENTURY BUILDING LOCKED OFF. THERE'S TROUBLE.
THE ONLY TROUBLE HERE IS THE IMMINENT TROUBLE BETWEEN MY BOOT AND YOUR BLACK ARSE, YOU ABO BASTARD--
I WOULD'VE SHAGGED YOUR DAUGHTER, SARGE, BUT YOUR WIFE GOT JEALOUS.

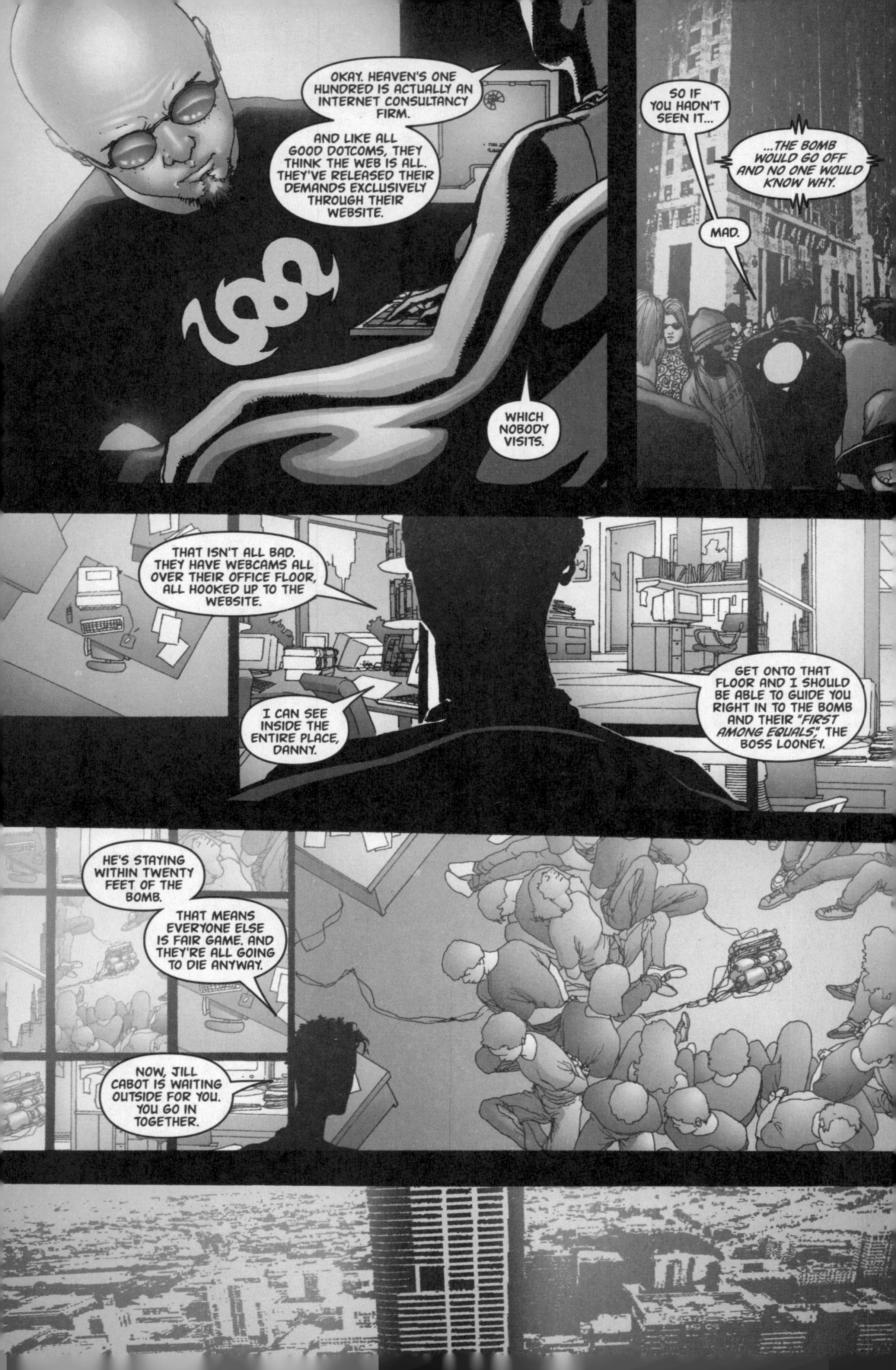
OKAY. HEAVEN'S ONE HUNDRED IS ACTUALLY AN INTERNET CONSULTANCY FIRM.
AND LIKE ALL GOOD DOTCOMS, THEY THINK THE WEB IS ALL. THEY'VE RELEASED THEIR DEMANDS EXCLUSIVELY THROUGH THEIR WEBSITE.
WHICH NOBODY VISITS.
SO IF YOU HADN'T SEEN IT...
...THE BOMB WOULD GO OFF AND NO ONE WOULD KNOW WHY.
MAD.
THAT ISN'T ALL BAD. THEY HAVE WEBCAMS ALL OVER THEIR OFFICE FLOOR, ALL HOOKED UP TO THE WEBSITE.
I CAN SEE INSIDE THE ENTIRE PLACE, DANNY.
GET ONTO THAT FLOOR AND I SHOULD BE ABLE TO GUIDE YOU RIGHT IN TO THE BOMB AND THEIR "FIRST AMONG EQUALS," THE BOSS LOONEY.
HE'S STAYING WITHIN TWENTY FEET OF THE BOMB.
THAT MEANS EVERYONE ELSE IS FAIR GAME. AND THEY'RE ALL GOING TO DIE ANYWAY.
NOW, JILL CABOT IS WAITING OUTSIDE FOR YOU. YOU GO IN TOGETHER.

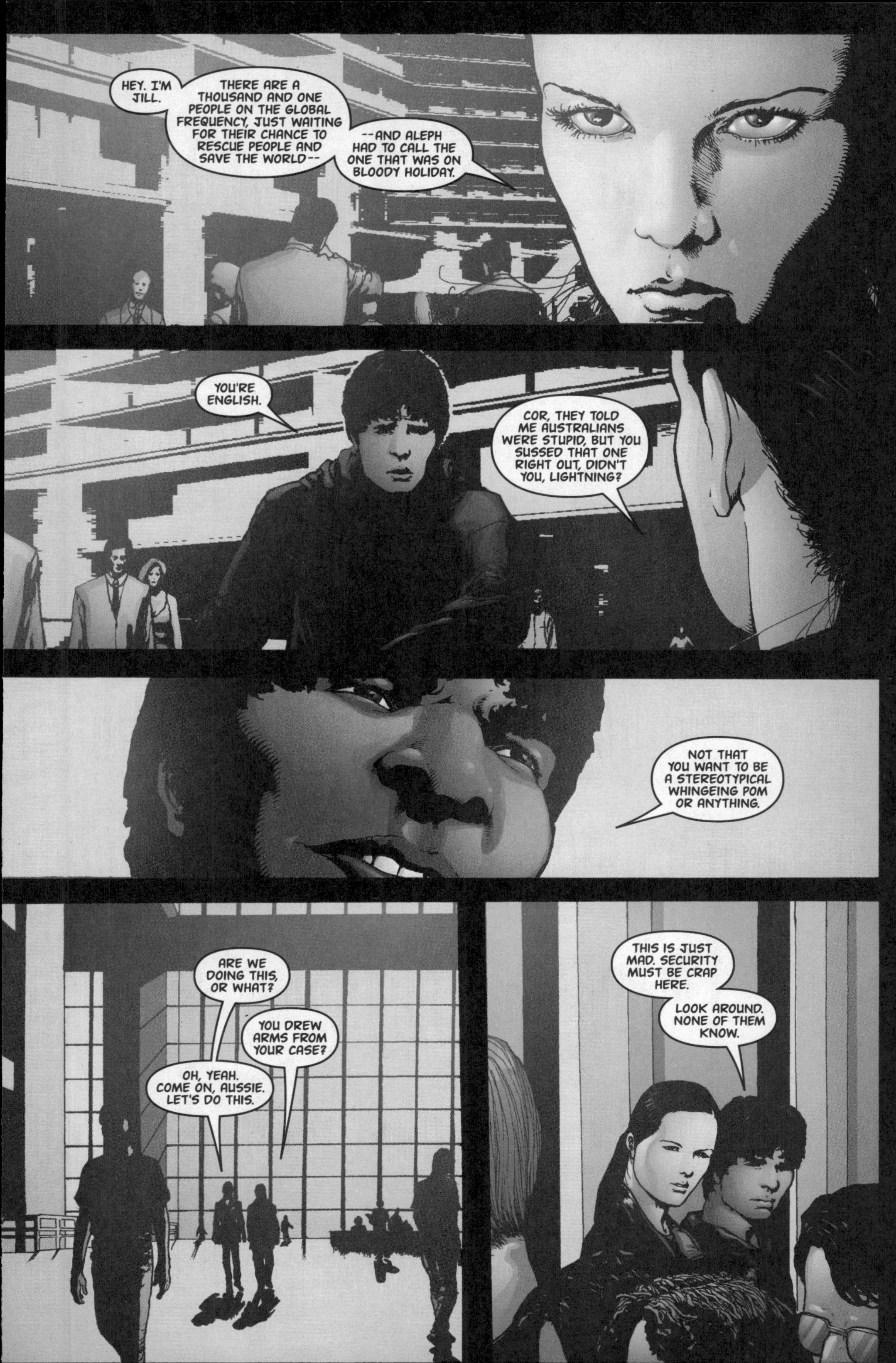
HEY. I'M JILL.
THERE ARE A THOUSAND AND ONE PEOPLE ON THE GLOBAL FREQUENCY, JUST WAITING FOR THEIR CHANCE TO RESCUE PEOPLE AND SAVE THE WORLD--
--AND ALEPH HAD TO CALL THE ONE THAT WAS ON BLOODY HOLIDAY.
YOU'RE ENGLISH.
COR, THEY TOLD ME AUSTRALIANS WERE STUPID, BUT YOU SUSSED THAT ONE RIGHT OUT, DIDN'T YOU, LIGHTNING?
NOT THAT YOU WANT TO BE A STEREOTYPICAL WHINGEING POM OR ANYTHING.
ARE WE DOING THIS, OR WHAT?
YOU DREW ARMS FROM YOUR CASE?
OH, YEAH. COME ON, AUSSIE. LET'S DO THIS.
THIS IS JUST MAD. SECURITY MUST BE CRAP HERE.
LOOK AROUND. NONE OF THEM KNOW.

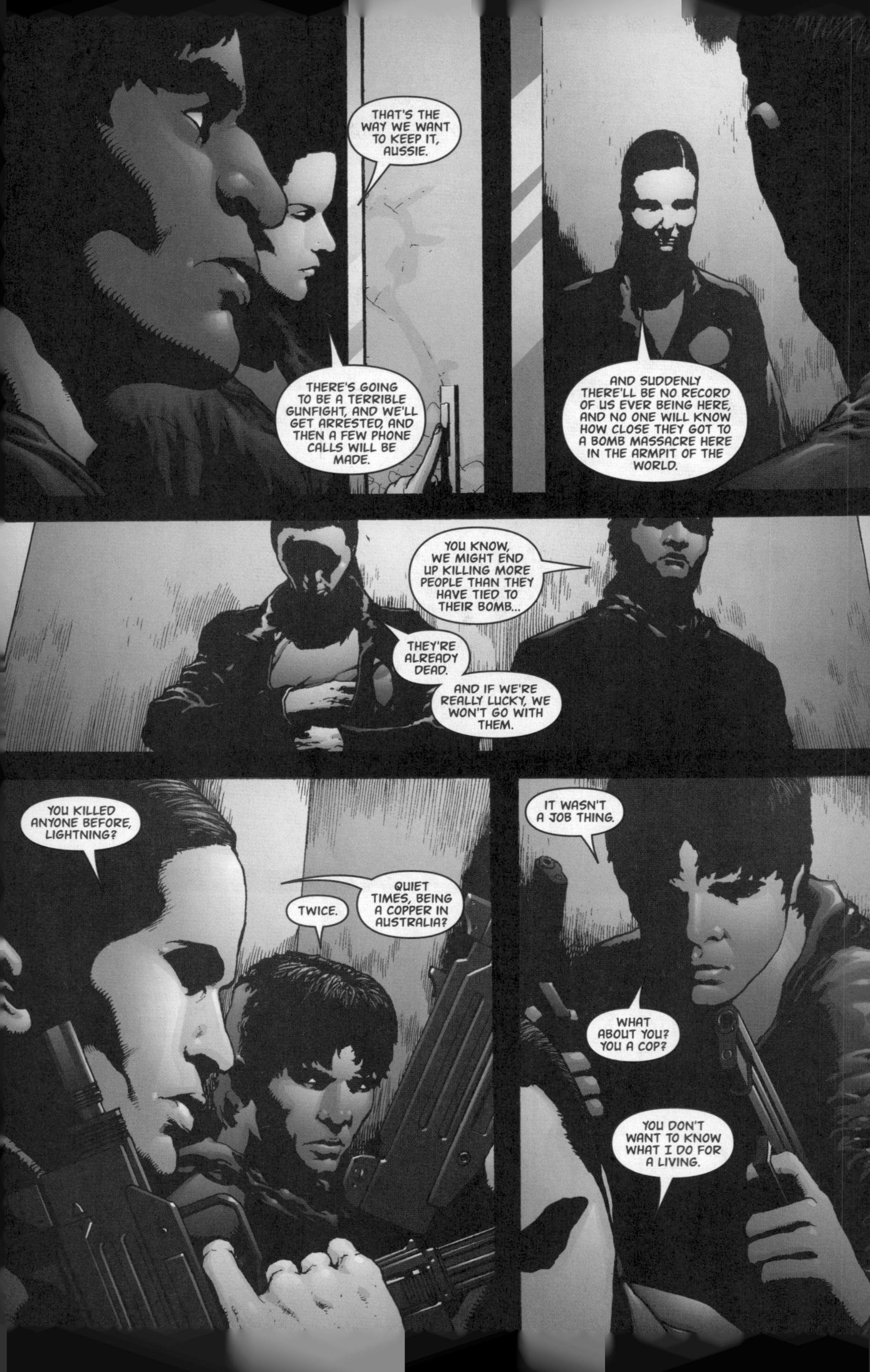
THAT'S THE WAY WE WANT TO KEEP IT, AUSSIE.
THERE'S GOING TO BE A TERRIBLE GUNFIGHT, AND WE'LL GET ARRESTED, AND THEN A FEW PHONE CALLS WILL BE MADE.
AND SUDDENLY THERE'LL BE NO RECORD OF US EVER BEING HERE, AND NO ONE WILL KNOW HOW CLOSE THEY GOT TO A BOMB MASSACRE HERE IN THE ARMPIT OF THE WORLD.
YOU KNOW, WE MIGHT END UP KILLING MORE PEOPLE THAN THEY HAVE TIED TO THEIR BOMB...
THEY'RE ALREADY DEAD.
AND IF WE'RE REALLY LUCKY, WE WON'T GO WITH THEM.
YOU KILLED ANYONE BEFORE, LIGHTNING?
TWICE.
QUIET TIMES, BEING A COPPER IN AUSTRALIA?
IT WASN'T A JOB THING.
WHAT ABOUT YOU? YOU A COP?
YOU DON'T WANT TO KNOW WHAT I DO FOR A LIVING.

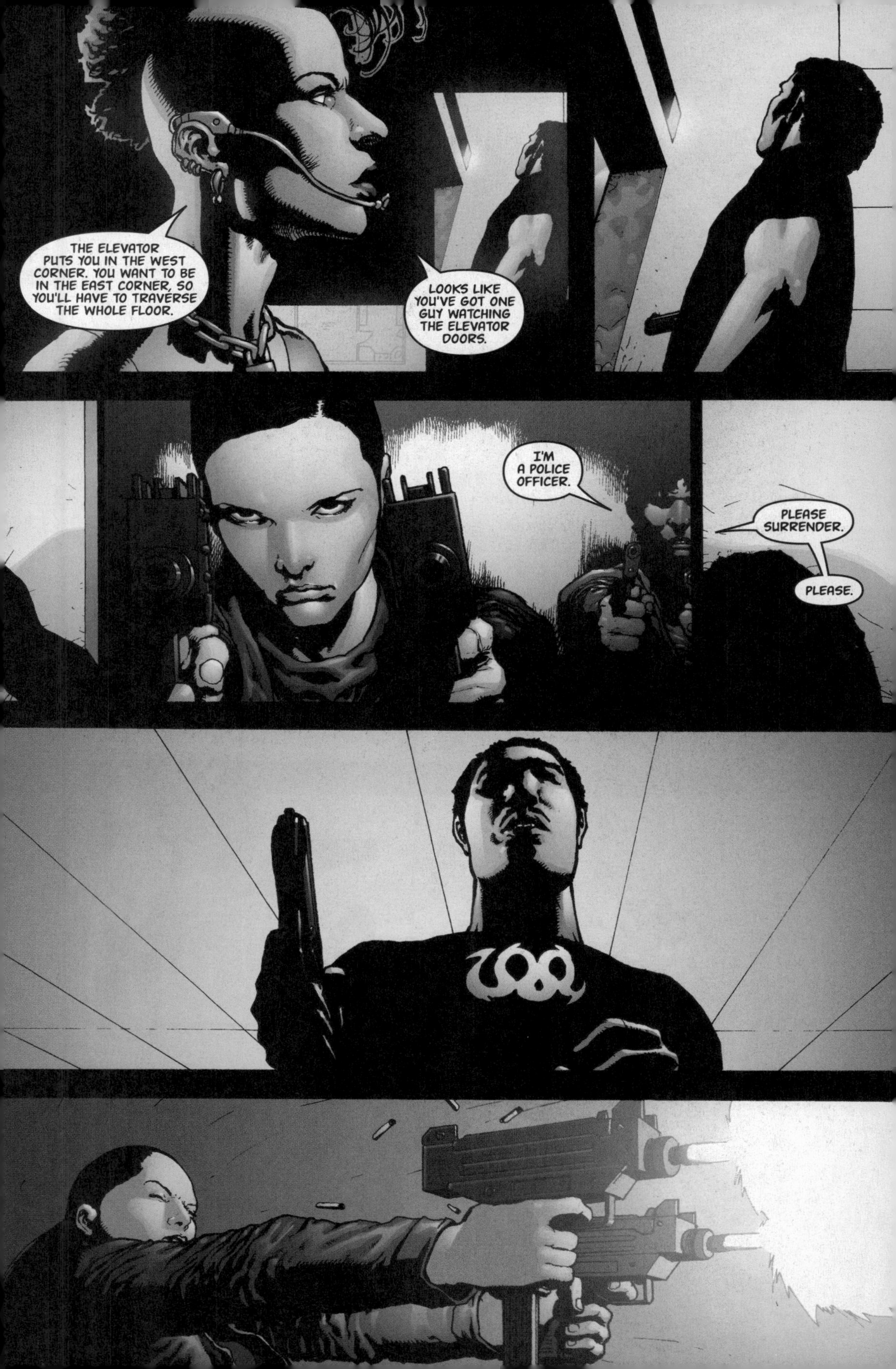
THE ELEVATOR PUTS YOU IN THE WEST CORNER. YOU WANT TO BE IN THE EAST CORNER, SO YOU'LL HAVE TO TRAVERSE THE WHOLE FLOOR.
LOOKS LIKE YOU'VE GOT ONE GUY WATCHING THE ELEVATOR DOORS.
I'M A POLICE OFFICER.
PLEASE SURRENDER.
PLEASE.

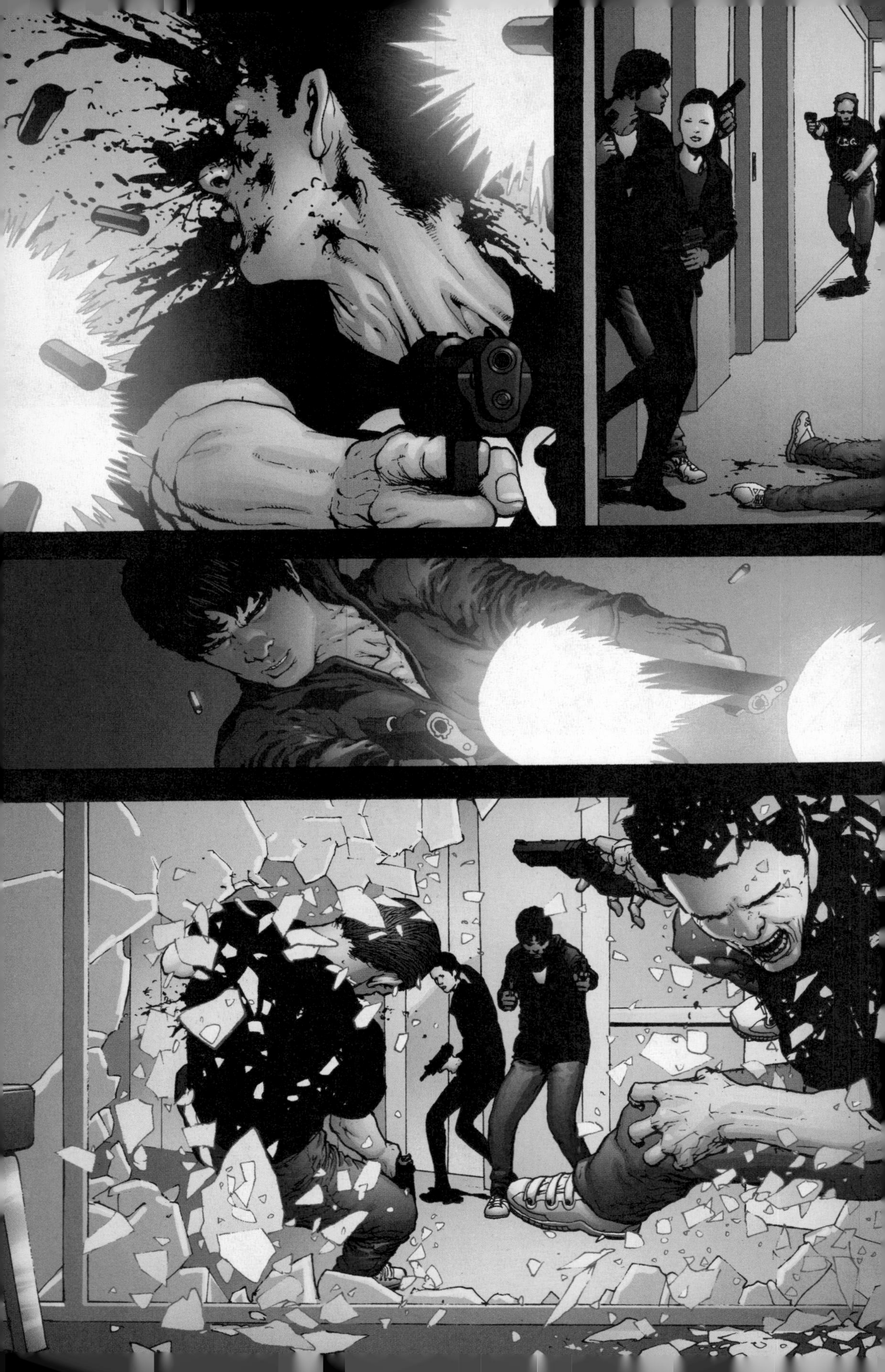

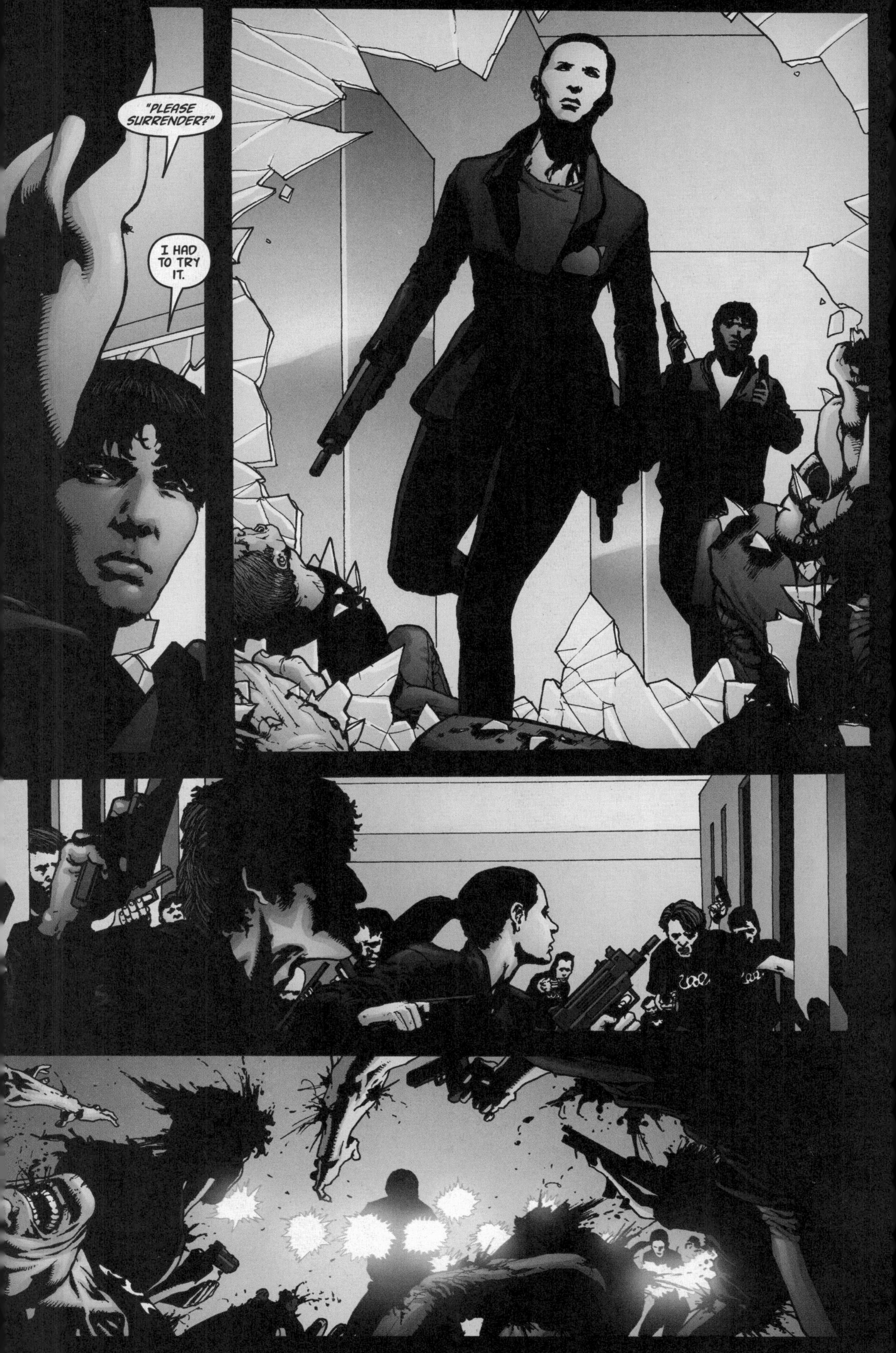
"PLEASE SURRENDER?"
I HAD TO TRY IT.

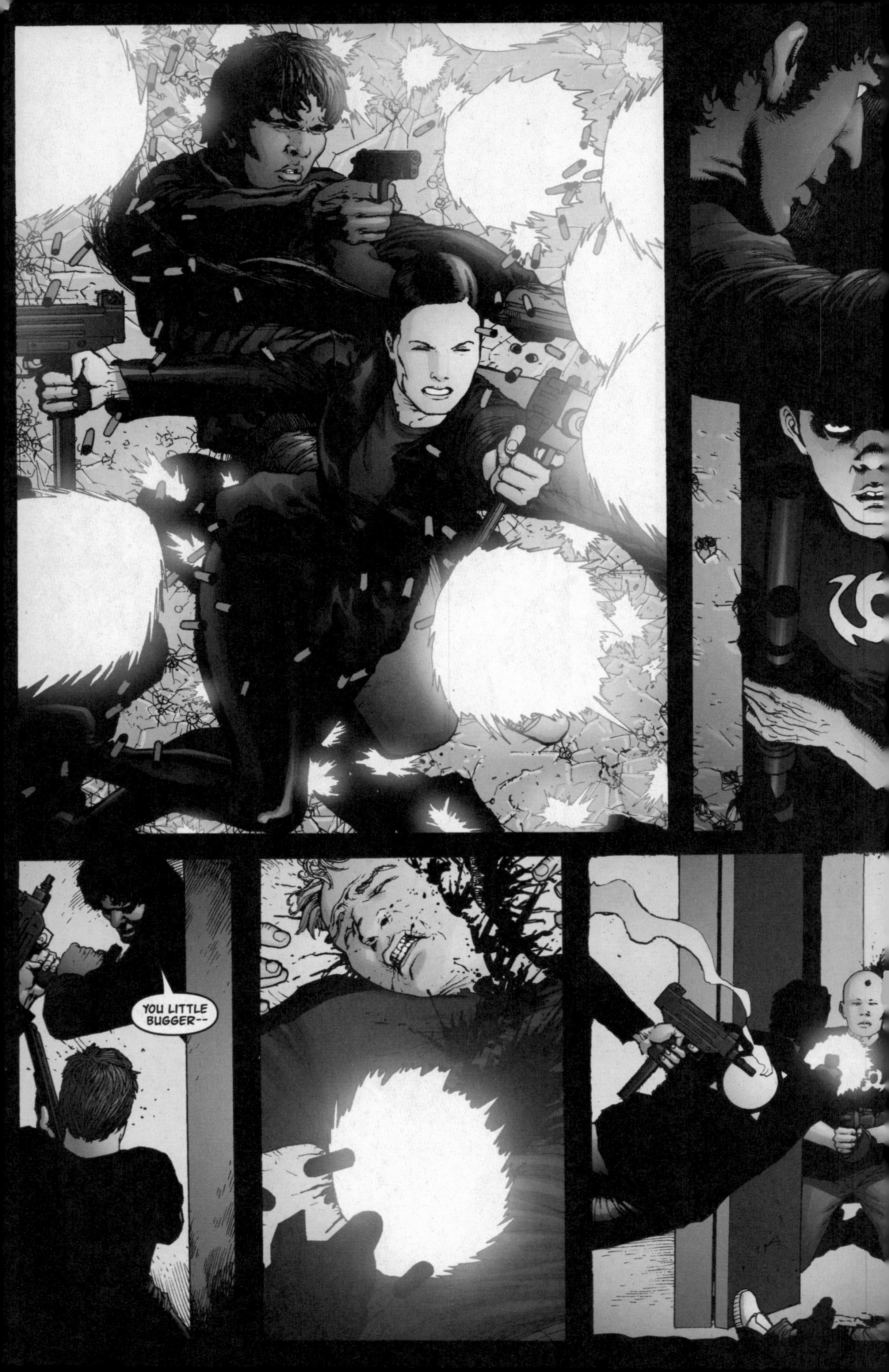
YOU LITTLE BUGGER--

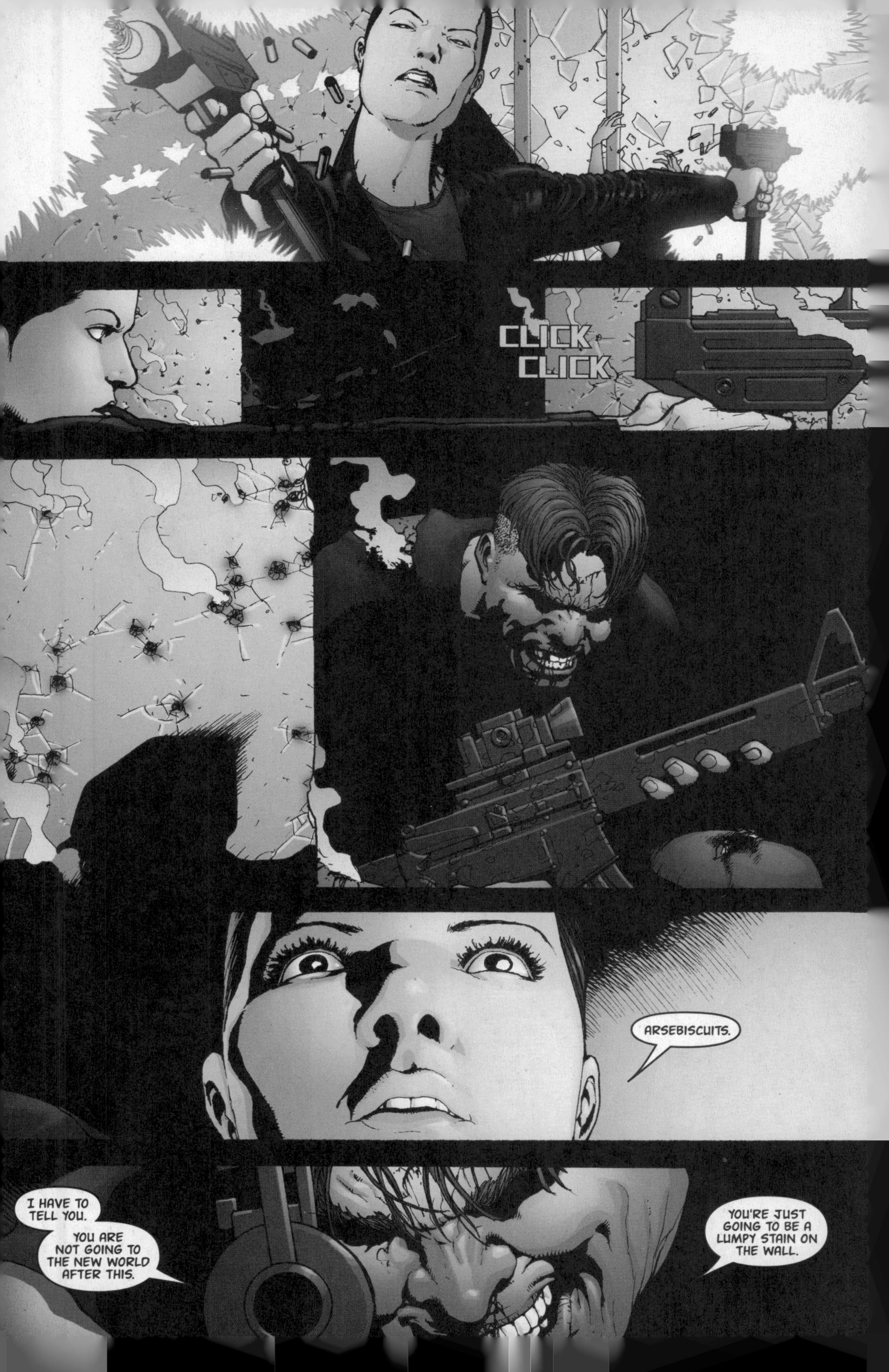

CLICK
CLICK
ARSEBISCUITS.
I HAVE TO TELL YOU.
YOU ARE NOT GOING TO THE NEW WORLD AFTER THIS.
YOU'RE JUST GOING TO BE A LUMPY STAIN ON THE WALL.

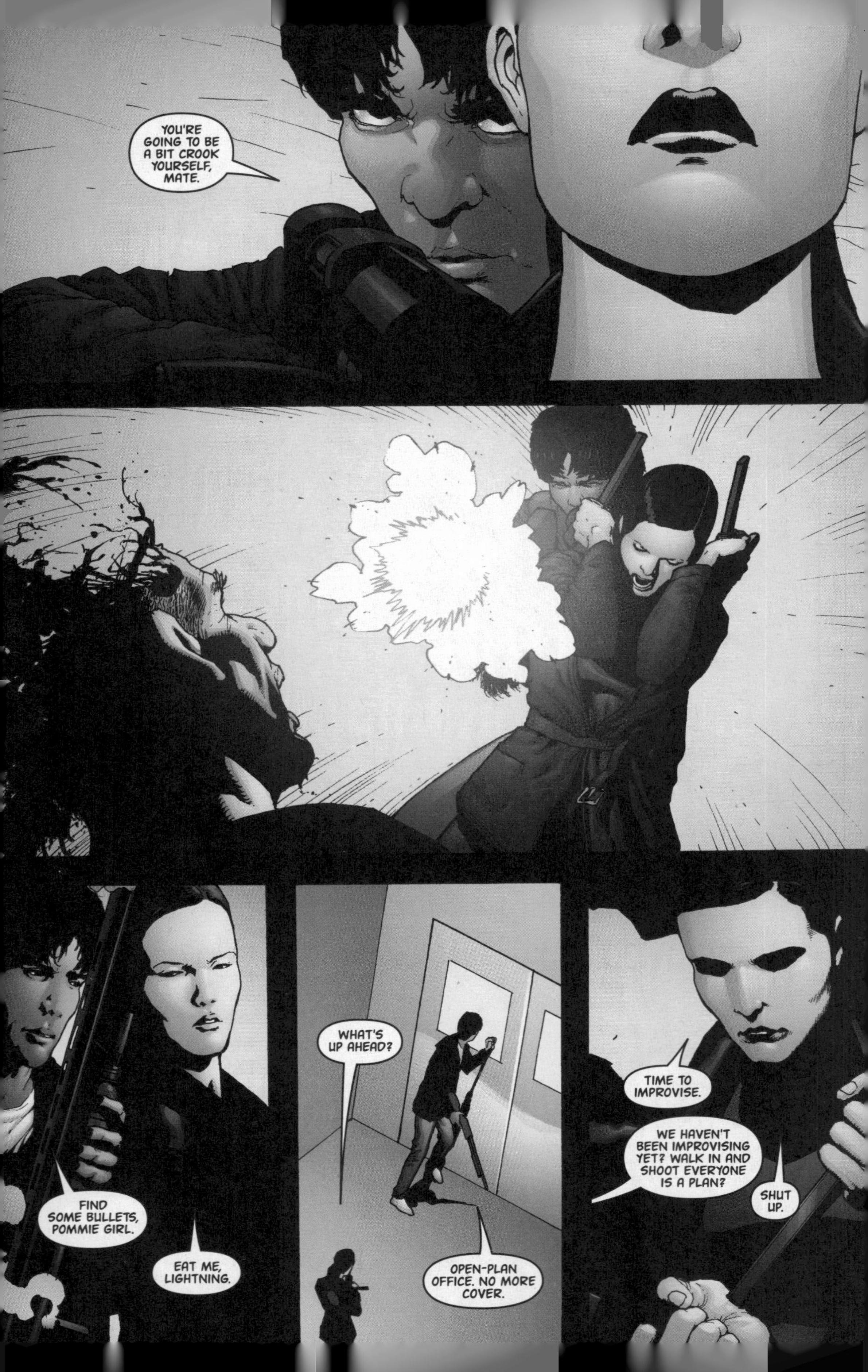
YOU'RE GOING TO BE A BIT CROOK YOURSELF, MATE.
FIND SOME BULLETS, POMMIE GIRL.
EAT ME, LIGHTNING.
WHAT'S UP AHEAD?
OPEN-PLAN OFFICE. NO MORE COVER.
TIME TO IMPROVISE.
WE HAVEN'T BEEN IMPROVISING YET? WALK IN AND SHOOT EVERYONE IS A PLAN?
SHUT UP.

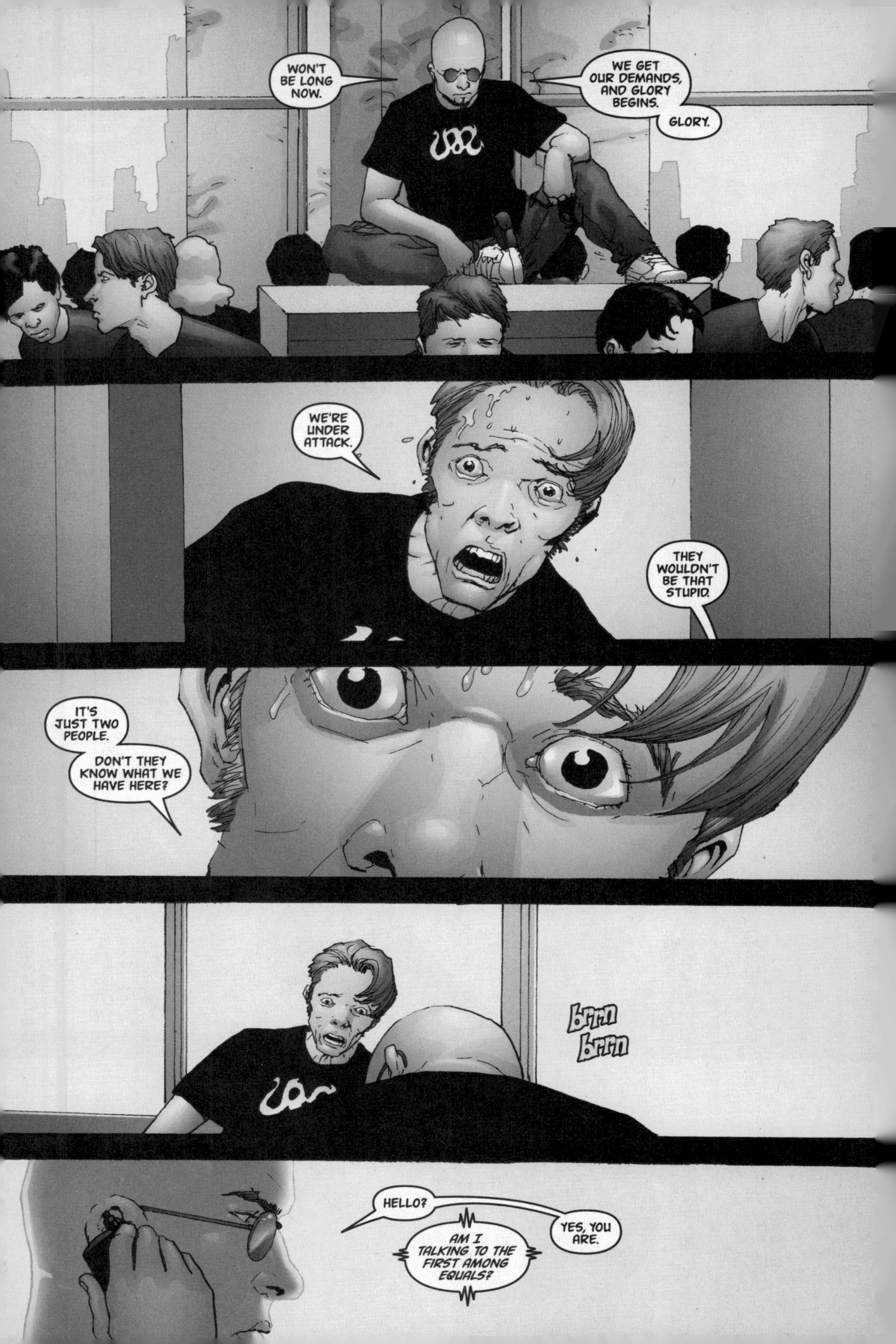
WON'T BE LONG NOW.
WE GET OUR DEMANDS, AND GLORY BEGINS.
GLORY.
WE'RE UNDER ATTACK.
THEY WOULDN'T BE THAT STUPID.
IT'S JUST TWO PEOPLE.
DON'T THEY KNOW WHAT WE HAVE HERE?
brrrn brrrn
HELLO?
AM I TALKING TO THE FIRST AMONG EQUALS?
YES, YOU ARE.

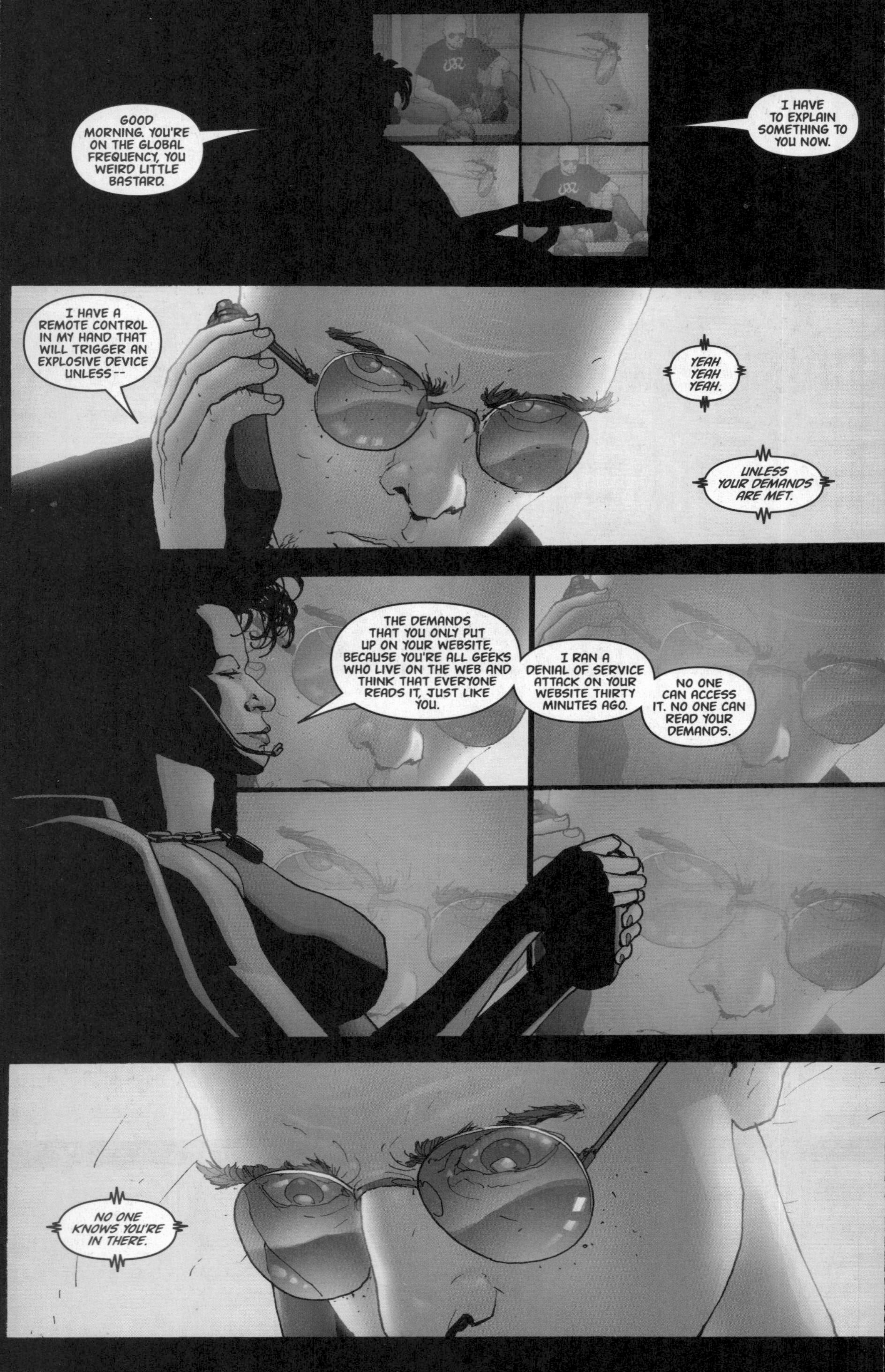
GOOD MORNING. YOU'RE ON THE GLOBAL FREQUENCY, YOU WEIRD LITTLE BASTARD.
I HAVE TO EXPLAIN SOMETHING TO YOU NOW.
I HAVE A REMOTE CONTROL IN MY HAND THAT WILL TRIGGER AN EXPLOSIVE DEVICE UNLESS--
YEAH YEAH YEAH.
UNLESS YOUR DEMANDS ARE MET.
THE DEMANDS THAT YOU ONLY PUT UP ON YOUR WEBSITE, BECAUSE YOU'RE ALL GEEKS WHO LIVE ON THE WEB AND THINK THAT EVERYONE READS IT, JUST LIKE YOU.
I RAN A DENIAL OF SERVICE ATTACK ON YOUR WEBSITE THIRTY MINUTES AGO.
NO ONE CAN ACCESS IT. NO ONE CAN READ YOUR DEMANDS.
NO ONE KNOWS YOU'RE IN THERE.

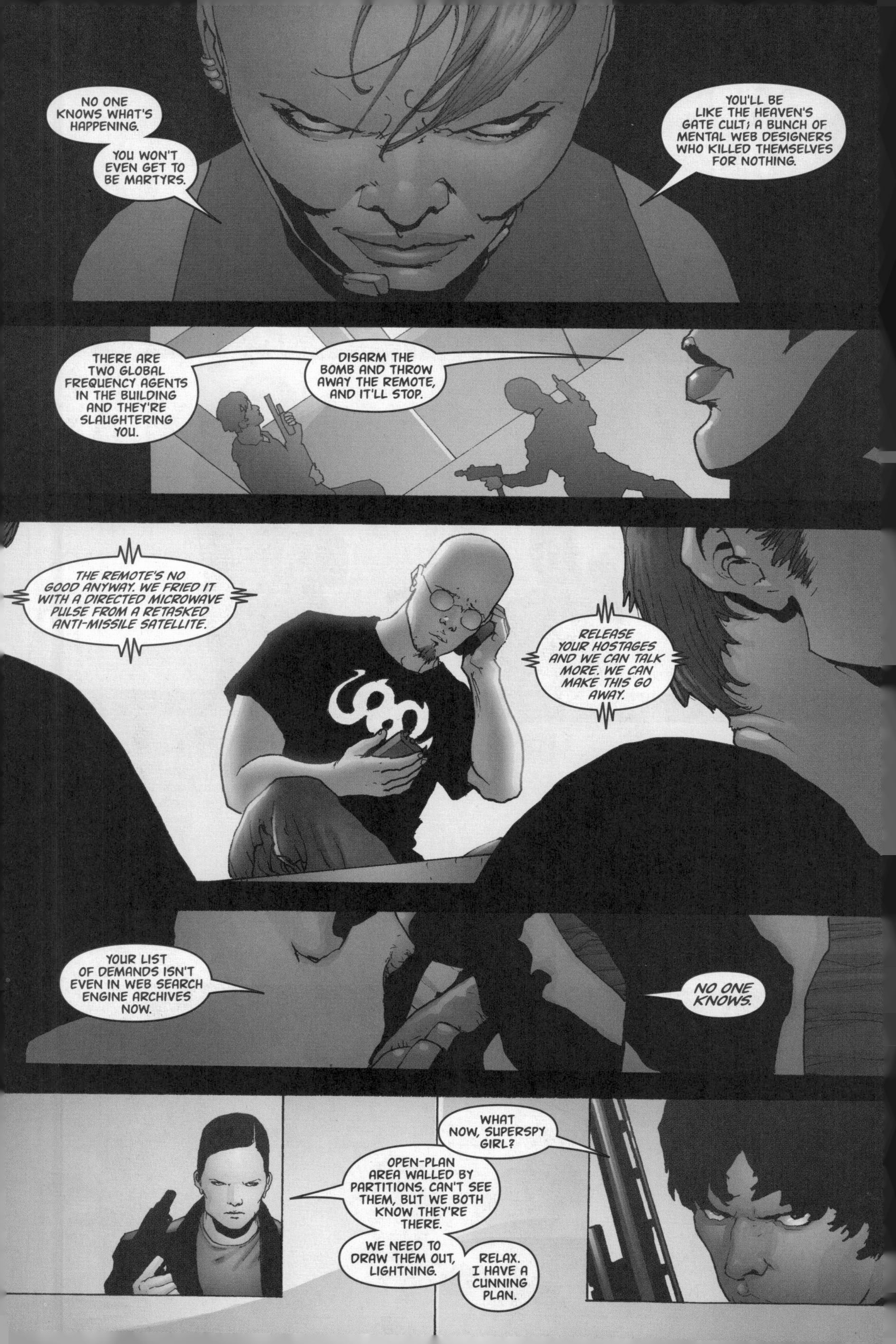
NO ONE KNOWS WHAT'S HAPPENING.
YOU WON'T EVEN GET TO BE MARTYRS.
YOU'LL BE LIKE THE HEAVEN'S GATE CULT; A BUNCH OF MENTAL WEB DESIGNERS WHO KILLED THEMSELVES FOR NOTHING.
THERE ARE TWO GLOBAL FREQUENCY AGENTS IN THE BUILDING AND THEY'RE SLAUGHTERING YOU.
DISARM THE BOMB AND THROW AWAY THE REMOTE, AND IT'LL STOP.
THE REMOTE'S NO GOOD ANYWAY. WE FRIED IT WITH A DIRECTED MICROWAVE PULSE FROM A RETASKED ANTI-MISSILE SATELLITE.
RELEASE YOUR HOSTAGES AND WE CAN TALK MORE. WE CAN MAKE THIS GO AWAY.
YOUR LIST OF DEMANDS ISN'T EVEN IN WEB SEARCH ENGINE ARCHIVES NOW.
NO ONE KNOWS.
WHAT NOW, SUPERSPY GIRL?
OPEN-PLAN AREA WALLED BY PARTITIONS. CAN'T SEE THEM, BUT WE BOTH KNOW THEY'RE THERE.
WE NEED TO DRAW THEM OUT, LIGHTNING.
RELAX. I HAVE A CUNNING PLAN.

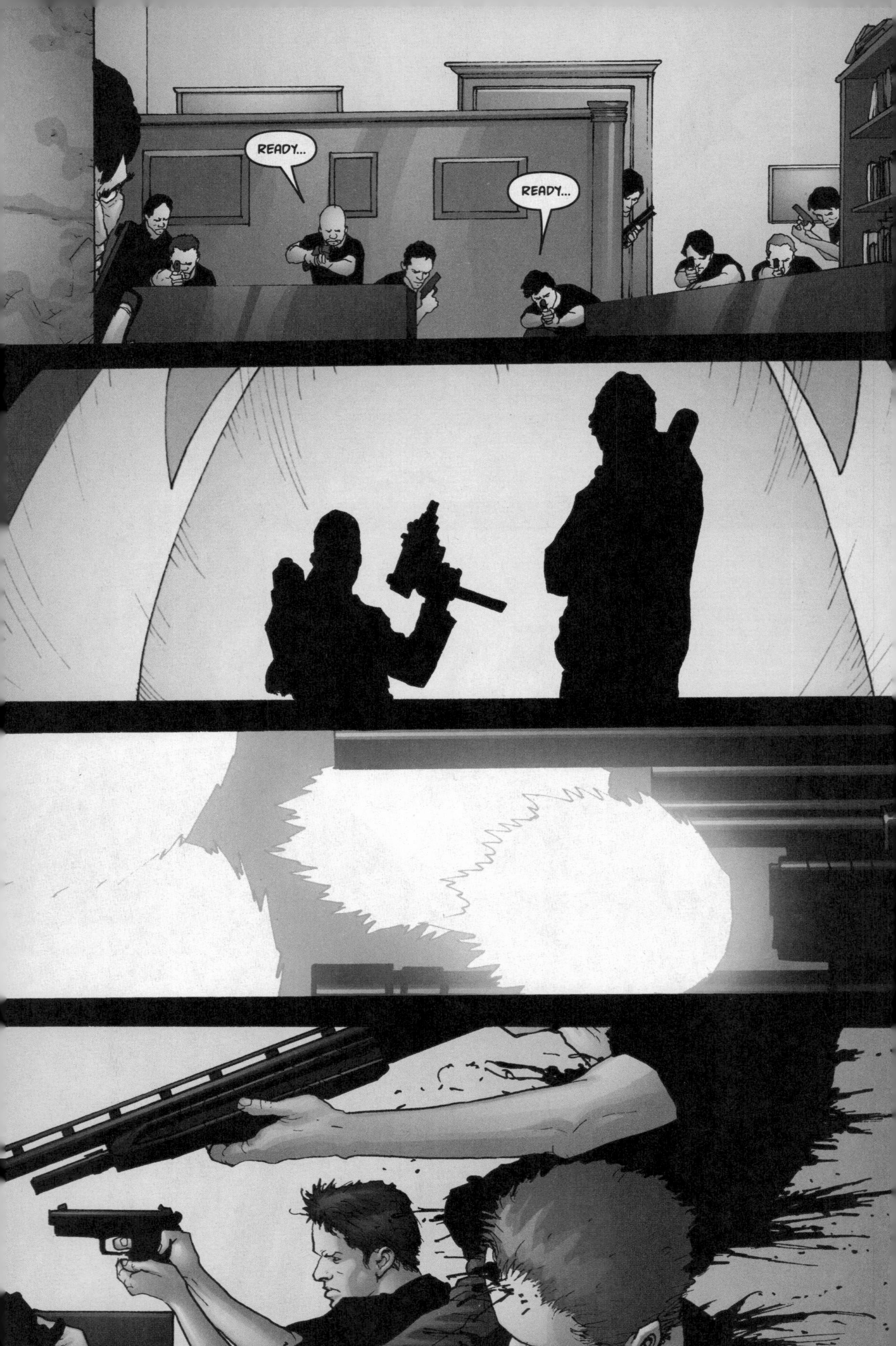
READY...
READY...

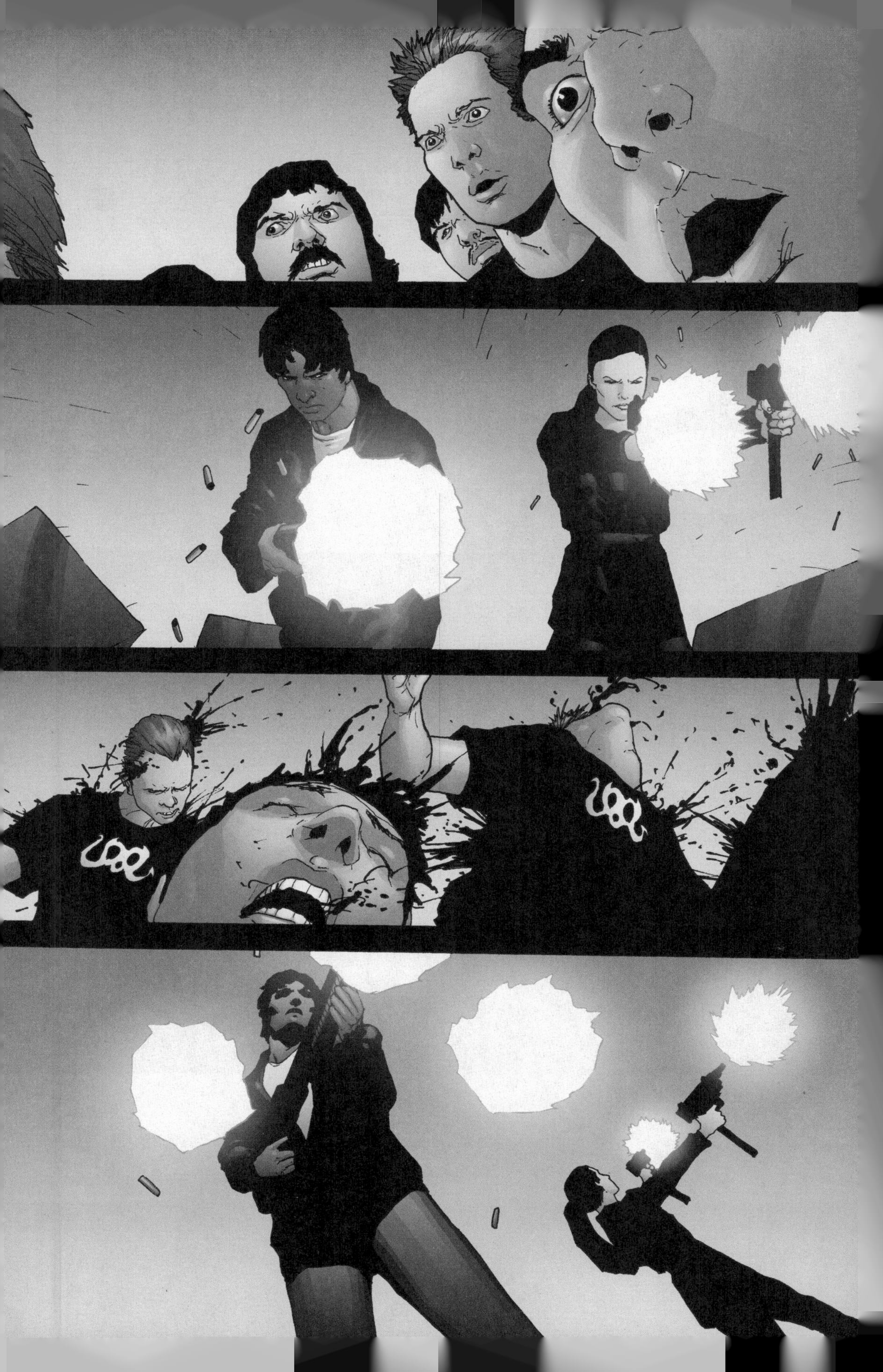

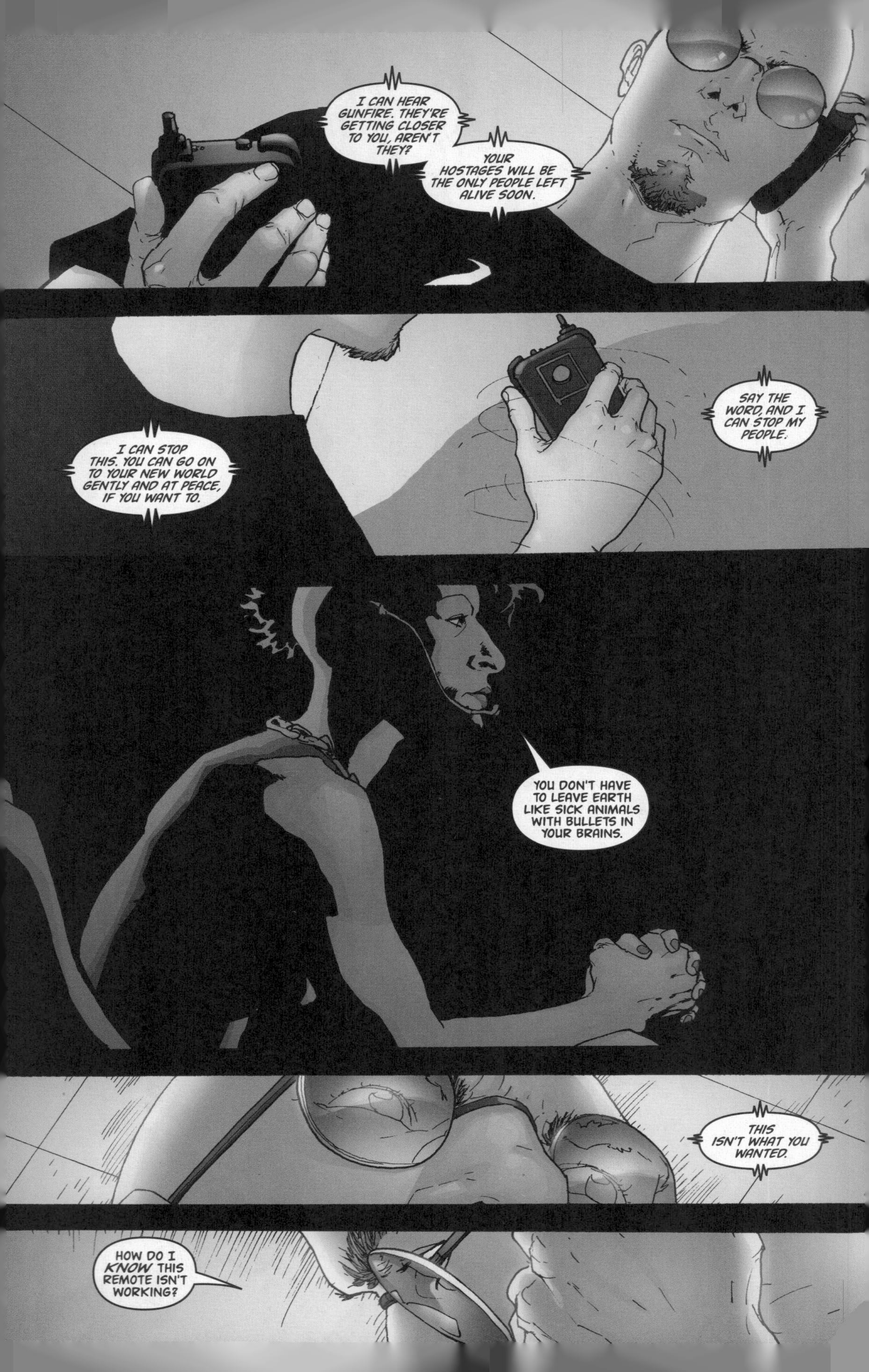
I CAN HEAR GUNFIRE. THEY'RE GETTING CLOSER TO YOU, AREN'T THEY?
YOUR HOSTAGES WILL BE THE ONLY PEOPLE LEFT ALIVE SOON.
I CAN STOP THIS. YOU CAN GO ON TO YOUR NEW WORLD GENTLY AND AT PEACE, IF YOU WANT TO.
SAY THE WORD, AND I CAN STOP MY PEOPLE.
YOU DON'T HAVE TO LEAVE EARTH LIKE SICK ANIMALS WITH BULLETS IN YOUR BRAINS.
THIS ISN'T WHAT YOU WANTED.
HOW DO I *KNOW* THIS REMOTE ISN'T WORKING?

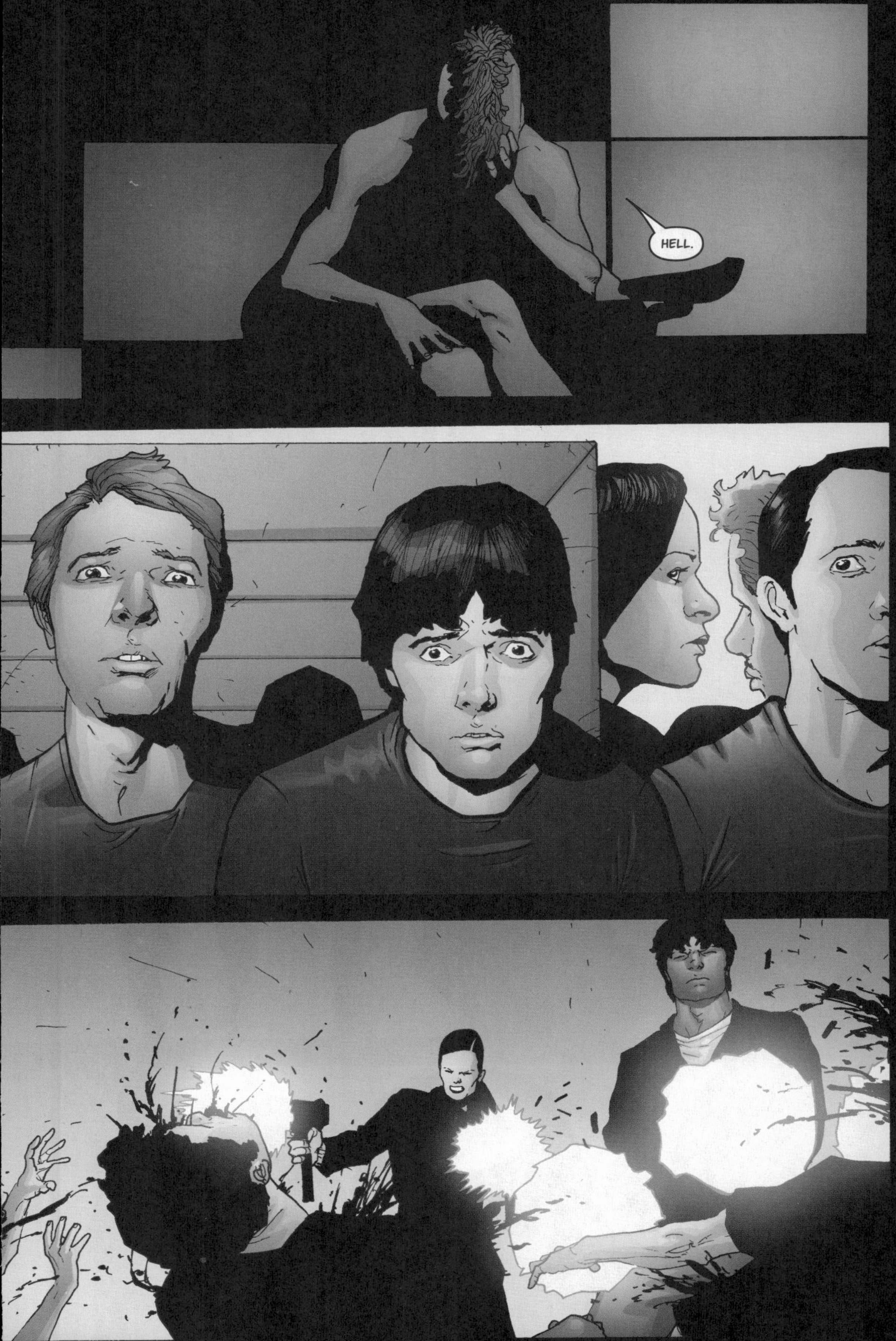
HELL.

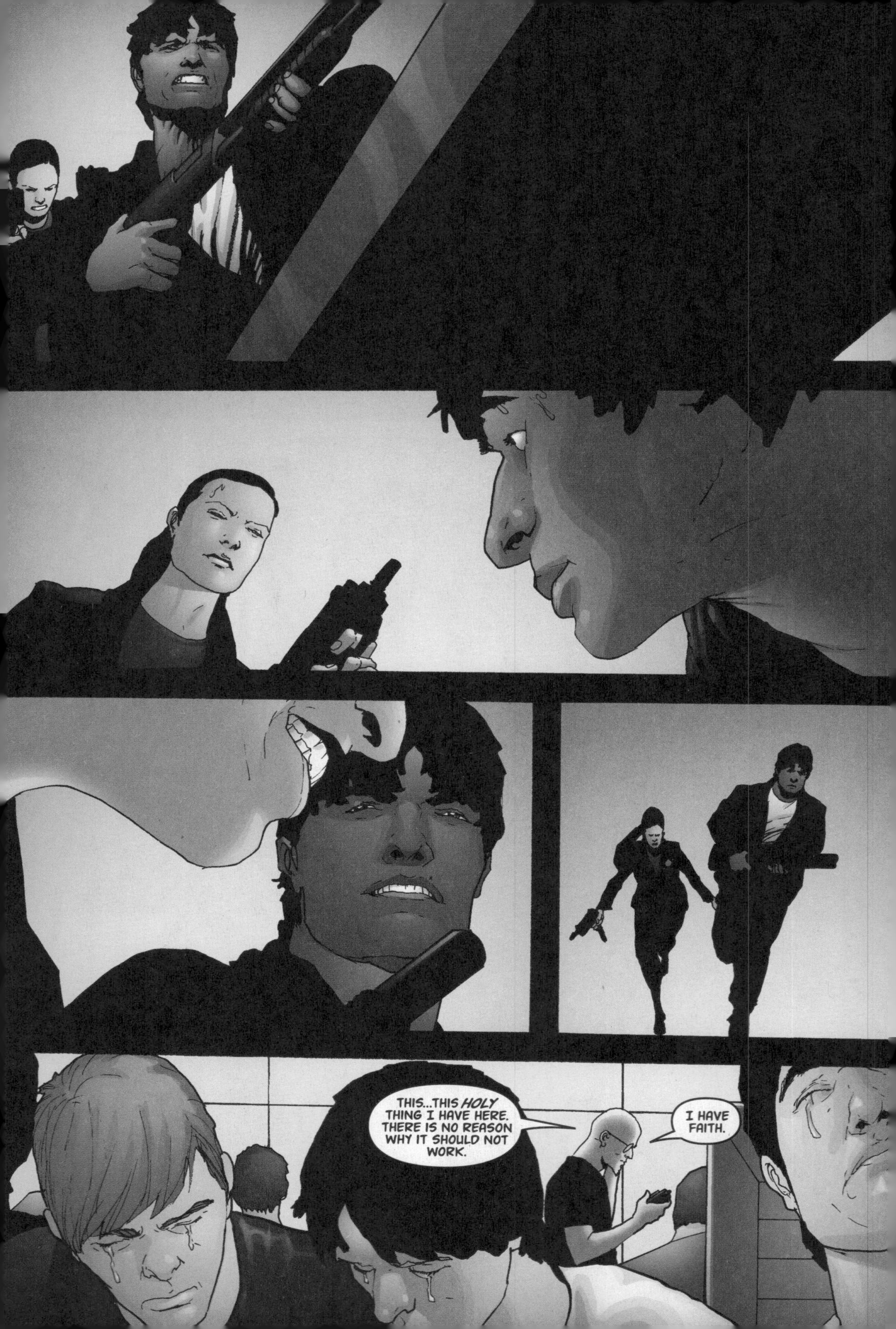
THIS...THIS *HOLY* THING I HAVE HERE. THERE IS NO REASON WHY IT SHOULD NOT WORK.
I HAVE FAITH.

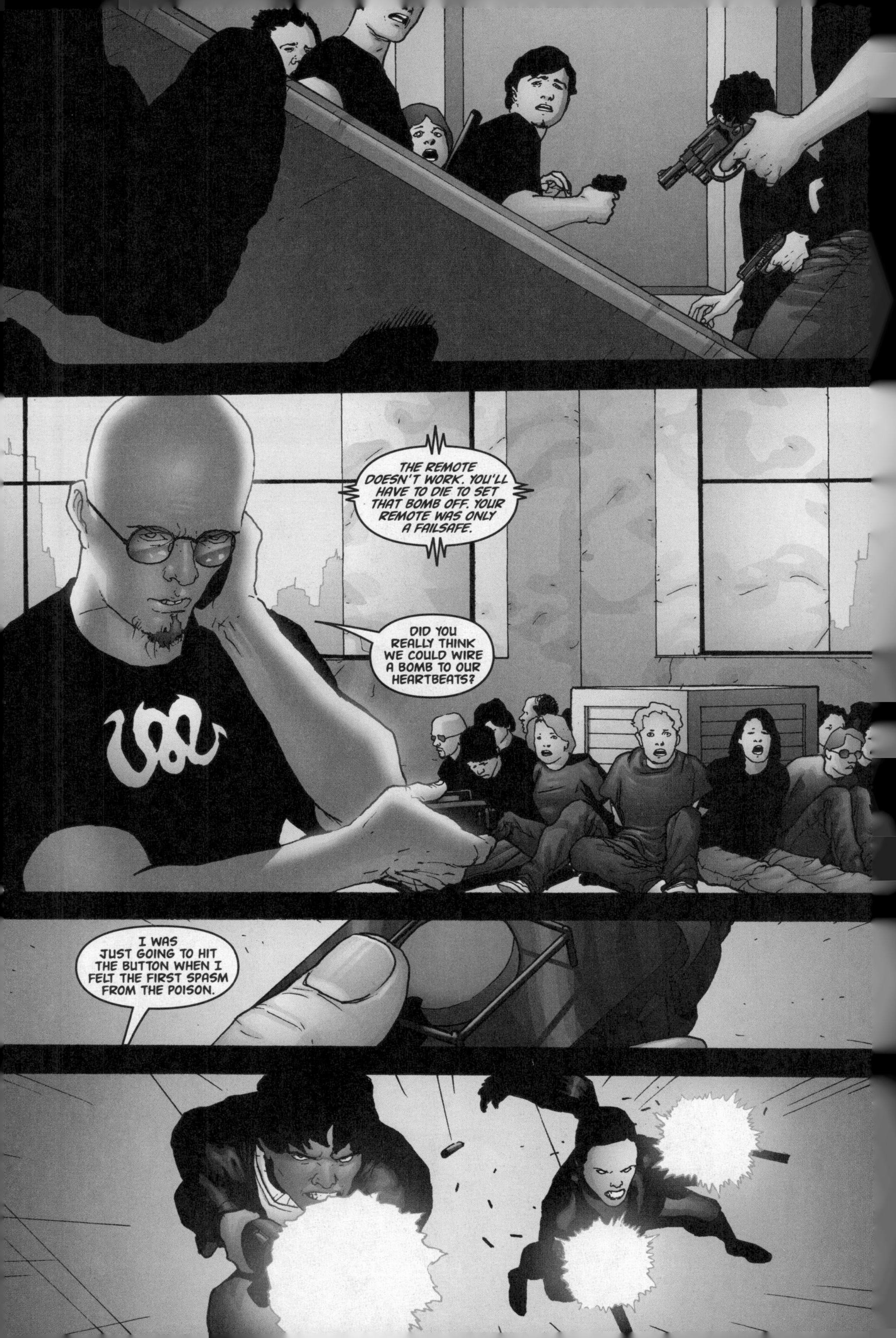
THE REMOTE DOESN'T WORK. YOU'LL HAVE TO DIE TO SET THAT BOMB OFF. YOUR REMOTE WAS ONLY A FAILSAFE.
DID YOU REALLY THINK WE COULD WIRE A BOMB TO OUR HEARTBEATS?
I WAS JUST GOING TO HIT THE BUTTON WHEN I FELT THE FIRST SPASM FROM THE POISON.

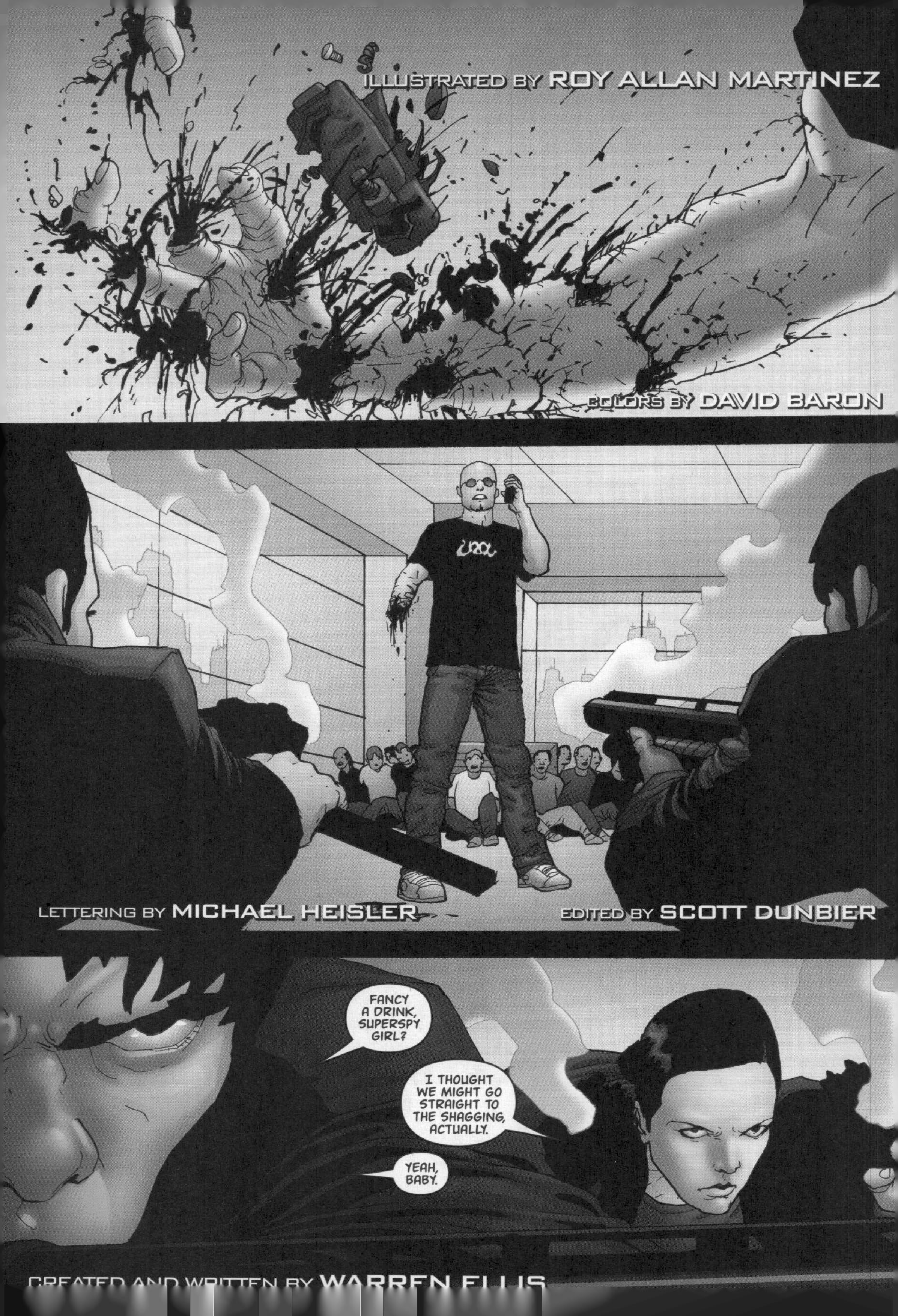

ILLUSTRATED BY ROY ALLAN MARTINEZ
COLORS BY DAVID BARON
LETTERING BY MICHAEL HEISLER
EDITED BY SCOTT DUNBIER
FANCY A DRINK, SUPERSPY GIRL?
I THOUGHT WE MIGHT GO STRAIGHT TO THE SHAGGING, ACTUALLY.
YEAH, BABY.
CREATED AND WRITTEN BY WARREN ELLIS

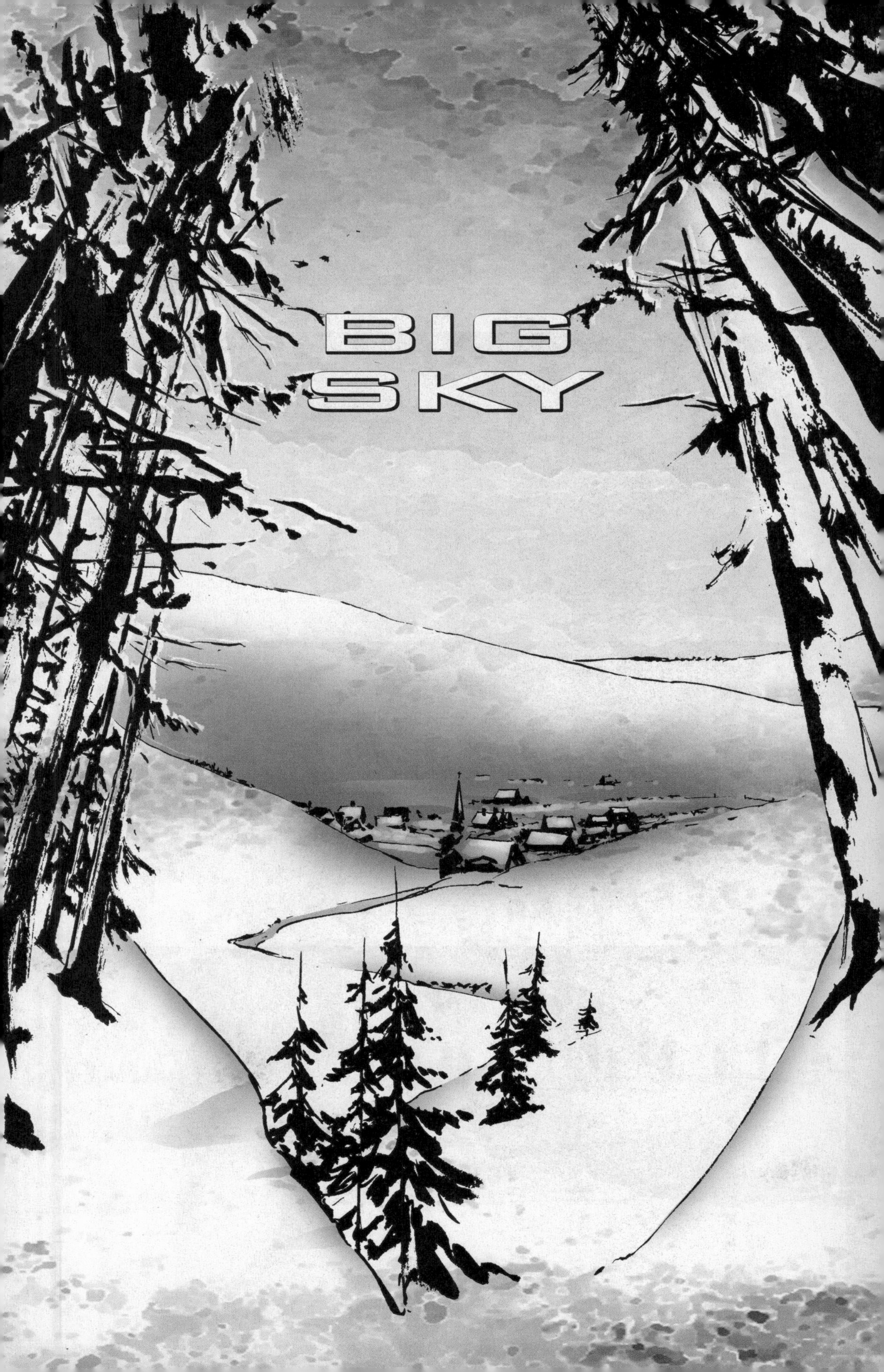
BIG
SKY

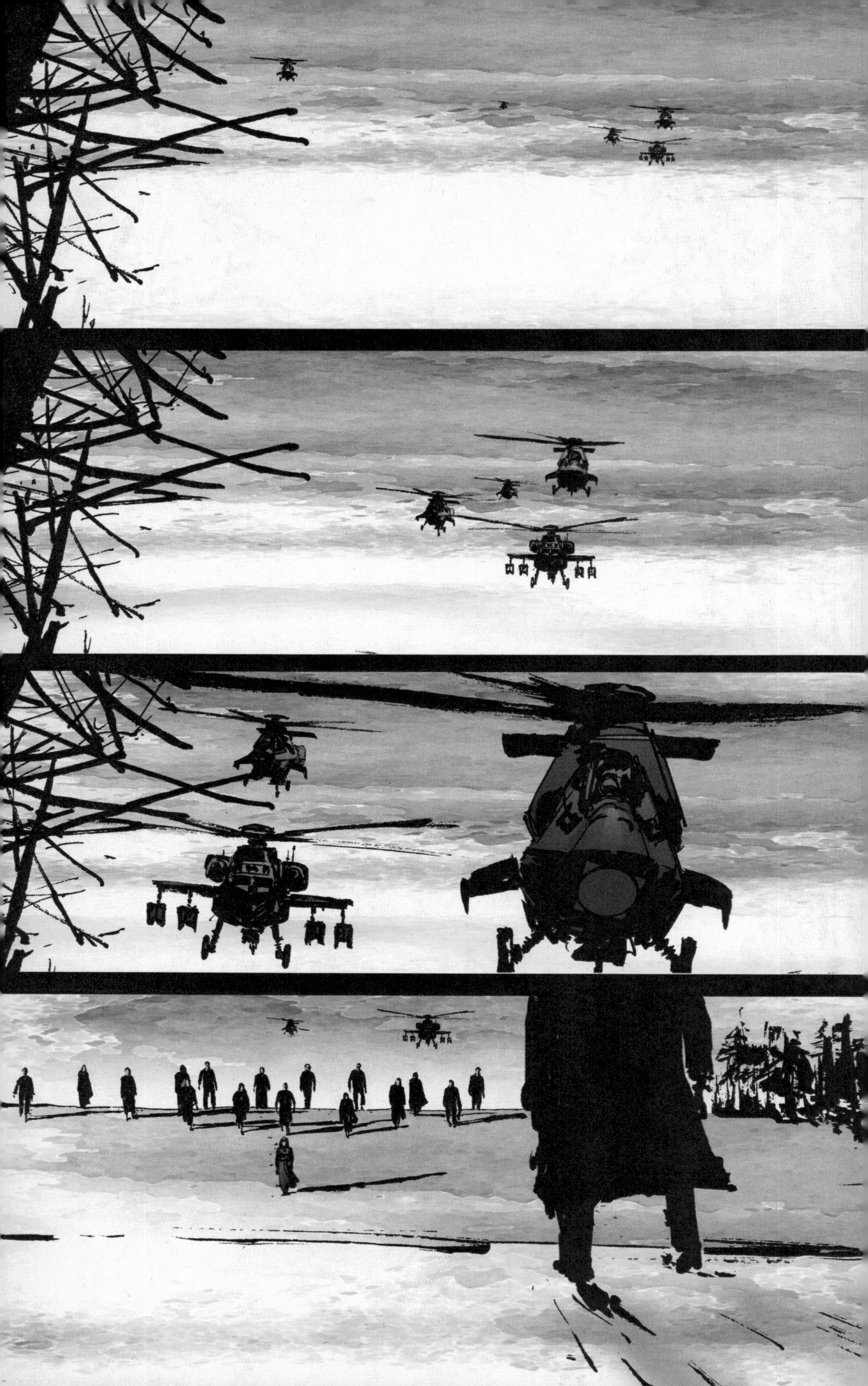

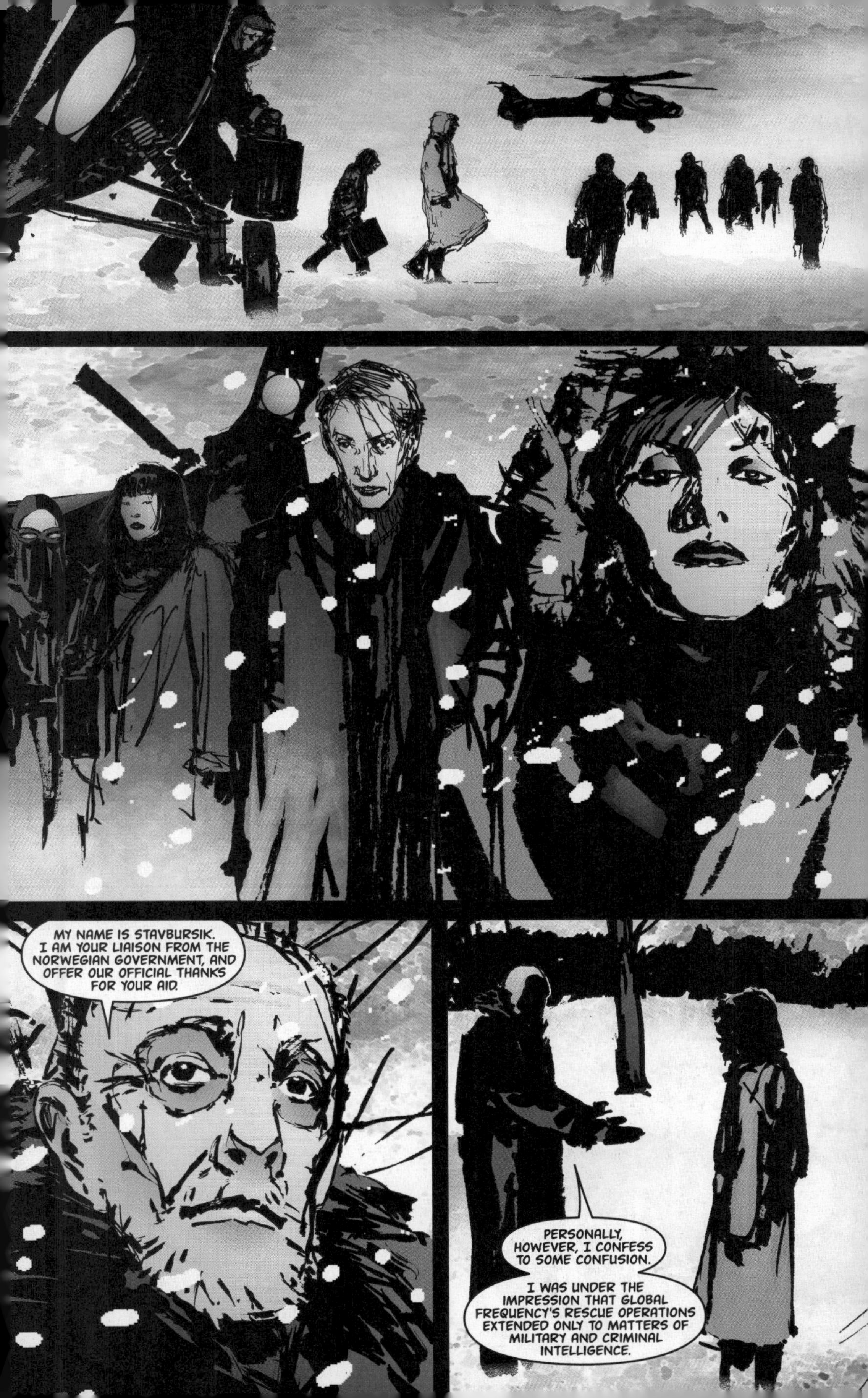
MY NAME IS STAVBURSIK. I AM YOUR LIAISON FROM THE NORWEGIAN GOVERNMENT, AND OFFER OUR OFFICIAL THANKS FOR YOUR AID.
PERSONALLY, HOWEVER, I CONFESS TO SOME CONFUSION.
I WAS UNDER THE IMPRESSION THAT GLOBAL FREQUENCY'S RESCUE OPERATIONS EXTENDED ONLY TO MATTERS OF MILITARY AND CRIMINAL INTELLIGENCE.

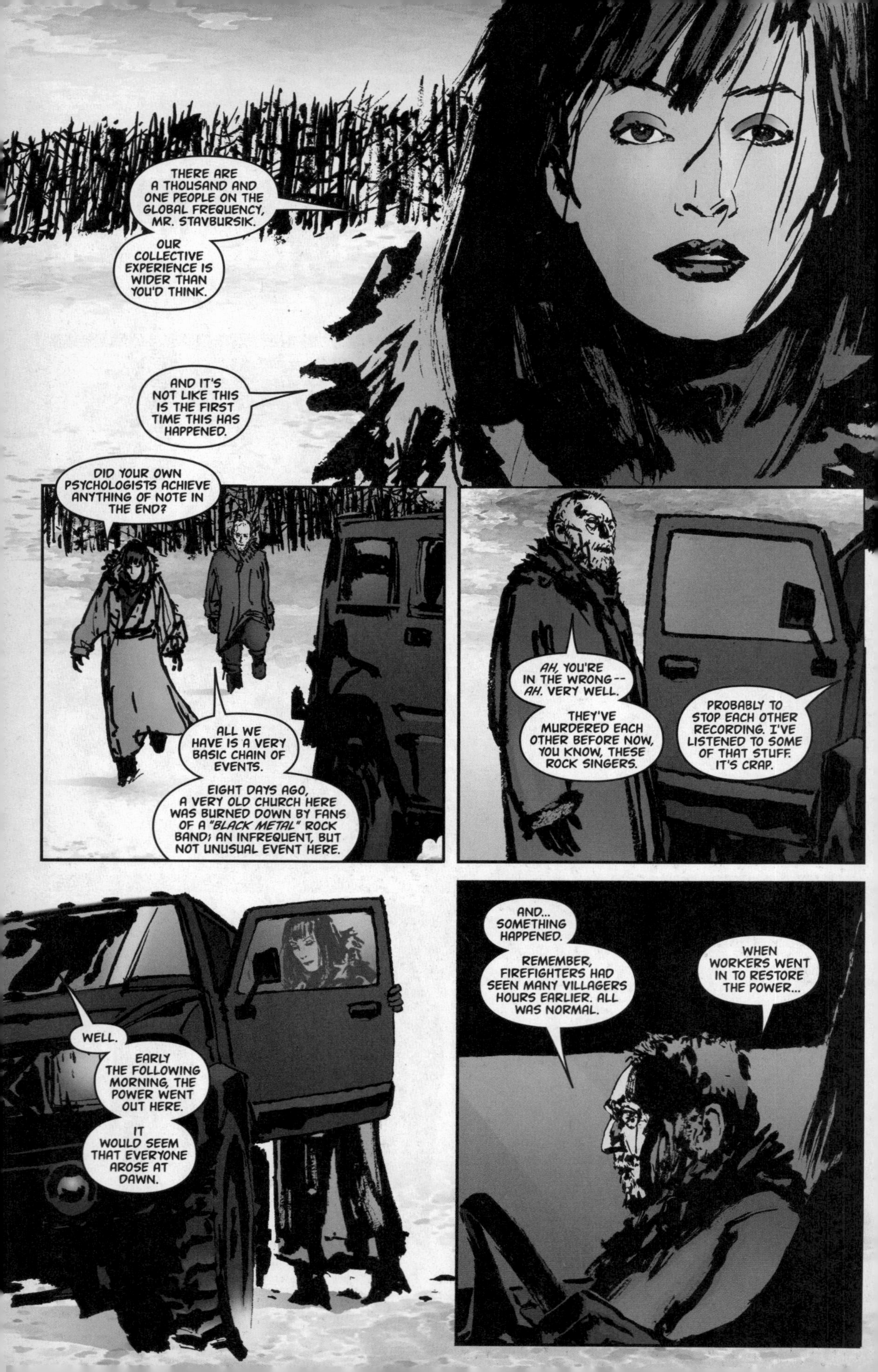
THERE ARE A THOUSAND AND ONE PEOPLE ON THE GLOBAL FREQUENCY, MR. STAVBURSIK.
OUR COLLECTIVE EXPERIENCE IS WIDER THAN YOU'D THINK.
AND IT'S NOT LIKE THIS IS THE FIRST TIME THIS HAS HAPPENED.
DID YOUR OWN PSYCHOLOGISTS ACHIEVE ANYTHING OF NOTE IN THE END?
ALL WE HAVE IS A VERY BASIC CHAIN OF EVENTS.
EIGHT DAYS AGO, A VERY OLD CHURCH HERE WAS BURNED DOWN BY FANS OF A *"BLACK METAL"* ROCK BAND; AN INFREQUENT, BUT NOT UNUSUAL EVENT HERE.
AH, YOU'RE IN THE WRONG-- *AH.* VERY WELL.
THEY'VE MURDERED EACH OTHER BEFORE NOW, YOU KNOW, THESE ROCK SINGERS.
PROBABLY TO STOP EACH OTHER RECORDING. I'VE LISTENED TO SOME OF THAT STUFF. IT'S CRAP.
WELL.
EARLY THE FOLLOWING MORNING, THE POWER WENT OUT HERE.
IT WOULD SEEM THAT EVERYONE AROSE AT DAWN.
AND... SOMETHING HAPPENED.
REMEMBER, FIREFIGHTERS HAD SEEN MANY VILLAGERS HOURS EARLIER. ALL WAS NORMAL.
WHEN WORKERS WENT IN TO RESTORE THE POWER...

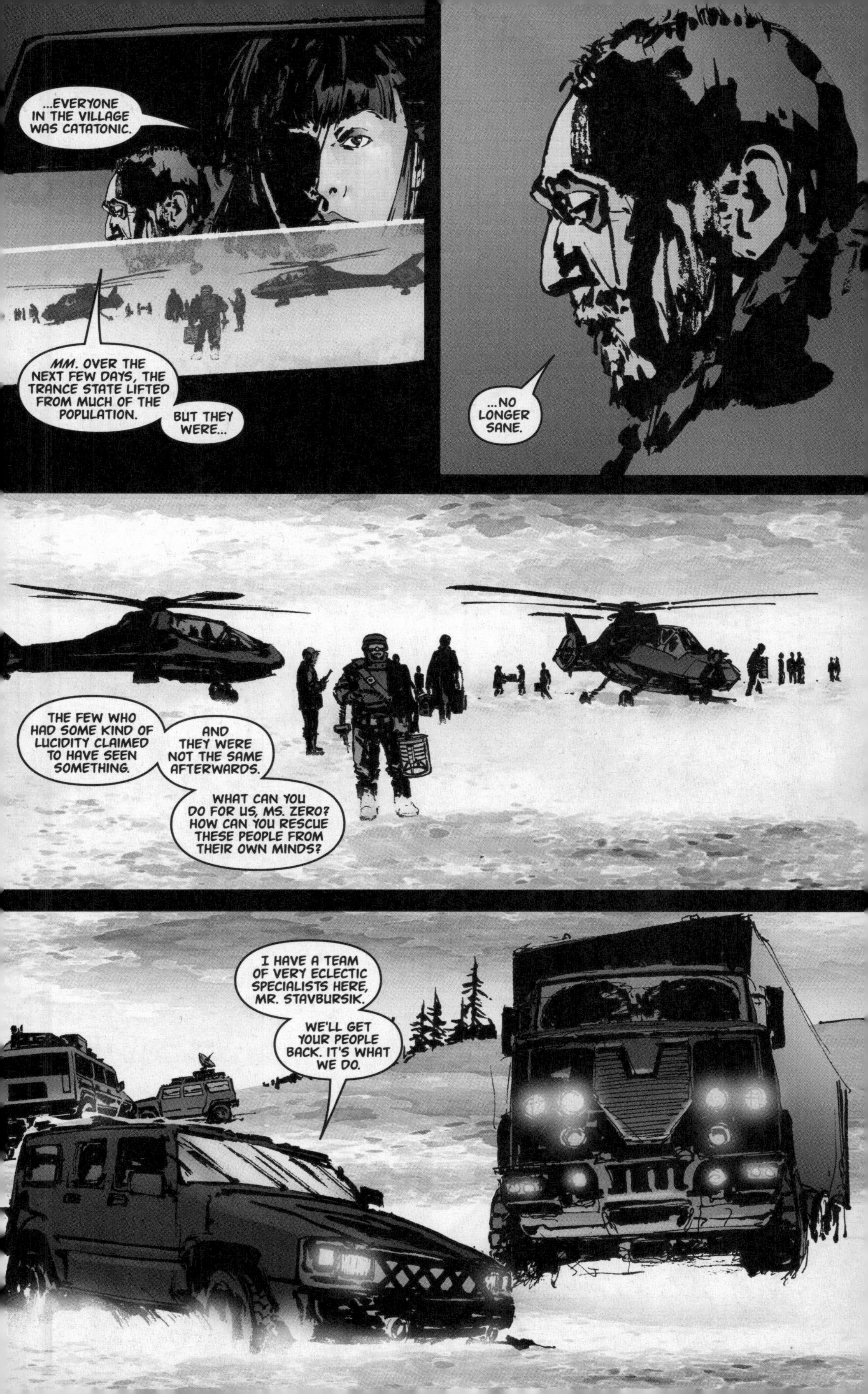
...EVERYONE IN THE VILLAGE WAS CATATONIC.
MM. OVER THE NEXT FEW DAYS, THE TRANCE STATE LIFTED FROM MUCH OF THE POPULATION.
BUT THEY WERE...
...NO LONGER SANE.
THE FEW WHO HAD SOME KIND OF LUCIDITY CLAIMED TO HAVE SEEN SOMETHING.
AND THEY WERE NOT THE SAME AFTERWARDS.
WHAT CAN YOU DO FOR US, MS. ZERO? HOW CAN YOU RESCUE THESE PEOPLE FROM THEIR OWN MINDS?
I HAVE A TEAM OF VERY ECLECTIC SPECIALISTS HERE, MR. STAVBURSIK.
WE'LL GET YOUR PEOPLE BACK. IT'S WHAT WE DO.

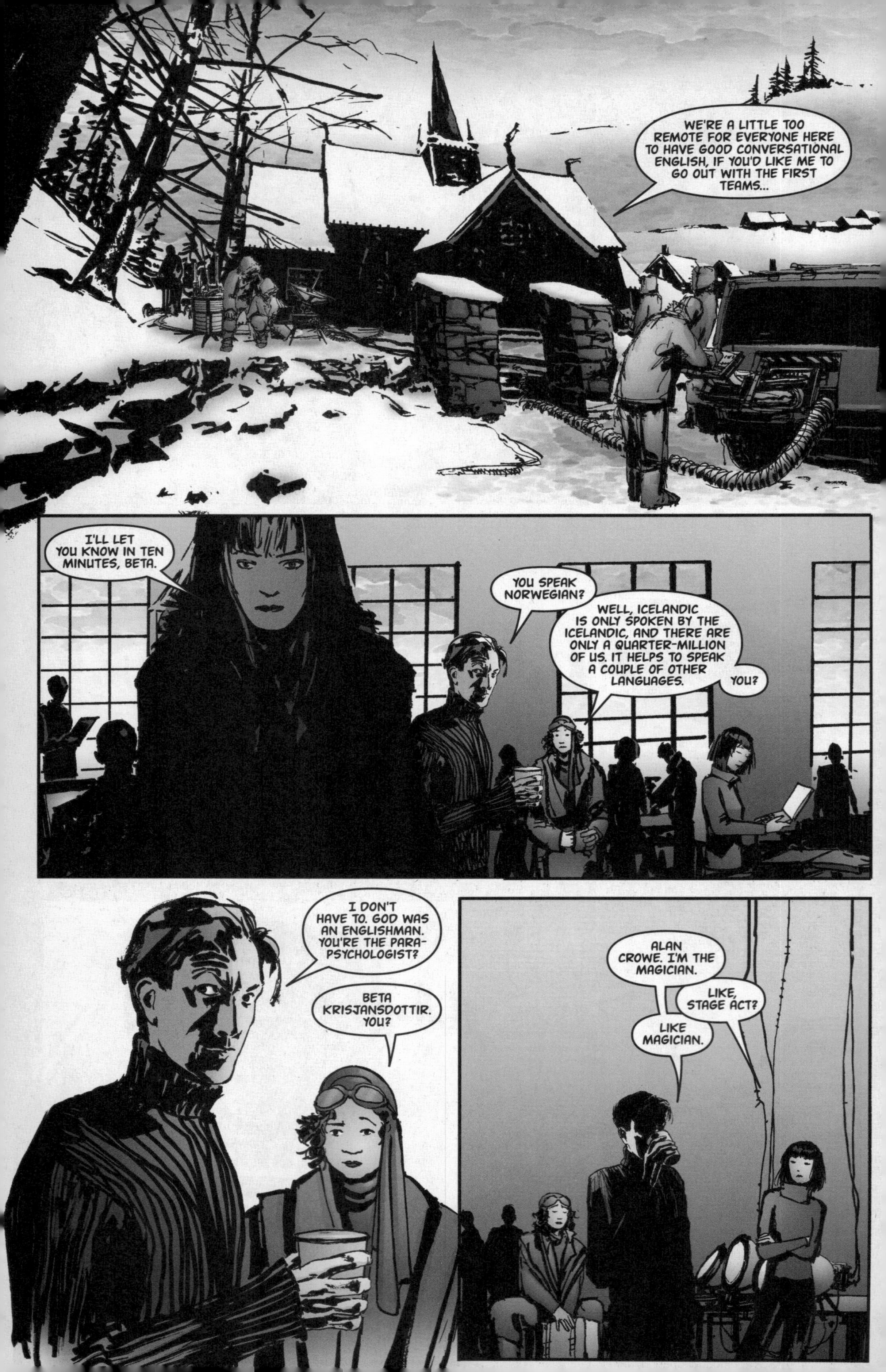
WE'RE A LITTLE TOO REMOTE FOR EVERYONE HERE TO HAVE GOOD CONVERSATIONAL ENGLISH, IF YOU'D LIKE ME TO GO OUT WITH THE FIRST TEAMS...
I'LL LET YOU KNOW IN TEN MINUTES, BETA.
YOU SPEAK NORWEGIAN?
WELL, ICELANDIC IS ONLY SPOKEN BY THE ICELANDIC, AND THERE ARE ONLY A QUARTER-MILLION OF US. IT HELPS TO SPEAK A COUPLE OF OTHER LANGUAGES.
YOU?
I DON'T HAVE TO. GOD WAS AN ENGLISHMAN. YOU'RE THE PARA-PSYCHOLOGIST?
BETA KRISJANSDOTTIR. YOU?
ALAN CROWE. I'M THE MAGICIAN.
LIKE, STAGE ACT?
LIKE MAGICIAN.

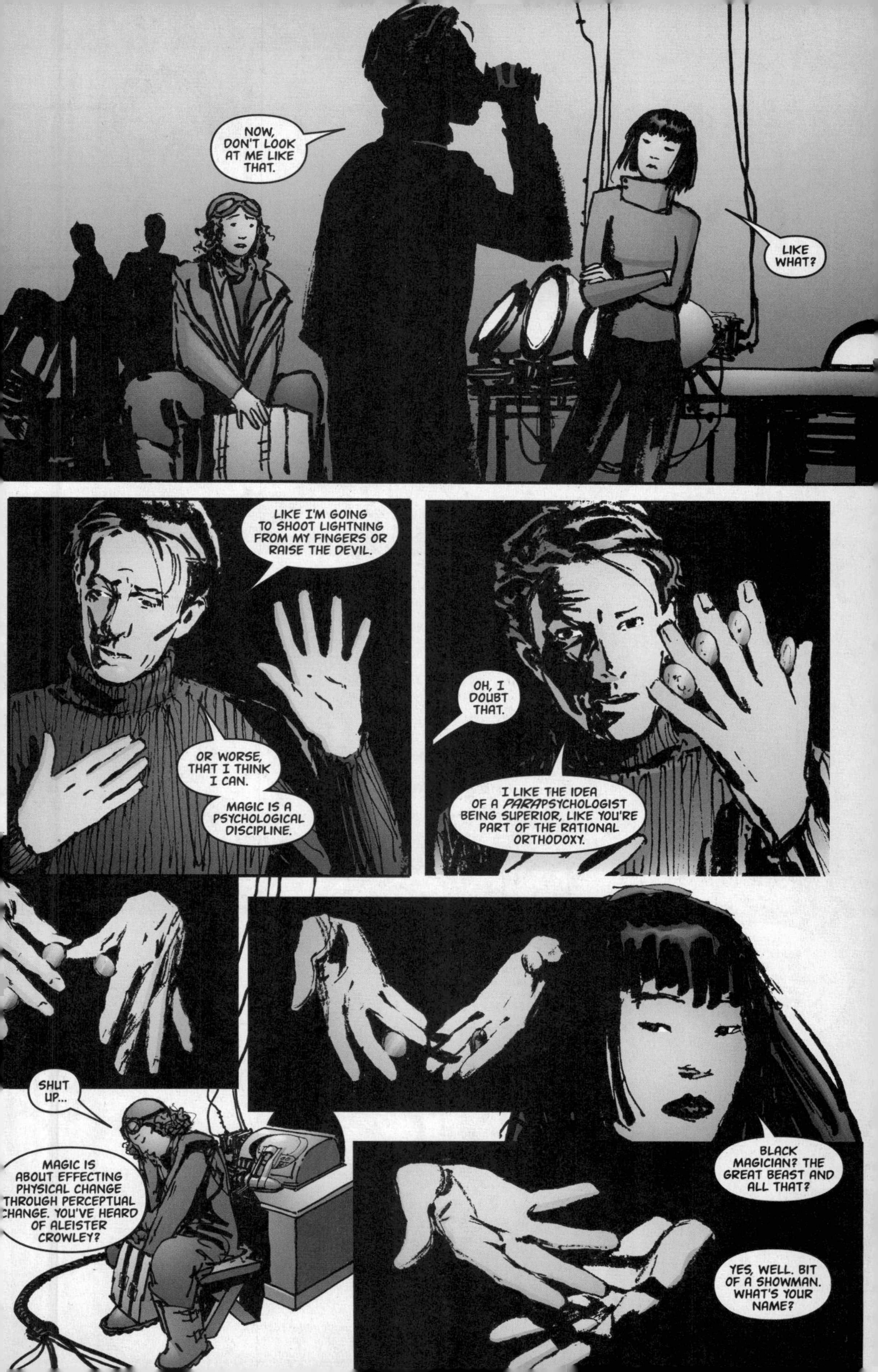
NOW, DON'T LOOK AT ME LIKE THAT.
LIKE WHAT?
LIKE I'M GOING TO SHOOT LIGHTNING FROM MY FINGERS OR RAISE THE DEVIL.
OR WORSE, THAT I THINK I CAN.
MAGIC IS A PSYCHOLOGICAL DISCIPLINE.
OH, I DOUBT THAT.
I LIKE THE IDEA OF A *PARA*PSYCHOLOGIST BEING SUPERIOR, LIKE YOU'RE PART OF THE RATIONAL ORTHODOXY.
SHUT UP...
MAGIC IS ABOUT EFFECTING PHYSICAL CHANGE THROUGH PERCEPTUAL CHANGE. YOU'VE HEARD OF ALEISTER CROWLEY?
BLACK MAGICIAN? THE GREAT BEAST AND ALL THAT?
YES, WELL. BIT OF A SHOWMAN. WHAT'S YOUR NAME?

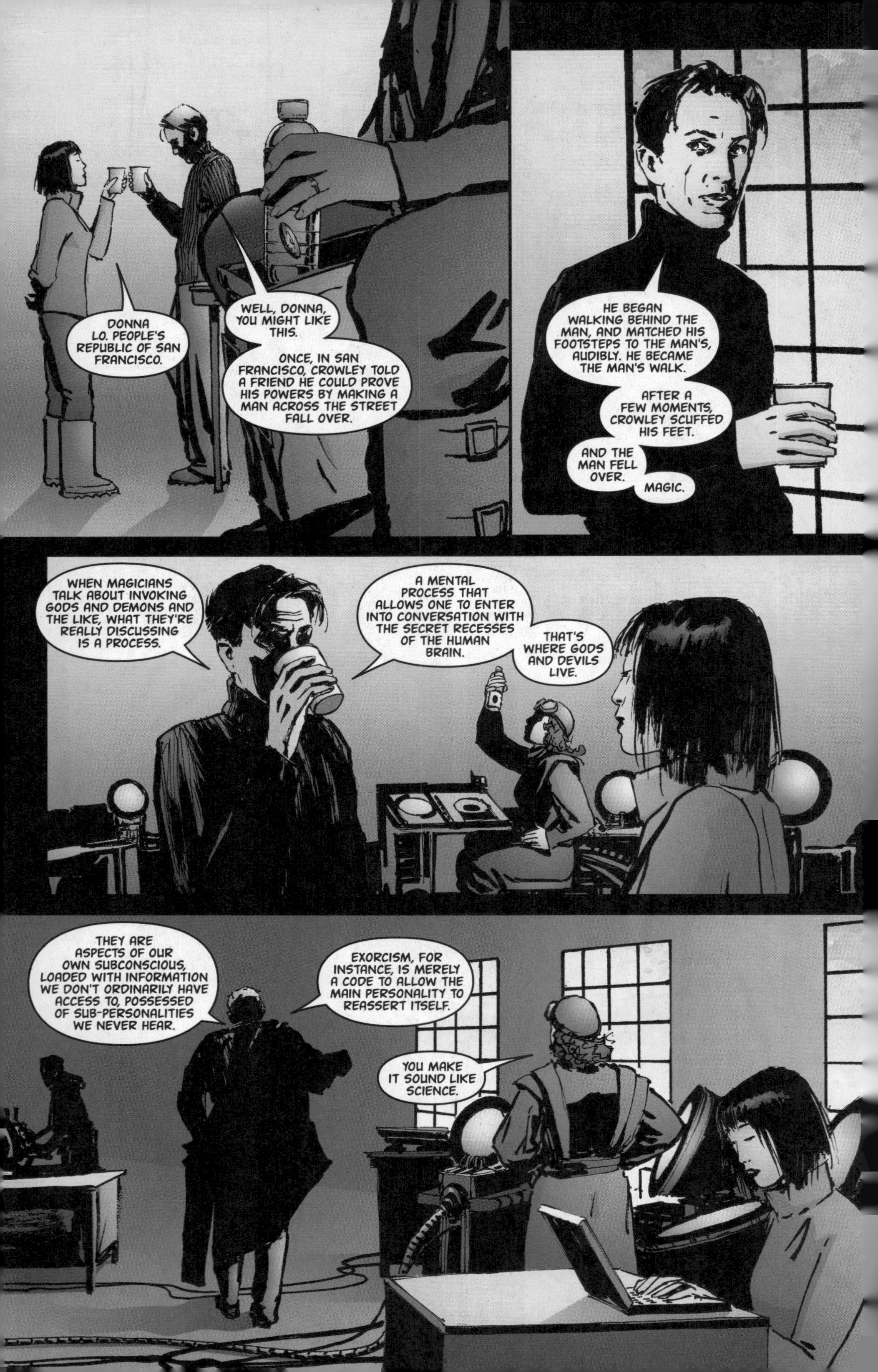
DONNA LO. PEOPLE'S REPUBLIC OF SAN FRANCISCO.
WELL, DONNA, YOU MIGHT LIKE THIS.
ONCE, IN SAN FRANCISCO, CROWLEY TOLD A FRIEND HE COULD PROVE HIS POWERS BY MAKING A MAN ACROSS THE STREET FALL OVER.
HE BEGAN WALKING BEHIND THE MAN, AND MATCHED HIS FOOTSTEPS TO THE MAN'S, AUDIBLY. HE BECAME THE MAN'S WALK.
AFTER A FEW MOMENTS, CROWLEY SCUFFED HIS FEET.
AND THE MAN FELL OVER.
MAGIC.
WHEN MAGICIANS TALK ABOUT INVOKING GODS AND DEMONS AND THE LIKE, WHAT THEY'RE REALLY DISCUSSING IS A PROCESS.
A MENTAL PROCESS THAT ALLOWS ONE TO ENTER INTO CONVERSATION WITH THE SECRET RECESSES OF THE HUMAN BRAIN.
THAT'S WHERE GODS AND DEVILS LIVE.
THEY ARE ASPECTS OF OUR OWN SUBCONSCIOUS, LOADED WITH INFORMATION WE DON'T ORDINARILY HAVE ACCESS TO, POSSESSED OF SUB-PERSONALITIES WE NEVER HEAR.
EXORCISM, FOR INSTANCE, IS MERELY A CODE TO ALLOW THE MAIN PERSONALITY TO REASSERT ITSELF.
YOU MAKE IT SOUND LIKE SCIENCE.

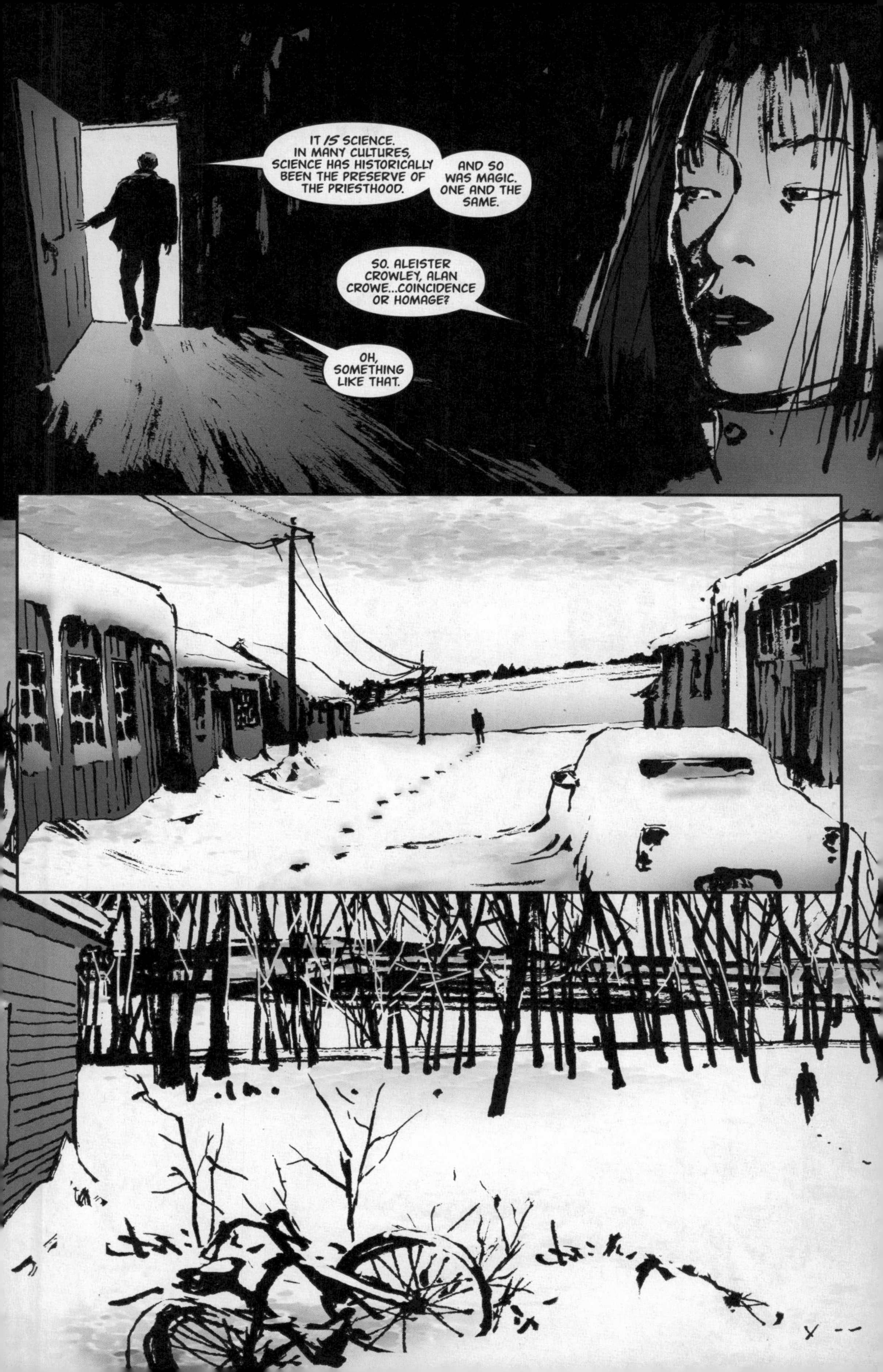
IT IS SCIENCE. IN MANY CULTURES, SCIENCE HAS HISTORICALLY BEEN THE PRESERVE OF THE PRIESTHOOD.
AND SO WAS MAGIC. ONE AND THE SAME.
SO. ALEISTER CROWLEY, ALAN CROWE...COINCIDENCE OR HOMAGE?
OH, SOMETHING LIKE THAT.

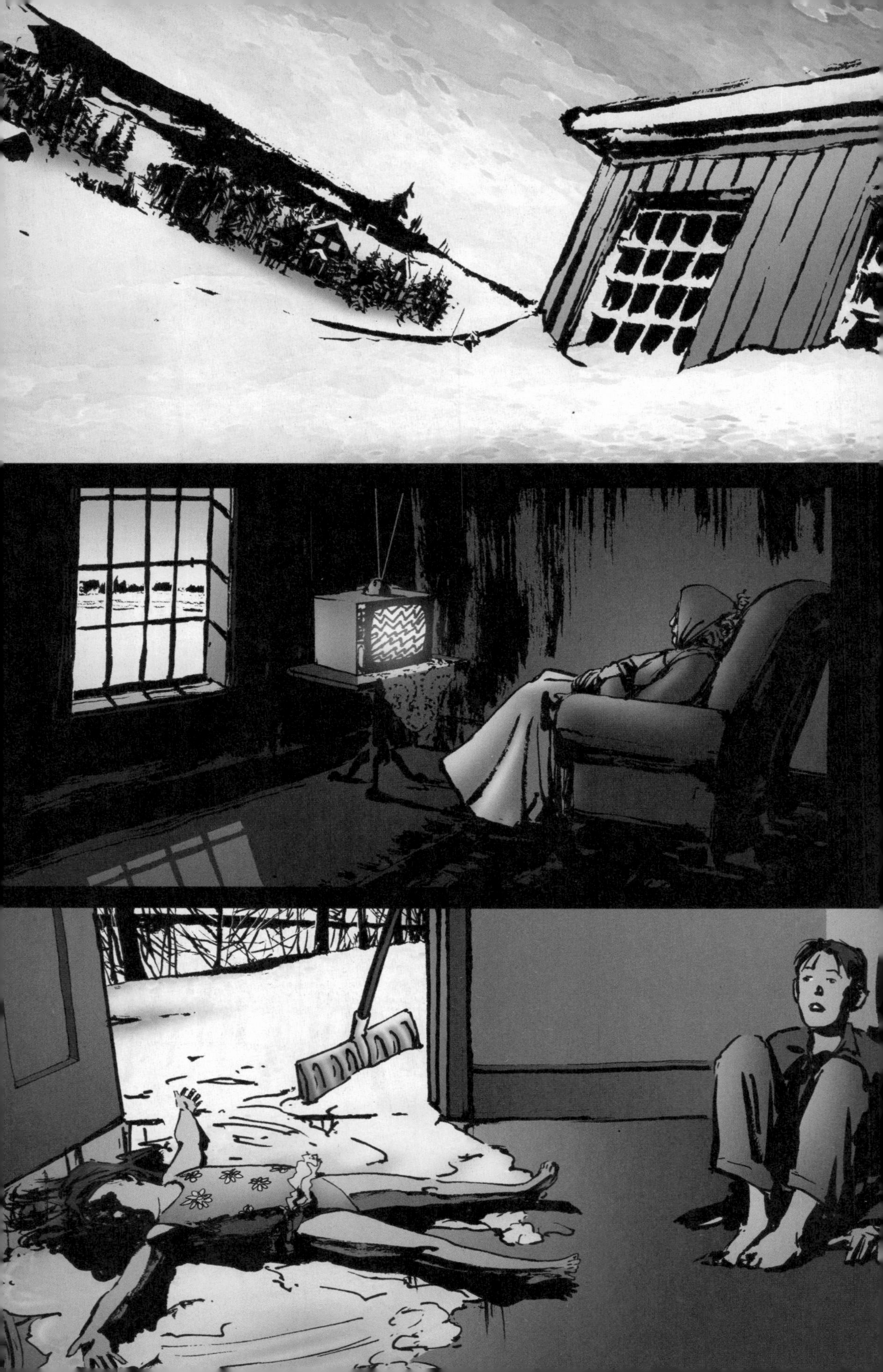

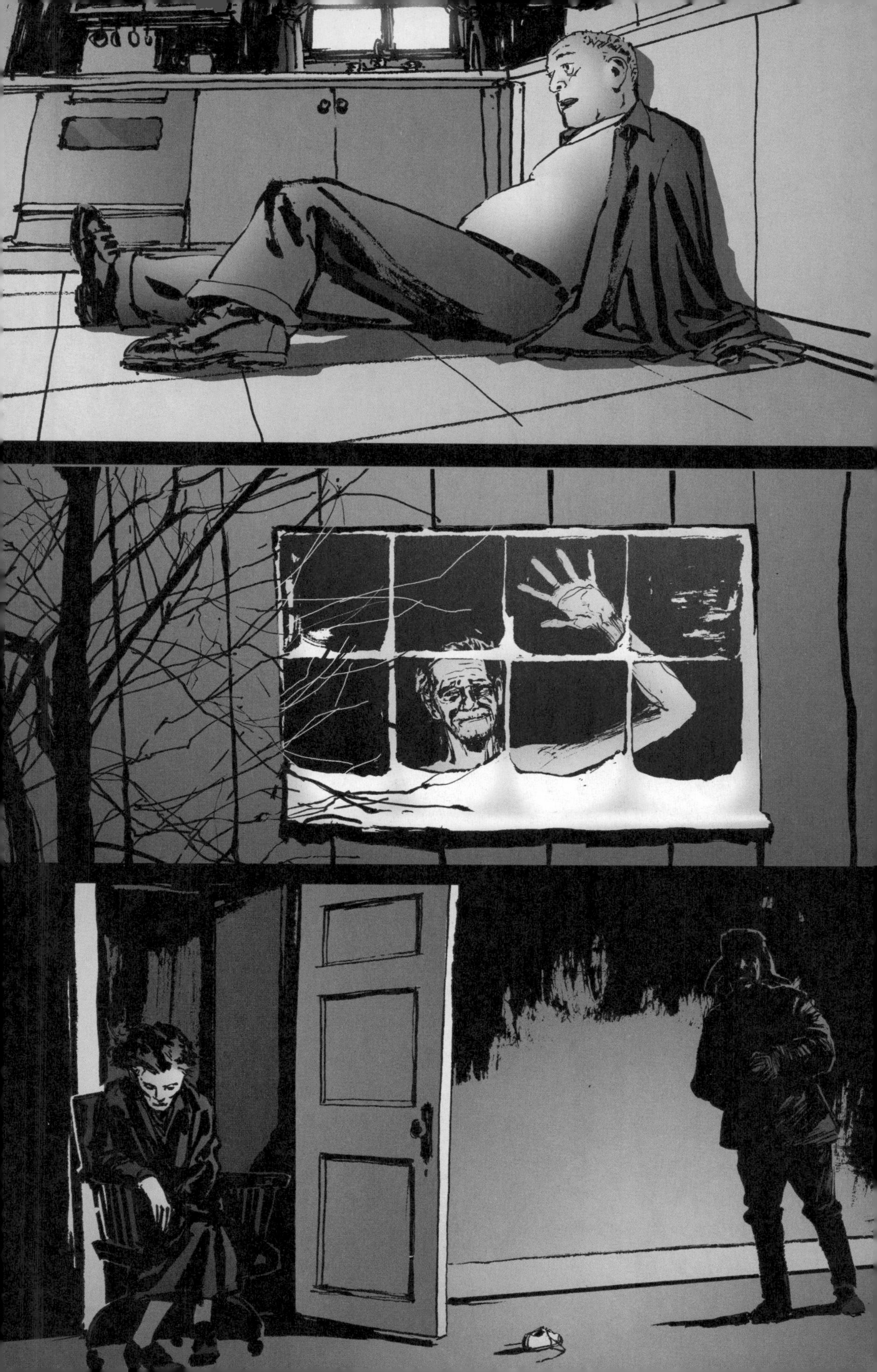

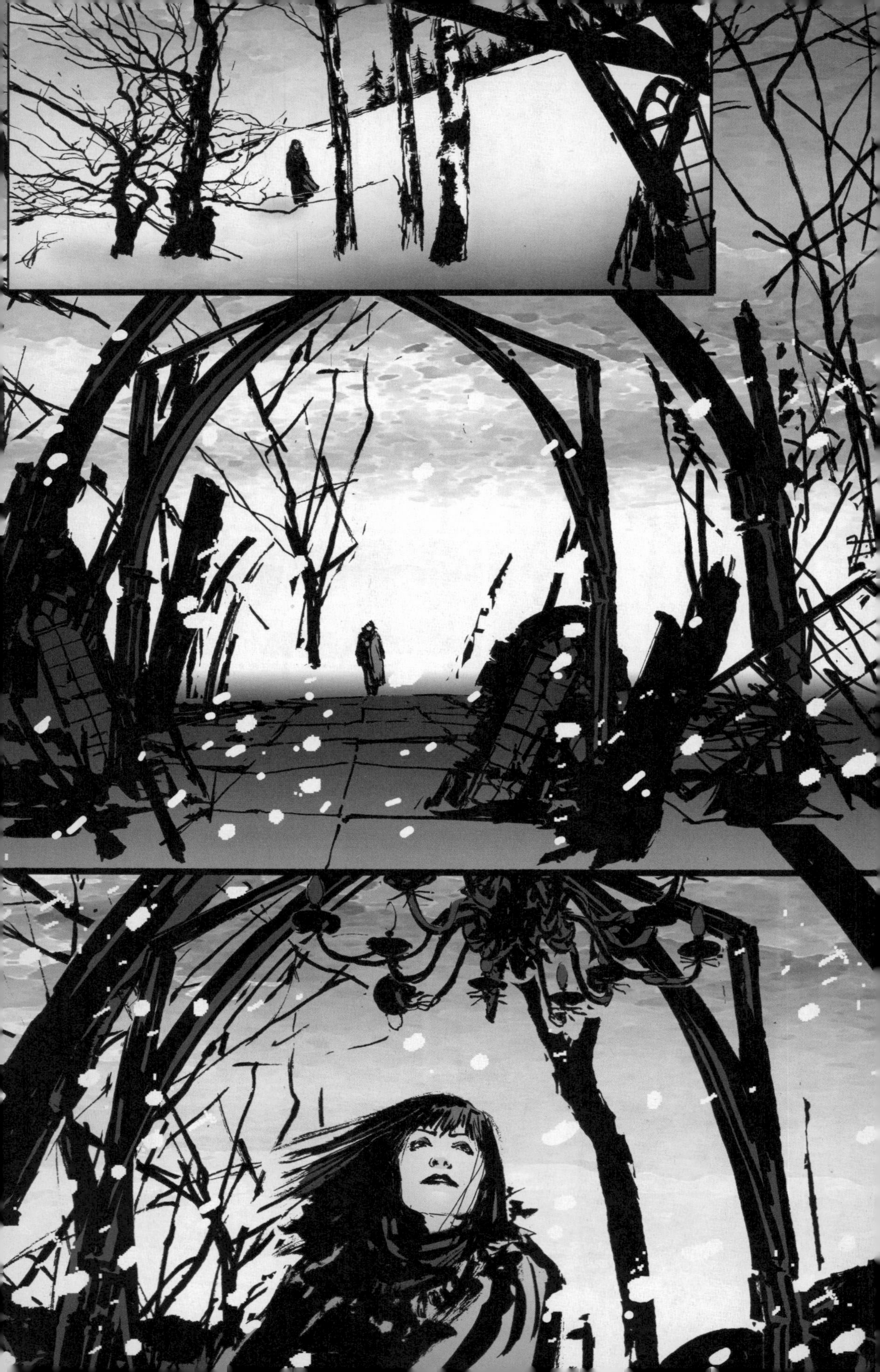

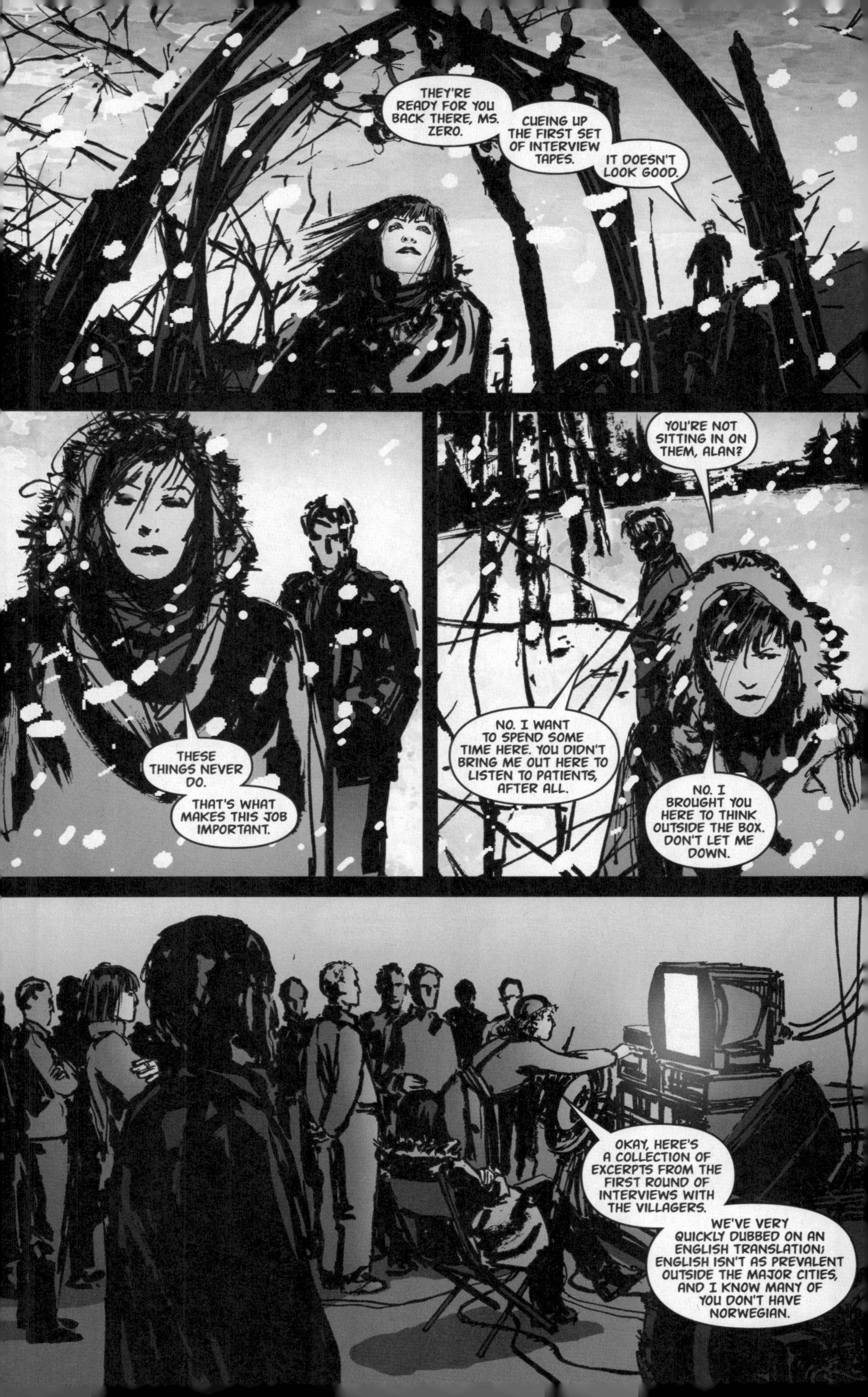
THEY'RE READY FOR YOU BACK THERE, MS. ZERO.
CUEING UP THE FIRST SET OF INTERVIEW TAPES.
IT DOESN'T LOOK GOOD.
THESE THINGS NEVER DO.
THAT'S WHAT MAKES THIS JOB IMPORTANT.
YOU'RE NOT SITTING IN ON THEM, ALAN?
NO. I WANT TO SPEND SOME TIME HERE. YOU DIDN'T BRING ME OUT HERE TO LISTEN TO PATIENTS, AFTER ALL.
NO. I BROUGHT YOU HERE TO THINK OUTSIDE THE BOX. DON'T LET ME DOWN.
OKAY, HERE'S A COLLECTION OF EXCERPTS FROM THE FIRST ROUND OF INTERVIEWS WITH THE VILLAGERS.
WE'VE VERY QUICKLY DUBBED ON AN ENGLISH TRANSLATION; ENGLISH ISN'T AS PREVALENT OUTSIDE THE MAJOR CITIES, AND I KNOW MANY OF YOU DON'T HAVE NORWEGIAN.

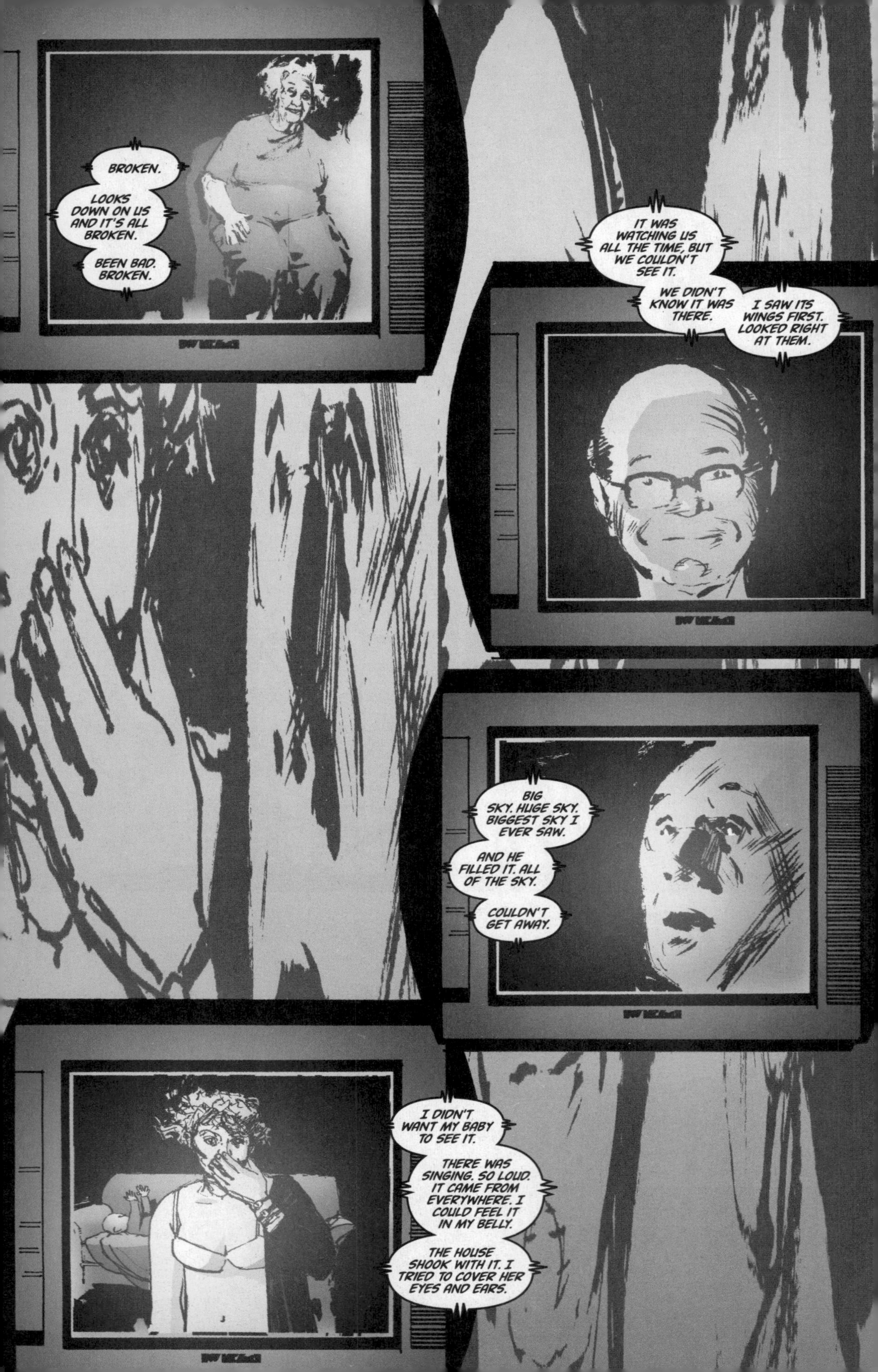
BROKEN.
LOOKS DOWN ON US AND IT'S ALL BROKEN.
BEEN BAD. BROKEN.
IT WAS WATCHING US ALL THE TIME, BUT WE COULDN'T SEE IT.
WE DIDN'T KNOW IT WAS THERE.
I SAW ITS WINGS FIRST. LOOKED RIGHT AT THEM.
BIG SKY. HUGE SKY. BIGGEST SKY I EVER SAW.
AND HE FILLED IT. ALL OF THE SKY.
COULDN'T GET AWAY.
I DIDN'T WANT MY BABY TO SEE IT.
THERE WAS SINGING. SO LOUD. IT CAME FROM EVERYWHERE. I COULD FEEL IT IN MY BELLY.
THE HOUSE SHOOK WITH IT. I TRIED TO COVER HER EYES AND EARS.

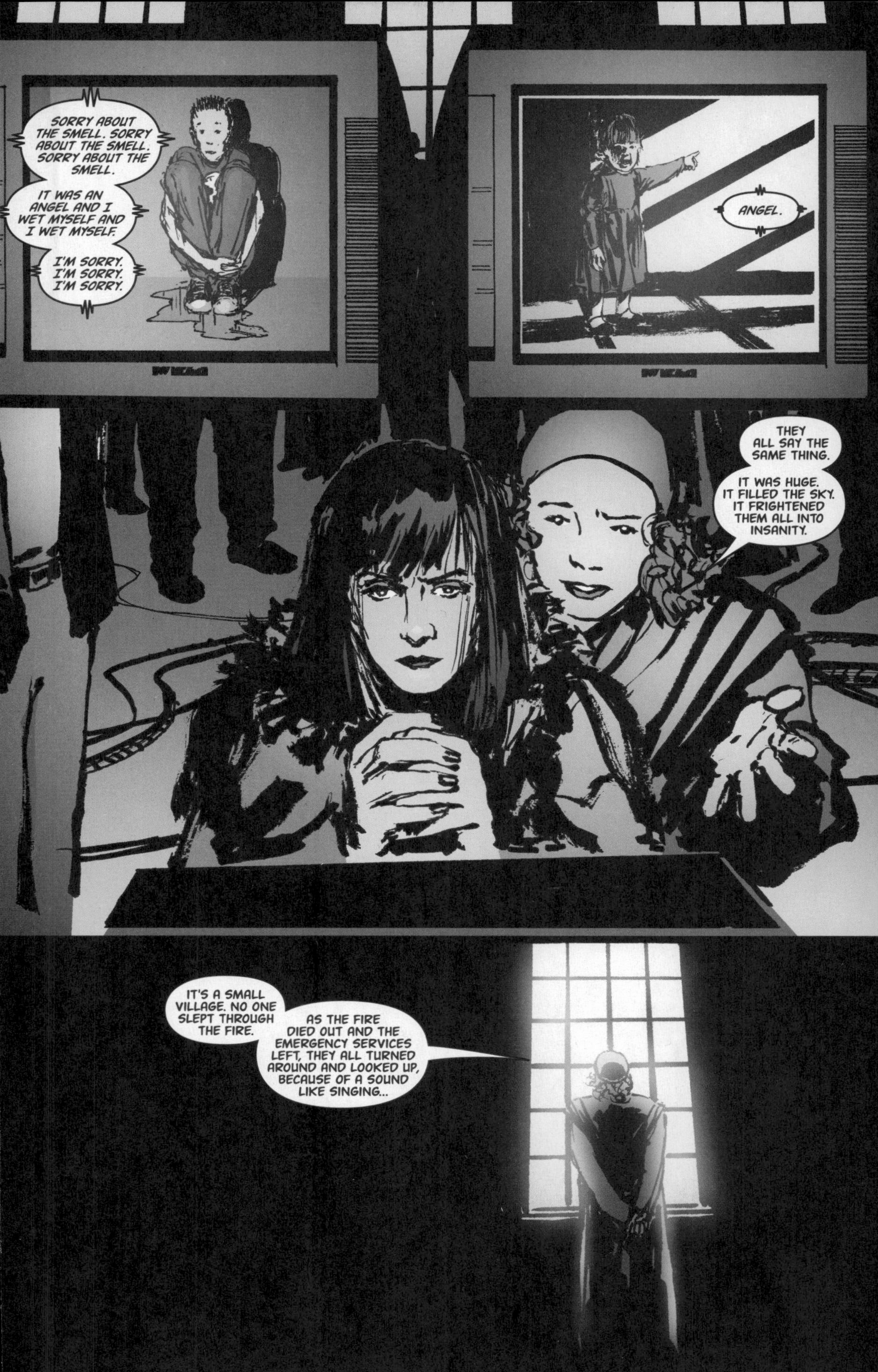
SORRY ABOUT THE SMELL. SORRY ABOUT THE SMELL. SORRY ABOUT THE SMELL.
IT WAS AN ANGEL AND I WET MYSELF AND I WET MYSELF.
I'M SORRY. I'M SORRY. I'M SORRY.
ANGEL.
THEY ALL SAY THE SAME THING.
IT WAS HUGE. IT FILLED THE SKY. IT FRIGHTENED THEM ALL INTO INSANITY.
IT'S A SMALL VILLAGE. NO ONE SLEPT THROUGH THE FIRE.
AS THE FIRE DIED OUT AND THE EMERGENCY SERVICES LEFT, THEY ALL TURNED AROUND AND LOOKED UP, BECAUSE OF A SOUND LIKE SINGING...

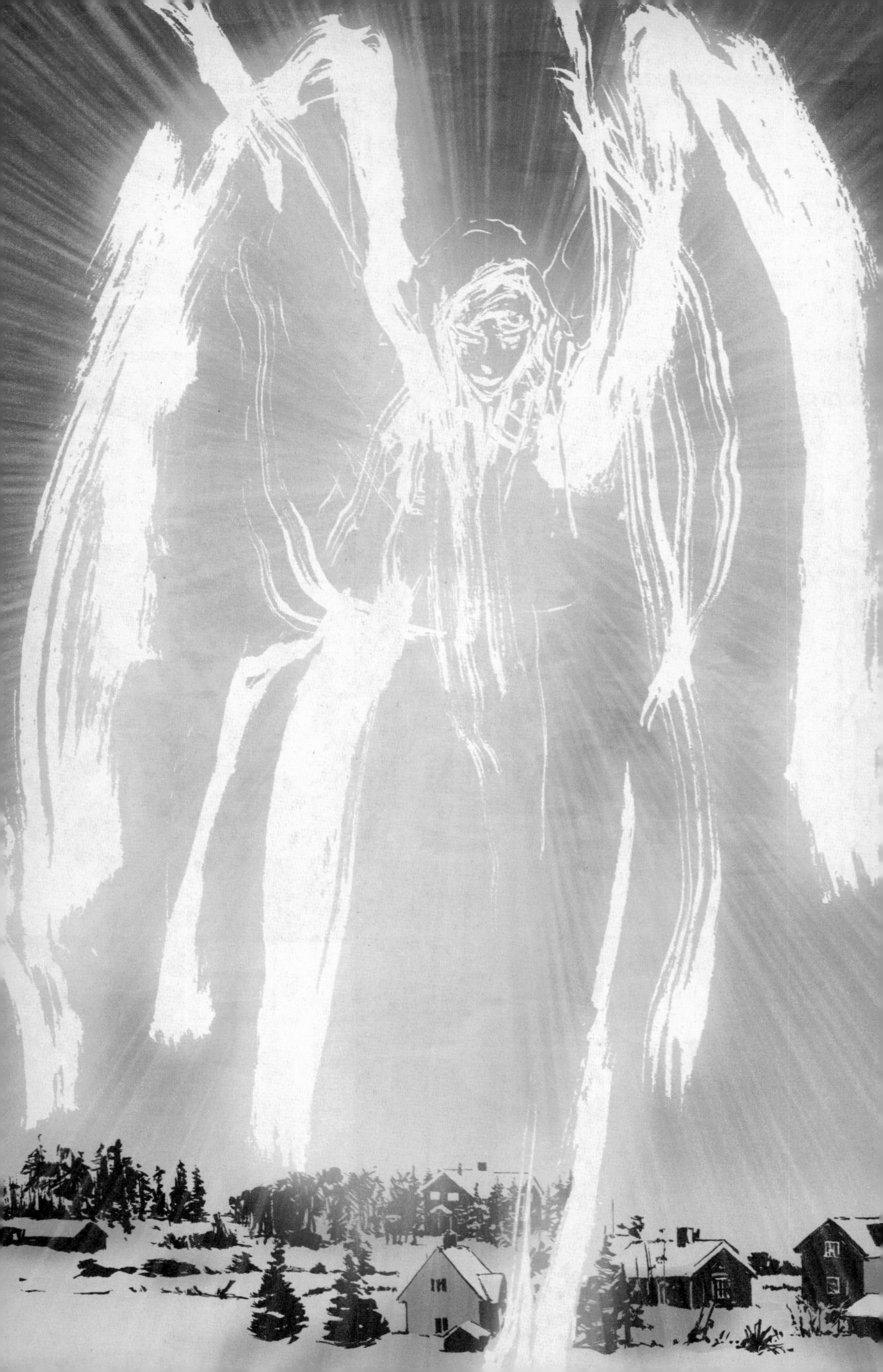

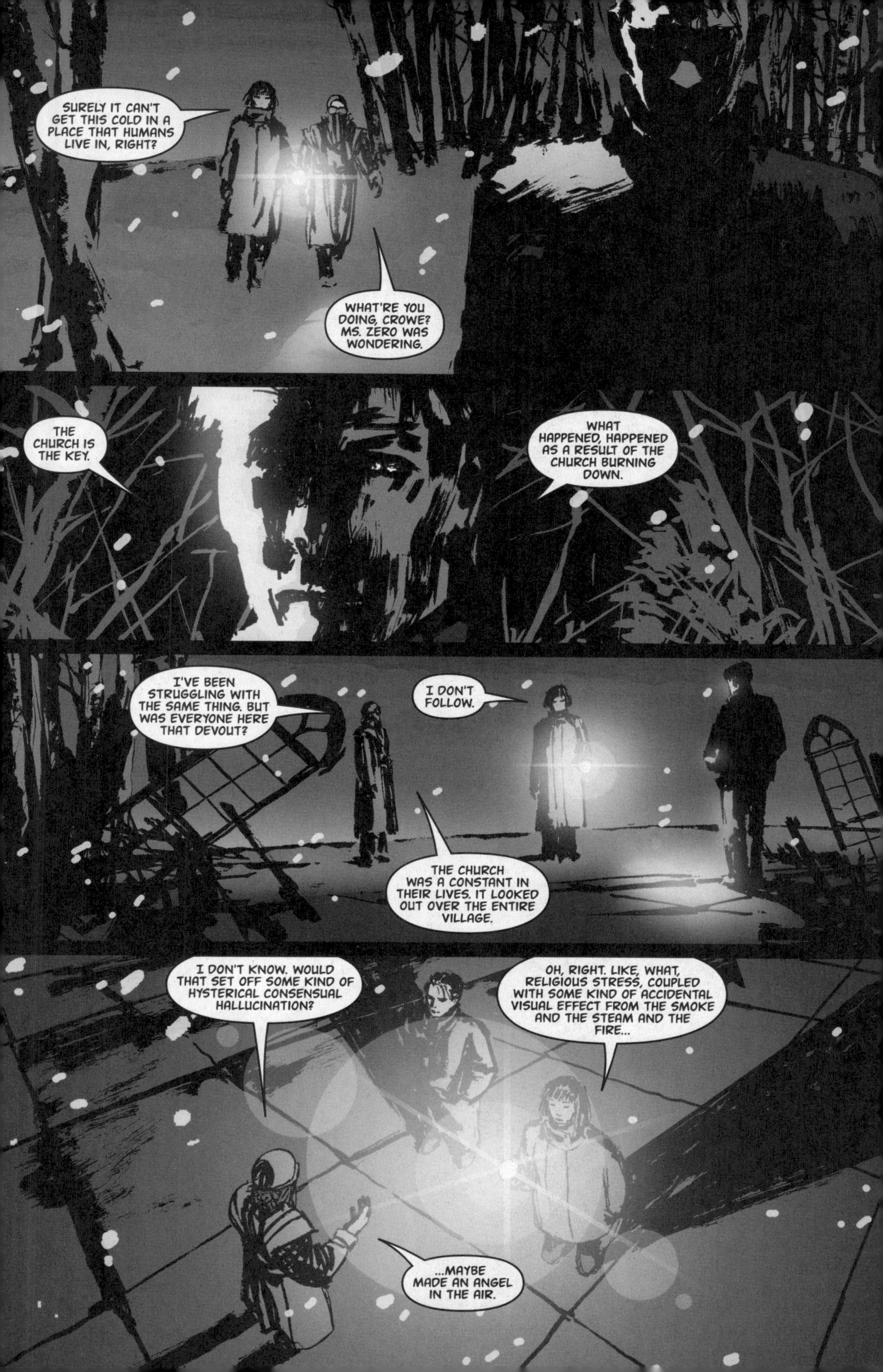
SURELY IT CAN'T GET THIS COLD IN A PLACE THAT HUMANS LIVE IN, RIGHT?
WHAT'RE YOU DOING, CROWE? MS. ZERO WAS WONDERING.
THE CHURCH IS THE KEY.
WHAT HAPPENED, HAPPENED AS A RESULT OF THE CHURCH BURNING DOWN.
I'VE BEEN STRUGGLING WITH THE SAME THING. BUT WAS EVERYONE HERE THAT DEVOUT?
I DON'T FOLLOW.
THE CHURCH WAS A CONSTANT IN THEIR LIVES. IT LOOKED OUT OVER THE ENTIRE VILLAGE.
I DON'T KNOW. WOULD THAT SET OFF SOME KIND OF HYSTERICAL CONSENSUAL HALLUCINATION?
OH, RIGHT. LIKE, WHAT, RELIGIOUS STRESS, COUPLED WITH SOME KIND OF ACCIDENTAL VISUAL EFFECT FROM THE SMOKE AND THE STEAM AND THE FIRE...
...MAYBE MADE AN ANGEL IN THE AIR.

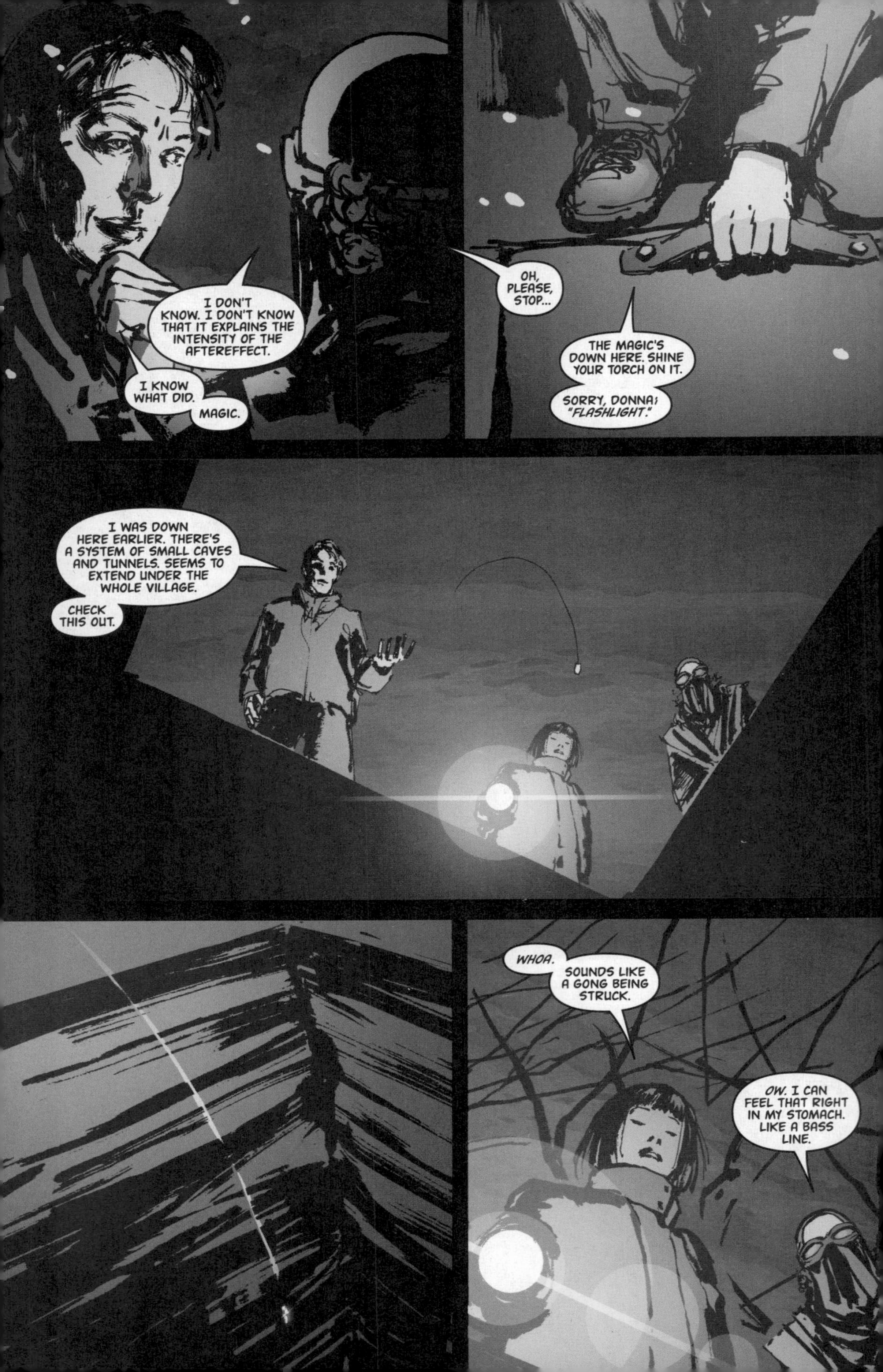
I DON'T KNOW. I DON'T KNOW THAT IT EXPLAINS THE INTENSITY OF THE AFTEREFFECT.
I KNOW WHAT DID.
MAGIC.
OH, PLEASE, STOP...
THE MAGIC'S DOWN HERE. SHINE YOUR TORCH ON IT.
SORRY, DONNA; "FLASHLIGHT."
I WAS DOWN HERE EARLIER. THERE'S A SYSTEM OF SMALL CAVES AND TUNNELS. SEEMS TO EXTEND UNDER THE WHOLE VILLAGE.
CHECK THIS OUT.
WHOA.
SOUNDS LIKE A GONG BEING STRUCK.
OW. I CAN FEEL THAT RIGHT IN MY STOMACH. LIKE A BASS LINE.

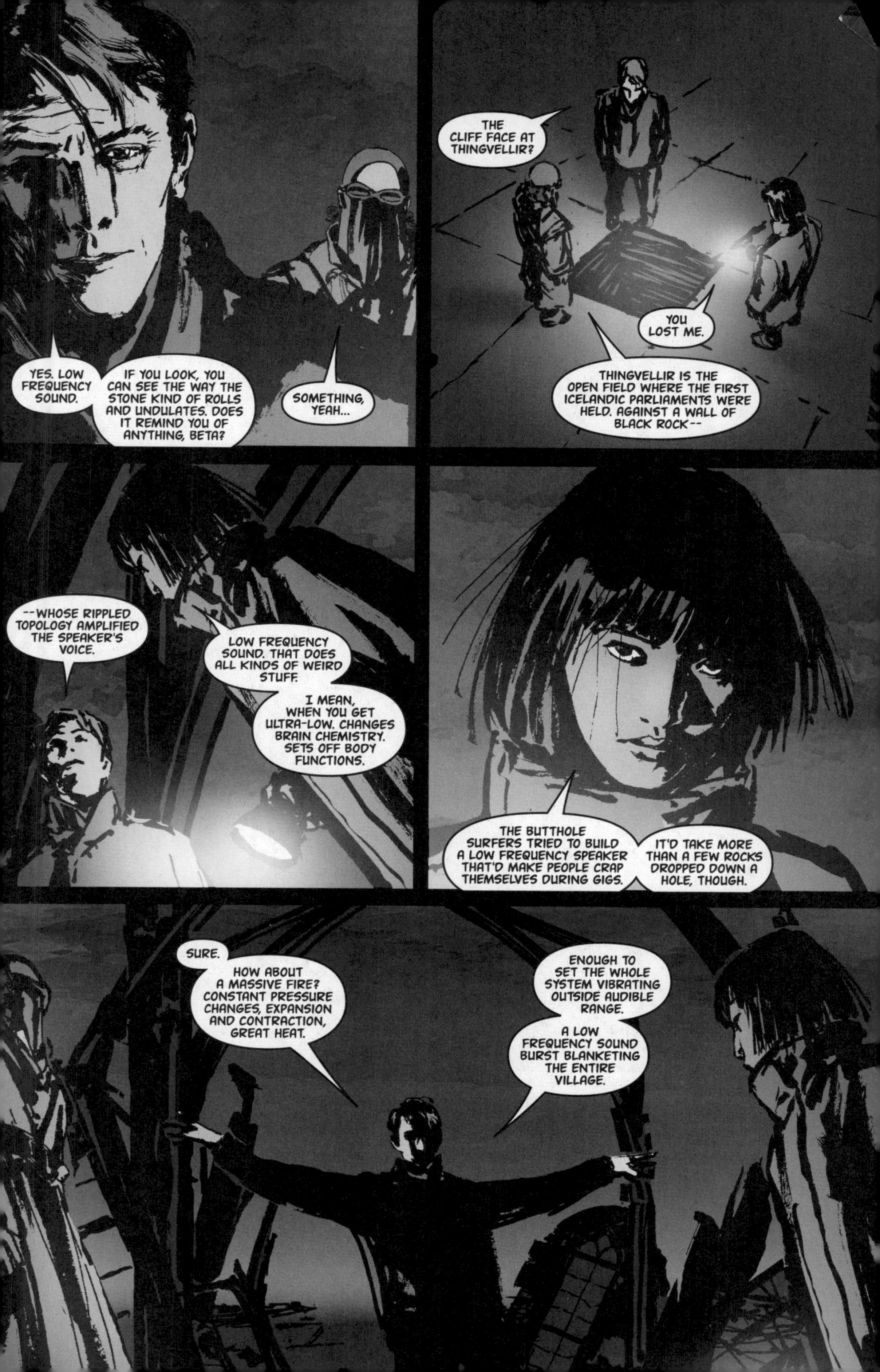
YES. LOW FREQUENCY SOUND.
IF YOU LOOK, YOU CAN SEE THE WAY THE STONE KIND OF ROLLS AND UNDULATES. DOES IT REMIND YOU OF ANYTHING, BETA?
SOMETHING, YEAH...
THE CLIFF FACE AT THINGVELLIR?
YOU LOST ME.
THINGVELLIR IS THE OPEN FIELD WHERE THE FIRST ICELANDIC PARLIAMENTS WERE HELD. AGAINST A WALL OF BLACK ROCK--
--WHOSE RIPPLED TOPOLOGY AMPLIFIED THE SPEAKER'S VOICE.
LOW FREQUENCY SOUND. THAT DOES ALL KINDS OF WEIRD STUFF.
I MEAN, WHEN YOU GET ULTRA-LOW. CHANGES BRAIN CHEMISTRY. SETS OFF BODY FUNCTIONS.
THE BUTTHOLE SURFERS TRIED TO BUILD A LOW FREQUENCY SPEAKER THAT'D MAKE PEOPLE CRAP THEMSELVES DURING GIGS.
IT'D TAKE MORE THAN A FEW ROCKS DROPPED DOWN A HOLE, THOUGH.
SURE.
HOW ABOUT A MASSIVE FIRE? CONSTANT PRESSURE CHANGES, EXPANSION AND CONTRACTION, GREAT HEAT.
ENOUGH TO SET THE WHOLE SYSTEM VIBRATING OUTSIDE AUDIBLE RANGE.
A LOW FREQUENCY SOUND BURST BLANKETING THE ENTIRE VILLAGE.

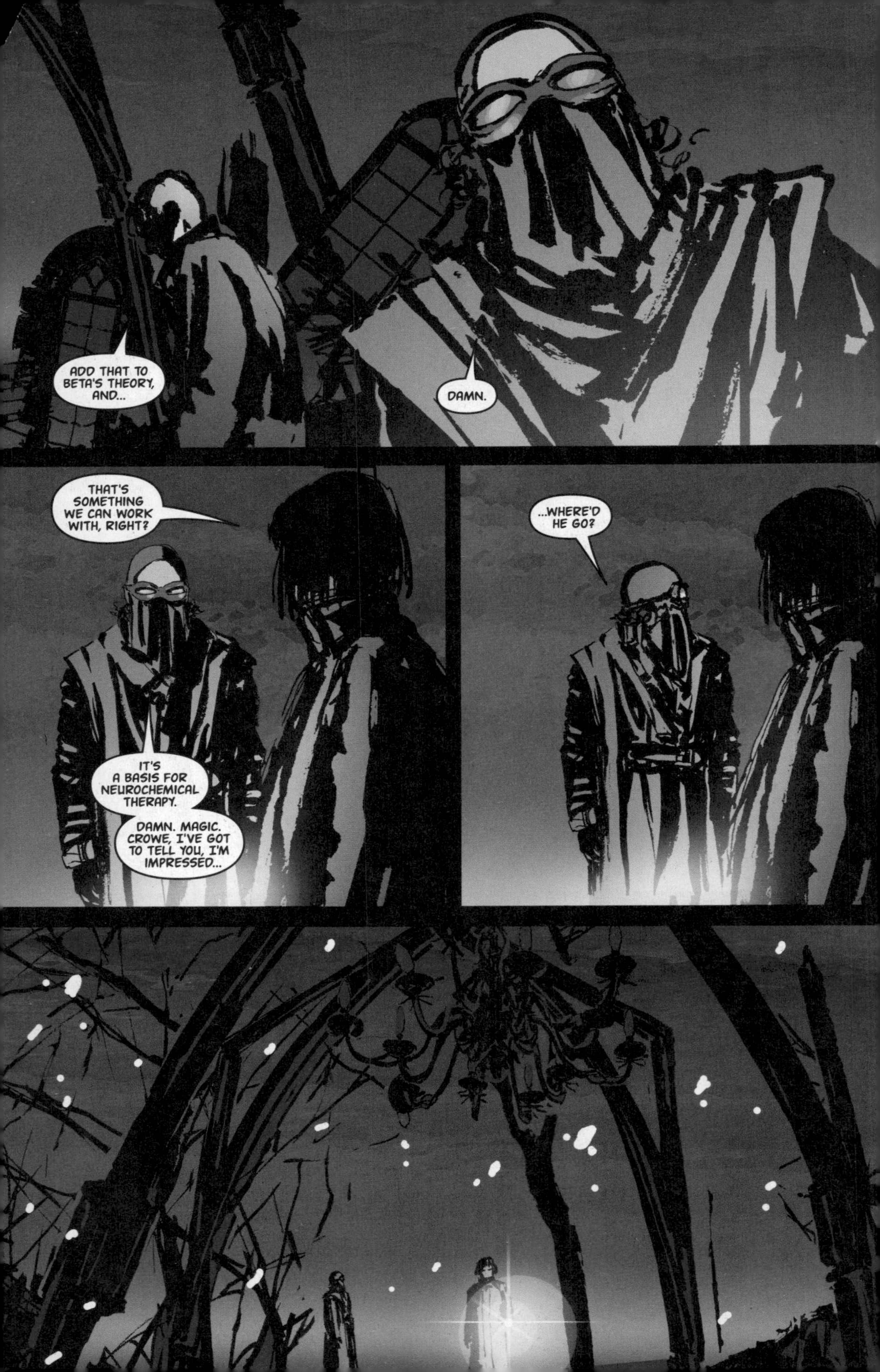
ADD THAT TO BETA'S THEORY, AND...
DAMN.
THAT'S SOMETHING WE CAN WORK WITH, RIGHT?
IT'S A BASIS FOR NEUROCHEMICAL THERAPY.
DAMN. MAGIC. CROWE, I'VE GOT TO TELL YOU, I'M IMPRESSED...
...WHERE'D HE GO?

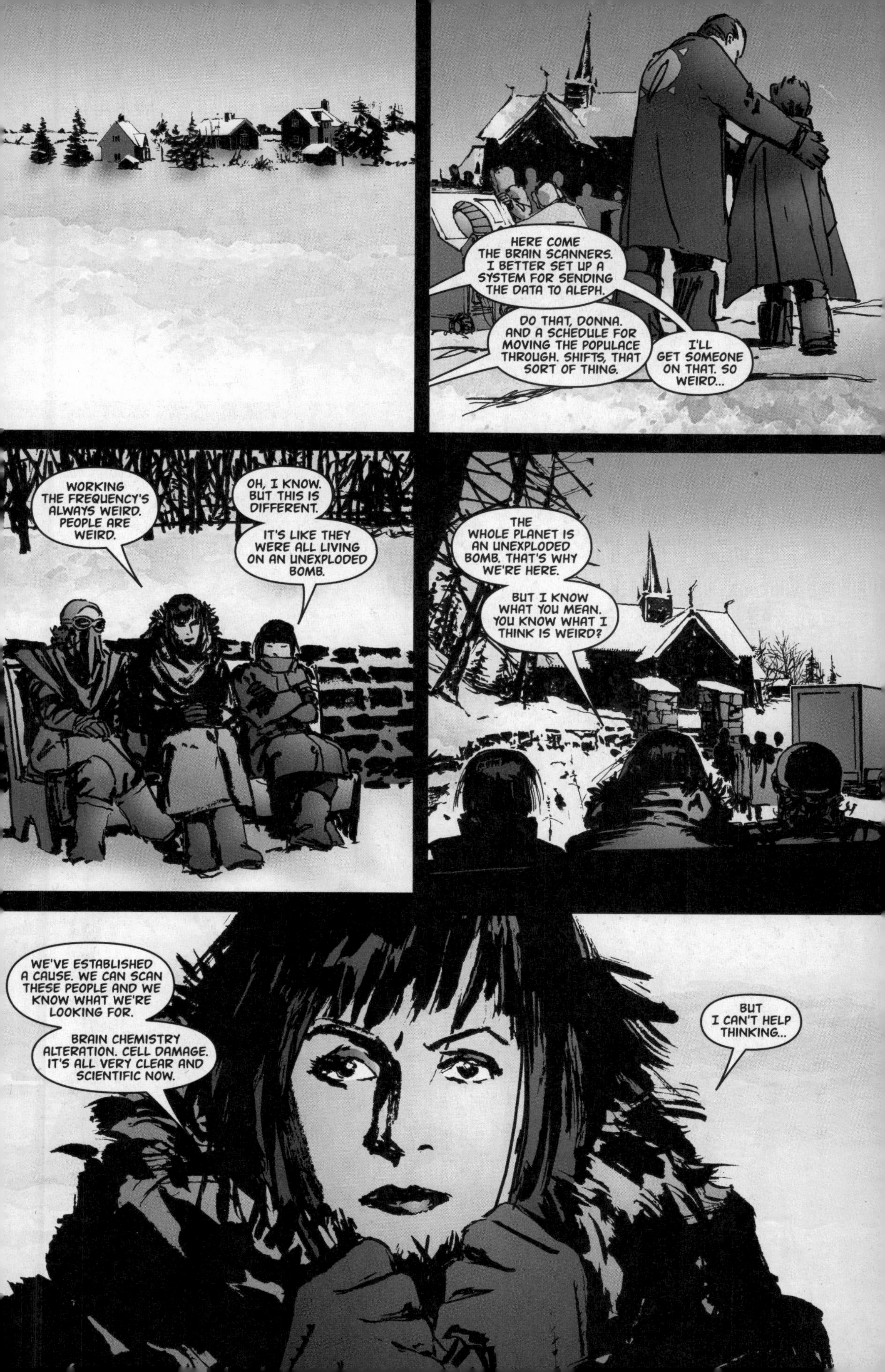
HERE COME THE BRAIN SCANNERS. I BETTER SET UP A SYSTEM FOR SENDING THE DATA TO ALEPH.
DO THAT, DONNA. AND A SCHEDULE FOR MOVING THE POPULACE THROUGH. SHIFTS, THAT SORT OF THING.
I'LL GET SOMEONE ON THAT. SO WEIRD...
WORKING THE FREQUENCY'S ALWAYS WEIRD. PEOPLE ARE WEIRD.
OH, I KNOW. BUT THIS IS DIFFERENT.
IT'S LIKE THEY WERE ALL LIVING ON AN UNEXPLODED BOMB.
THE WHOLE PLANET IS AN UNEXPLODED BOMB. THAT'S WHY WE'RE HERE.
BUT I KNOW WHAT YOU MEAN. YOU KNOW WHAT I THINK IS WEIRD?
WE'VE ESTABLISHED A CAUSE. WE CAN SCAN THESE PEOPLE AND WE KNOW WHAT WE'RE LOOKING FOR.
BRAIN CHEMISTRY ALTERATION. CELL DAMAGE. IT'S ALL VERY CLEAR AND SCIENTIFIC NOW.
BUT I CAN'T HELP THINKING...

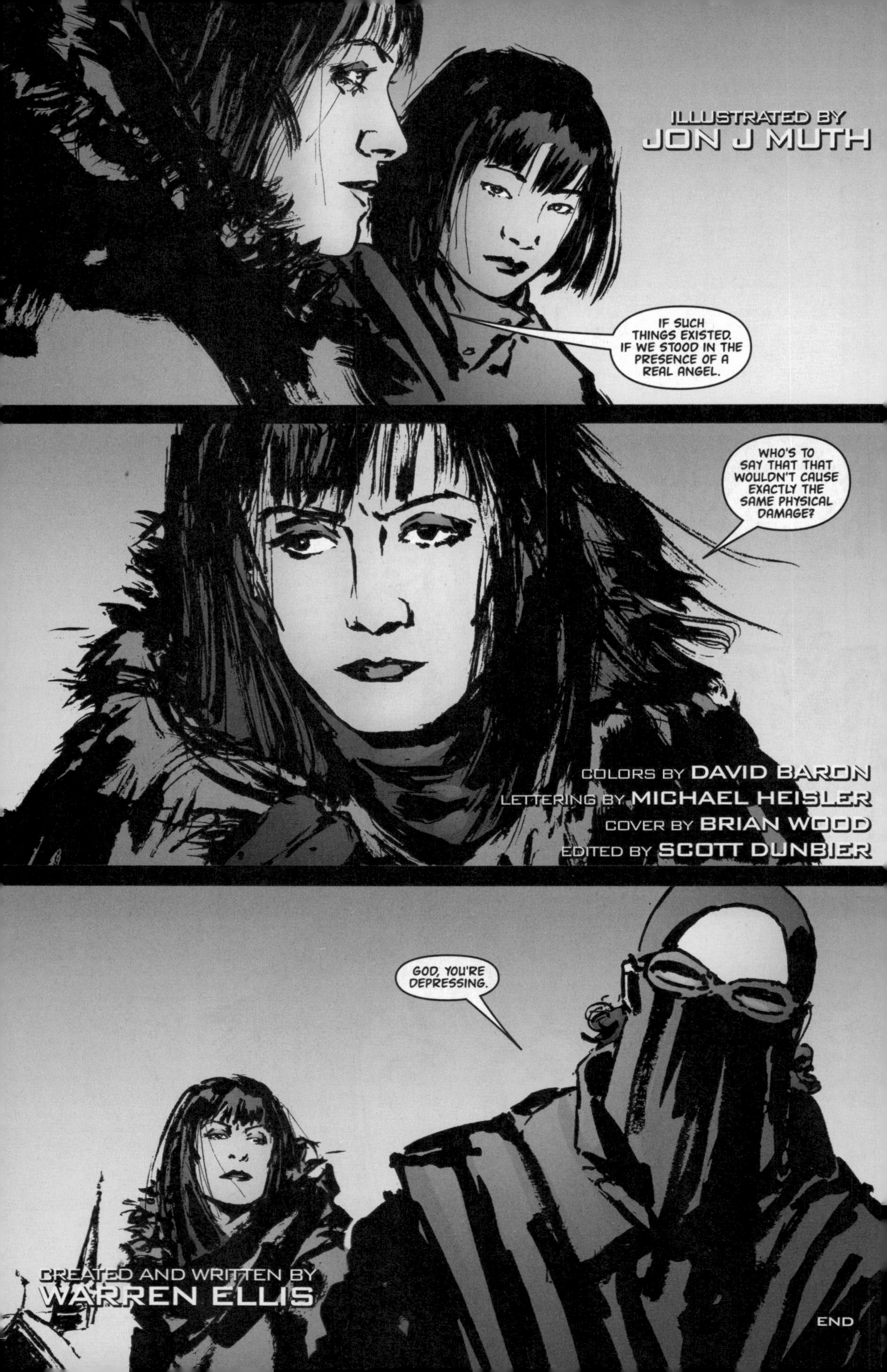
ILLUSTRATED BY
JON J MUTH
IF SUCH THINGS EXISTED. IF WE STOOD IN THE PRESENCE OF A REAL ANGEL.
WHO'S TO SAY THAT THAT WOULDN'T CAUSE EXACTLY THE SAME PHYSICAL DAMAGE?
COLORS BY DAVID BARON
LETTERING BY MICHAEL HEISLER
COVER BY BRIAN WOOD
EDITED BY SCOTT DUNBIER
GOD, YOU'RE DEPRESSING.
CREATED AND WRITTEN BY
WARREN ELLIS
END

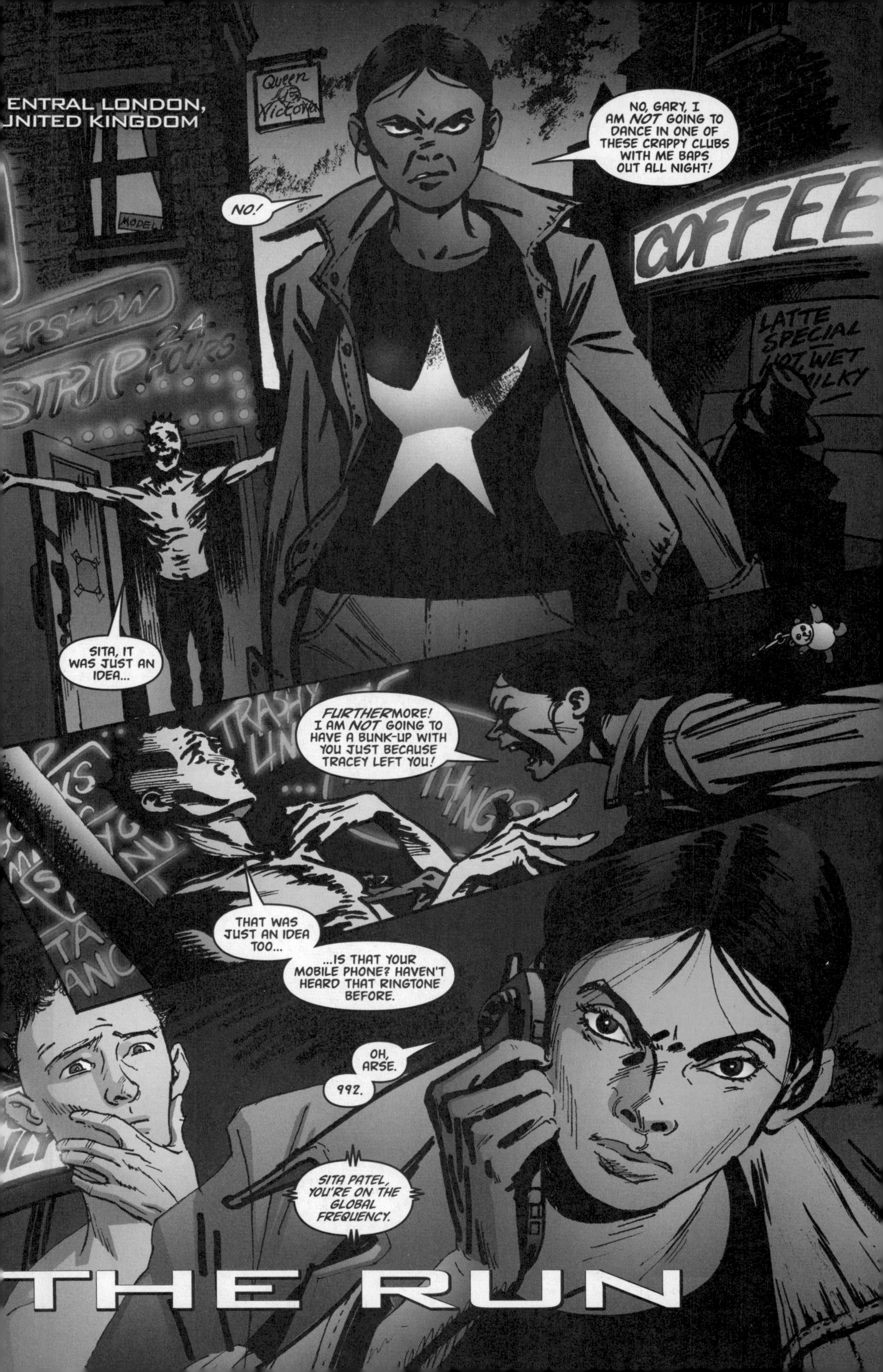
ENTRAL LONDON,
JNITED KINGDOM
NO, GARY, I AM NOT GOING TO DANCE IN ONE OF THESE CRAPPY CLUBS WITH ME BAPS OUT ALL NIGHT!
NO!
SITA, IT WAS JUST AN IDEA...
FURTHERMORE! I AM NOT GOING TO HAVE A BUNK-UP WITH YOU JUST BECAUSE TRACEY LEFT YOU!
THAT WAS JUST AN IDEA TOO...
...IS THAT YOUR MOBILE PHONE? HAVEN'T HEARD THAT RINGTONE BEFORE.
OH, ARSE.
992.
SITA PATEL, YOU'RE ON THE GLOBAL FREQUENCY.
THE RUN

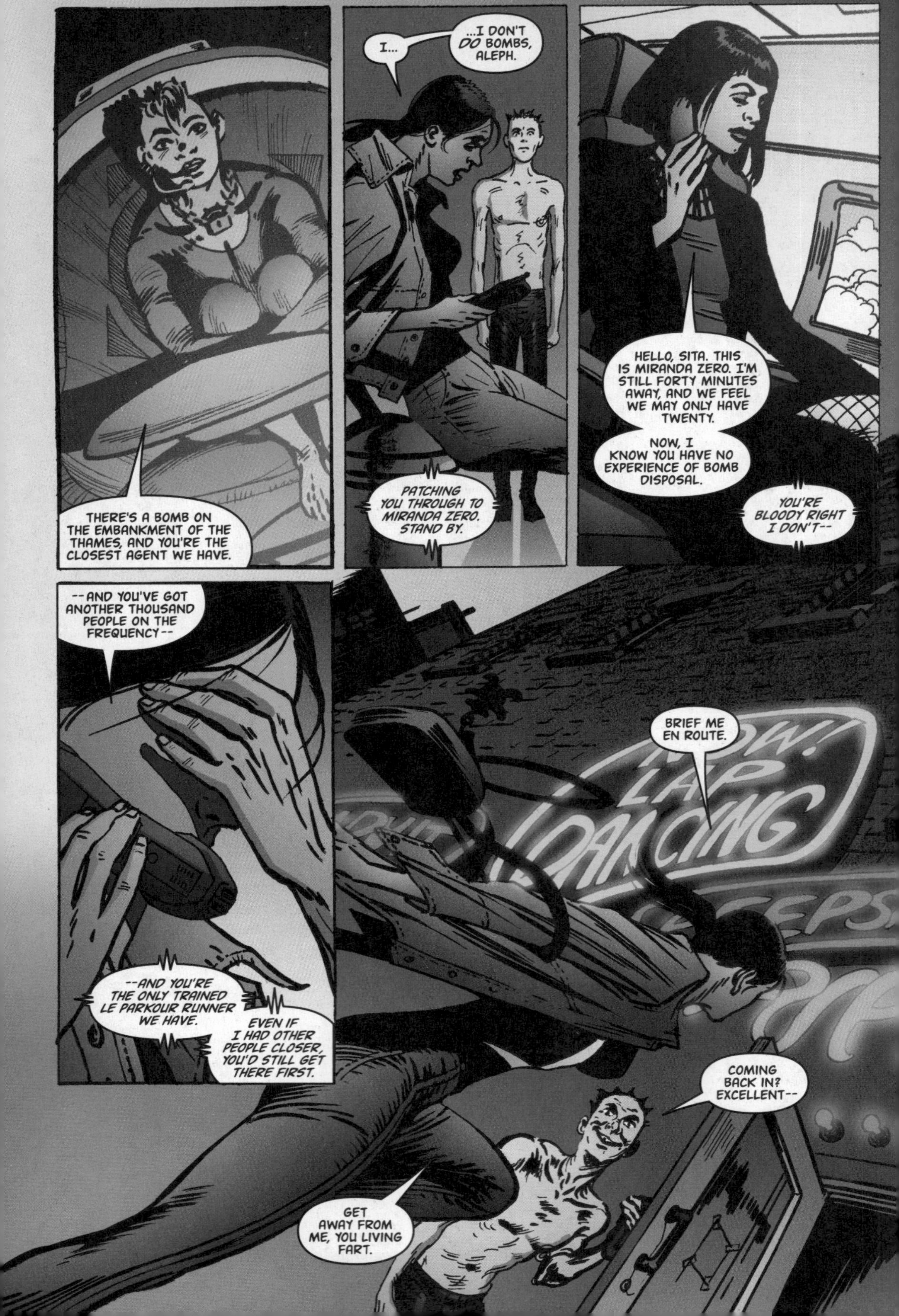
THERE'S A BOMB ON THE EMBANKMENT OF THE THAMES, AND YOU'RE THE CLOSEST AGENT WE HAVE.
I...
...I DON'T DO BOMBS, ALEPH.
PATCHING YOU THROUGH TO MIRANDA ZERO. STAND BY.
HELLO, SITA. THIS IS MIRANDA ZERO. I'M STILL FORTY MINUTES AWAY, AND WE FEEL WE MAY ONLY HAVE TWENTY.
NOW, I KNOW YOU HAVE NO EXPERIENCE OF BOMB DISPOSAL.
YOU'RE BLOODY RIGHT I DON'T--
--AND YOU'VE GOT ANOTHER THOUSAND PEOPLE ON THE FREQUENCY--
--AND YOU'RE THE ONLY TRAINED LE PARKOUR RUNNER WE HAVE.
EVEN IF I HAD OTHER PEOPLE CLOSER, YOU'D STILL GET THERE FIRST.
BRIEF ME EN ROUTE.
LAP DANCING
COMING BACK IN? EXCELLENT--
GET AWAY FROM ME, YOU LIVING FART.

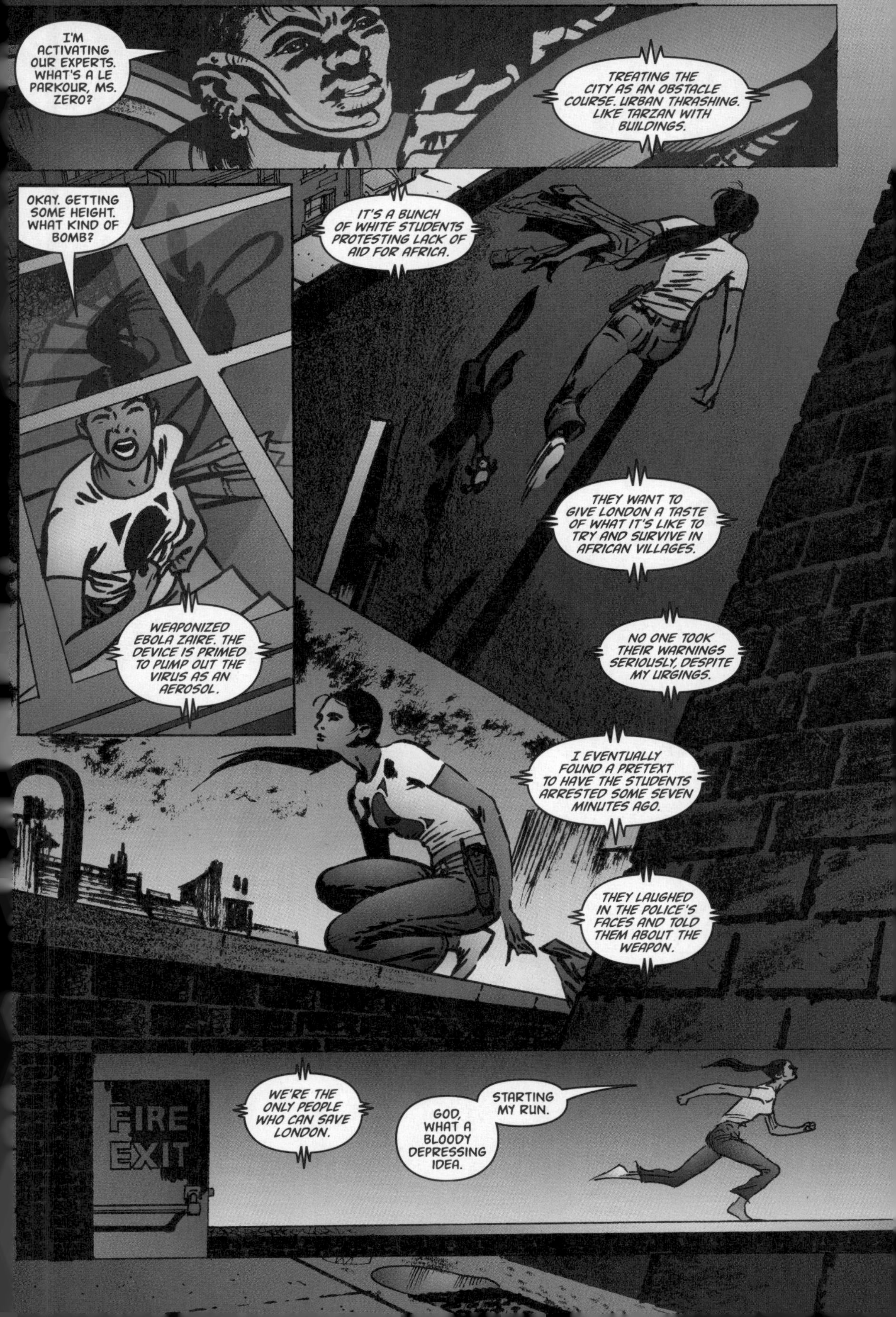
I'M ACTIVATING OUR EXPERTS. WHAT'S A LE PARKOUR, MS. ZERO?
TREATING THE CITY AS AN OBSTACLE COURSE. URBAN THRASHING. LIKE TARZAN WITH BUILDINGS.
OKAY. GETTING SOME HEIGHT. WHAT KIND OF BOMB?
IT'S A BUNCH OF WHITE STUDENTS PROTESTING LACK OF AID FOR AFRICA.
THEY WANT TO GIVE LONDON A TASTE OF WHAT IT'S LIKE TO TRY AND SURVIVE IN AFRICAN VILLAGES.
WEAPONIZED EBOLA ZAIRE. THE DEVICE IS PRIMED TO PUMP OUT THE VIRUS AS AN AEROSOL.
NO ONE TOOK THEIR WARNINGS SERIOUSLY, DESPITE MY URGINGS.
I EVENTUALLY FOUND A PRETEXT TO HAVE THE STUDENTS ARRESTED SOME SEVEN MINUTES AGO.
THEY LAUGHED IN THE POLICE'S FACES AND TOLD THEM ABOUT THE WEAPON.
FIRE EXIT
WE'RE THE ONLY PEOPLE WHO CAN SAVE LONDON.
STARTING MY RUN.
GOD, WHAT A BLOODY DEPRESSING IDEA.

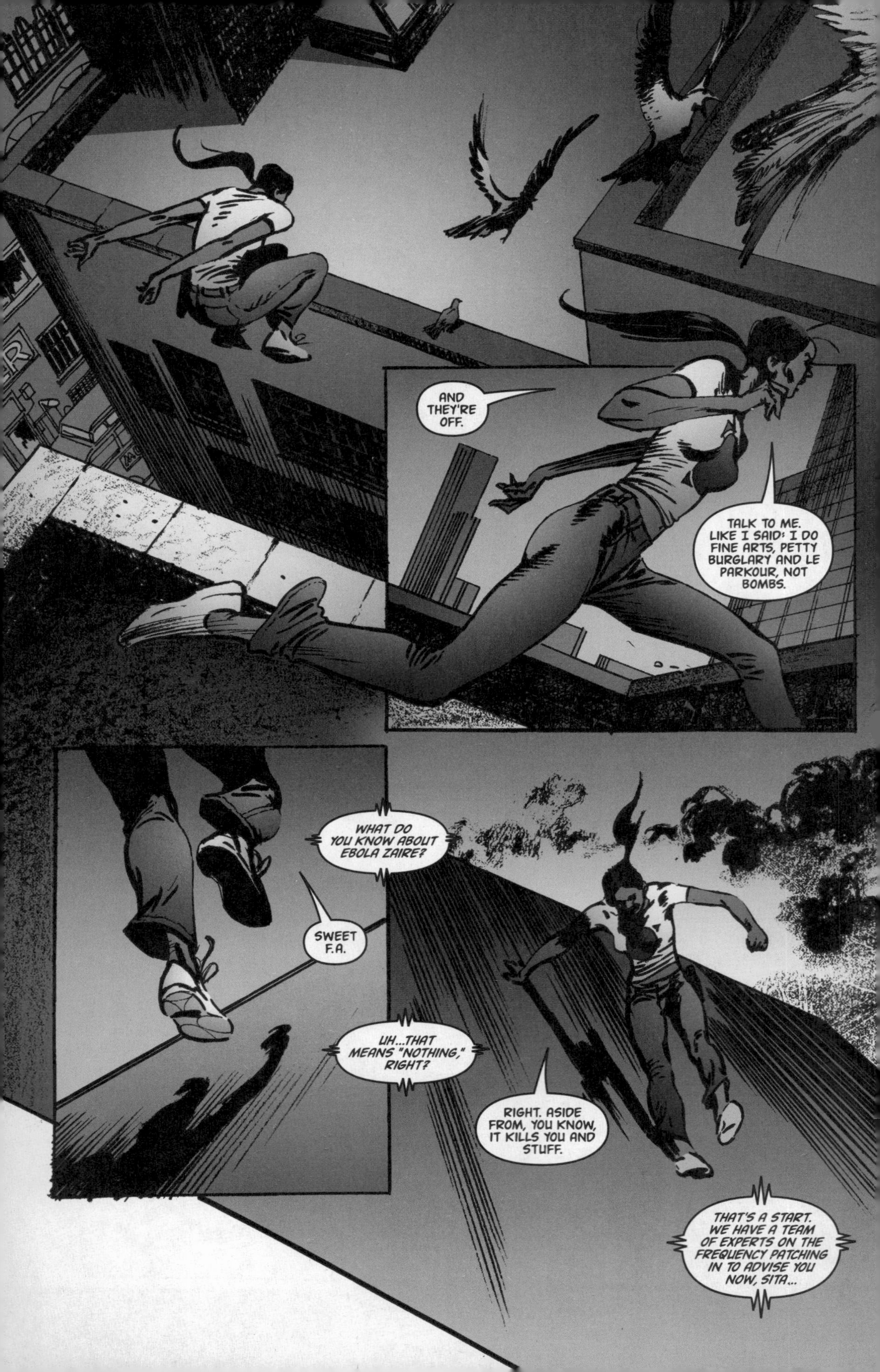
AND THEY'RE OFF.
TALK TO ME. LIKE I SAID: I DO FINE ARTS, PETTY BURGLARY AND LE PARKOUR, NOT BOMBS.
WHAT DO YOU KNOW ABOUT EBOLA ZAIRE?
SWEET F.A.
UH...THAT MEANS "NOTHING," RIGHT?
RIGHT. ASIDE FROM, YOU KNOW, IT KILLS YOU AND STUFF.
THAT'S A START. WE HAVE A TEAM OF EXPERTS ON THE FREQUENCY PATCHING IN TO ADVISE YOU NOW, SITA...

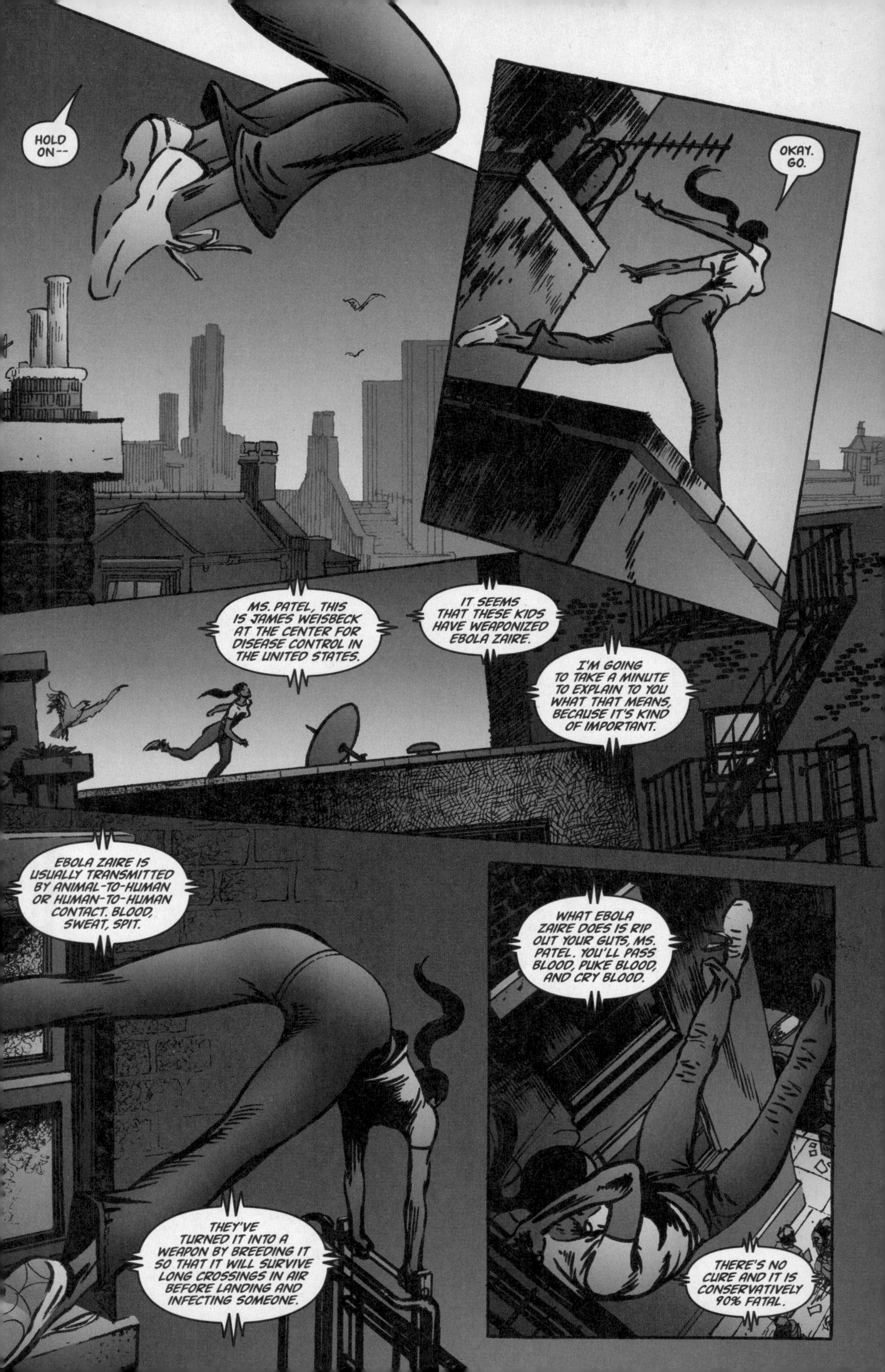
HOLD ON--
OKAY. GO.
MS. PATEL, THIS IS JAMES WEISBECK AT THE CENTER FOR DISEASE CONTROL IN THE UNITED STATES.
IT SEEMS THAT THESE KIDS HAVE WEAPONIZED EBOLA ZAIRE.
I'M GOING TO TAKE A MINUTE TO EXPLAIN TO YOU WHAT THAT MEANS, BECAUSE IT'S KIND OF IMPORTANT.
EBOLA ZAIRE IS USUALLY TRANSMITTED BY ANIMAL-TO-HUMAN OR HUMAN-TO-HUMAN CONTACT. BLOOD, SWEAT, SPIT.
THEY'VE TURNED IT INTO A WEAPON BY BREEDING IT SO THAT IT WILL SURVIVE LONG CROSSINGS IN AIR BEFORE LANDING AND INFECTING SOMEONE.
WHAT EBOLA ZAIRE DOES IS RIP OUT YOUR GUTS, MS. PATEL. YOU'LL PASS BLOOD, PUKE BLOOD, AND CRY BLOOD.
THERE'S NO CURE AND IT IS CONSERVATIVELY 90% FATAL.

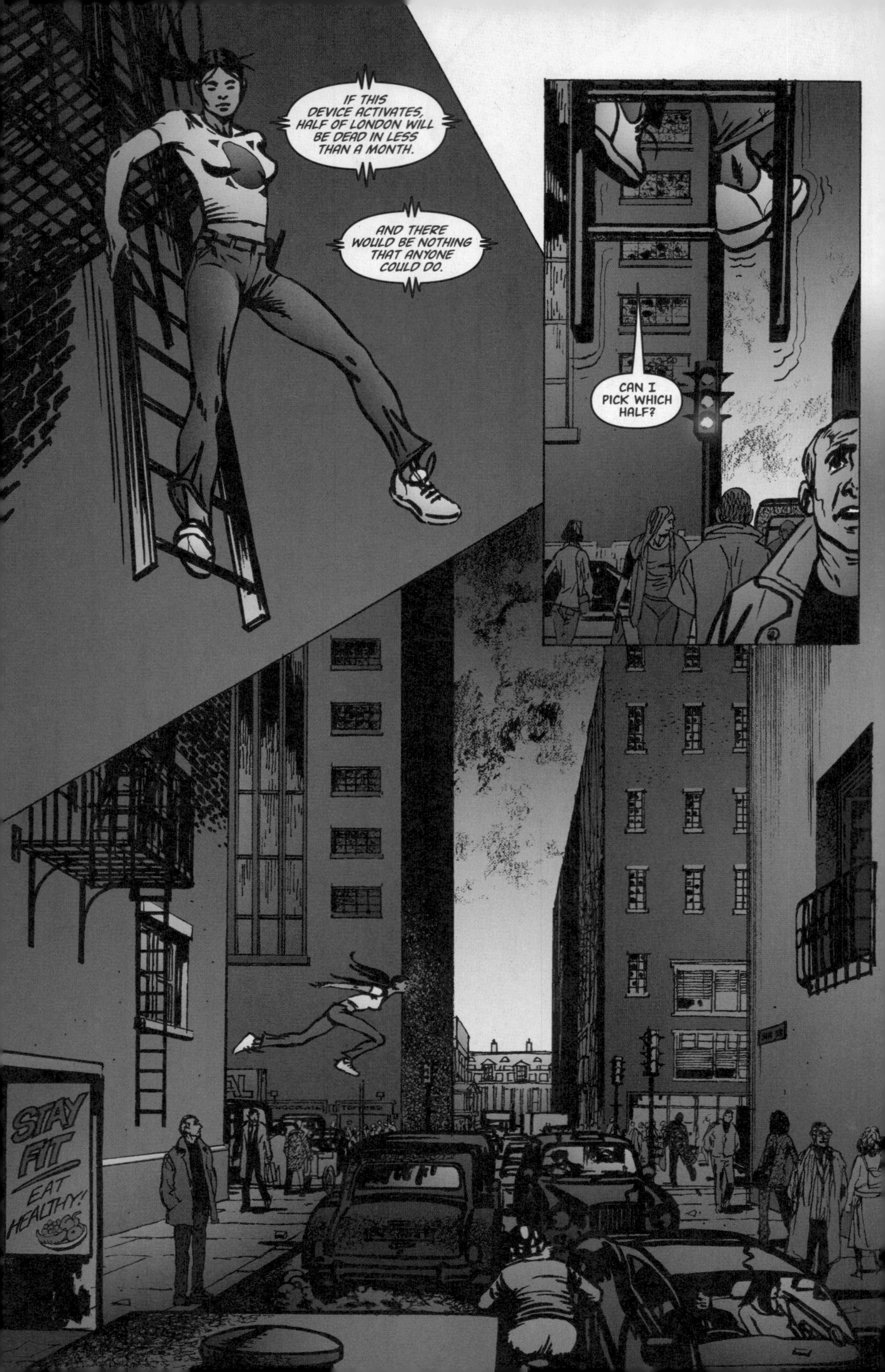
IF THIS DEVICE ACTIVATES, HALF OF LONDON WILL BE DEAD IN LESS THAN A MONTH.
AND THERE WOULD BE NOTHING THAT ANYONE COULD DO.
CAN I PICK WHICH HALF?
STAY FIT
EAT HEALTHY!

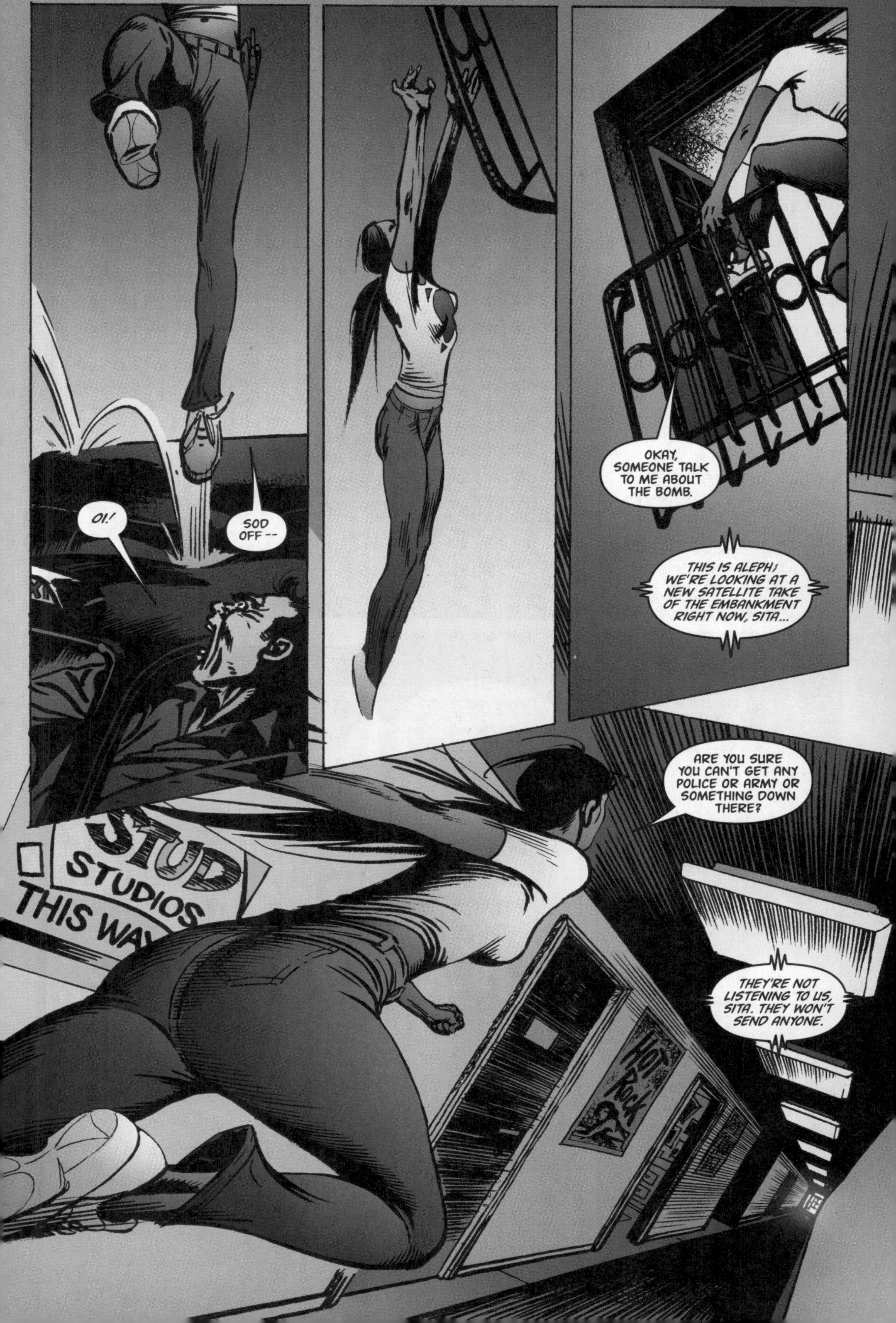
OI!
SOD OFF --
OKAY, SOMEONE TALK TO ME ABOUT THE BOMB.
THIS IS ALEPH; WE'RE LOOKING AT A NEW SATELLITE TAKE OF THE EMBANKMENT RIGHT NOW, SITA...
ARE YOU SURE YOU CAN'T GET ANY POLICE OR ARMY OR SOMETHING DOWN THERE?
STUD STUDIOS THIS WA
THEY'RE NOT LISTENING TO US, SITA. THEY WON'T SEND ANYONE.
HOT ROCK

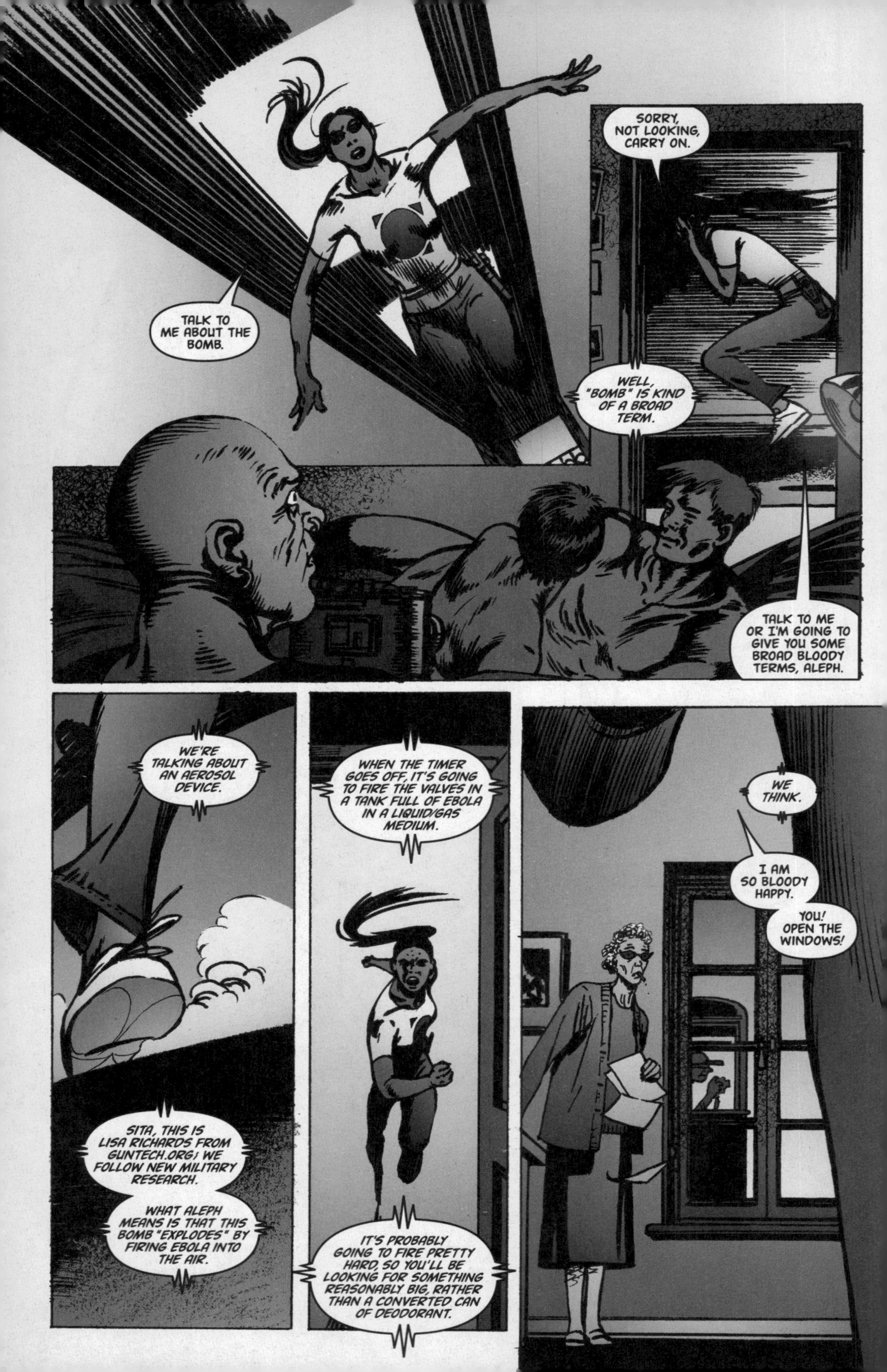
SORRY, NOT LOOKING, CARRY ON.
TALK TO ME ABOUT THE BOMB.
WELL, "BOMB" IS KIND OF A BROAD TERM.
TALK TO ME OR I'M GOING TO GIVE YOU SOME BROAD BLOODY TERMS, ALEPH.
WE'RE TALKING ABOUT AN AEROSOL DEVICE.
SITA, THIS IS LISA RICHARDS FROM GUNTECH.ORG; WE FOLLOW NEW MILITARY RESEARCH.
WHAT ALEPH MEANS IS THAT THIS BOMB "EXPLODES" BY FIRING EBOLA INTO THE AIR.
WHEN THE TIMER GOES OFF, IT'S GOING TO FIRE THE VALVES IN A TANK FULL OF EBOLA IN A LIQUID/GAS MEDIUM.
IT'S PROBABLY GOING TO FIRE PRETTY HARD, SO YOU'LL BE LOOKING FOR SOMETHING REASONABLY BIG, RATHER THAN A CONVERTED CAN OF DEODORANT.
WE THINK.
I AM SO BLOODY HAPPY.
YOU! OPEN THE WINDOWS!

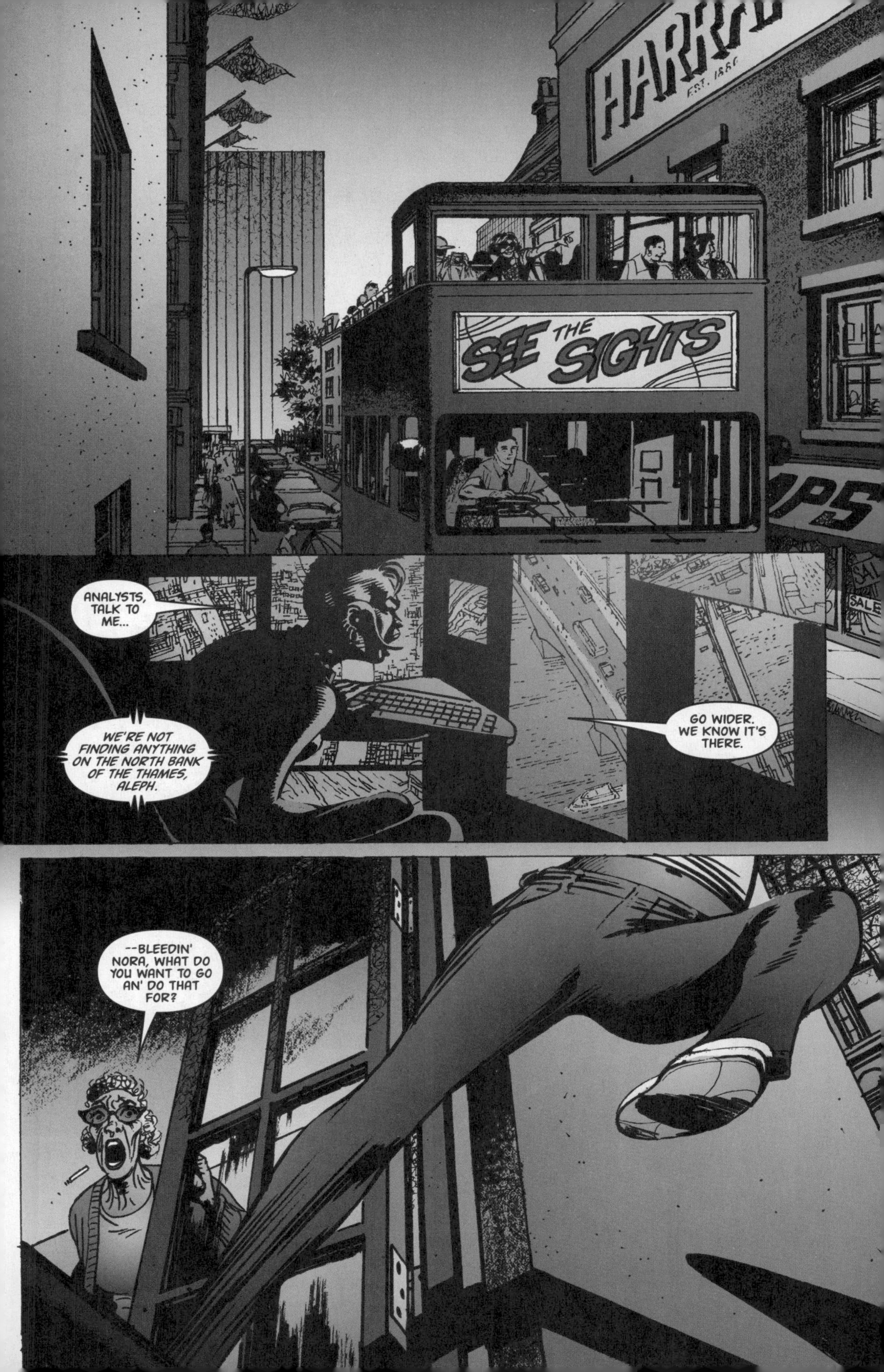
HARROD
EST. 1880
SEE THE SIGHTS
ANALYSTS, TALK TO ME...
WE'RE NOT FINDING ANYTHING ON THE NORTH BANK OF THE THAMES, ALEPH.
GO WIDER. WE KNOW IT'S THERE.
SALE
--BLEEDIN' NORA, WHAT DO YOU WANT TO GO AN' DO THAT FOR?

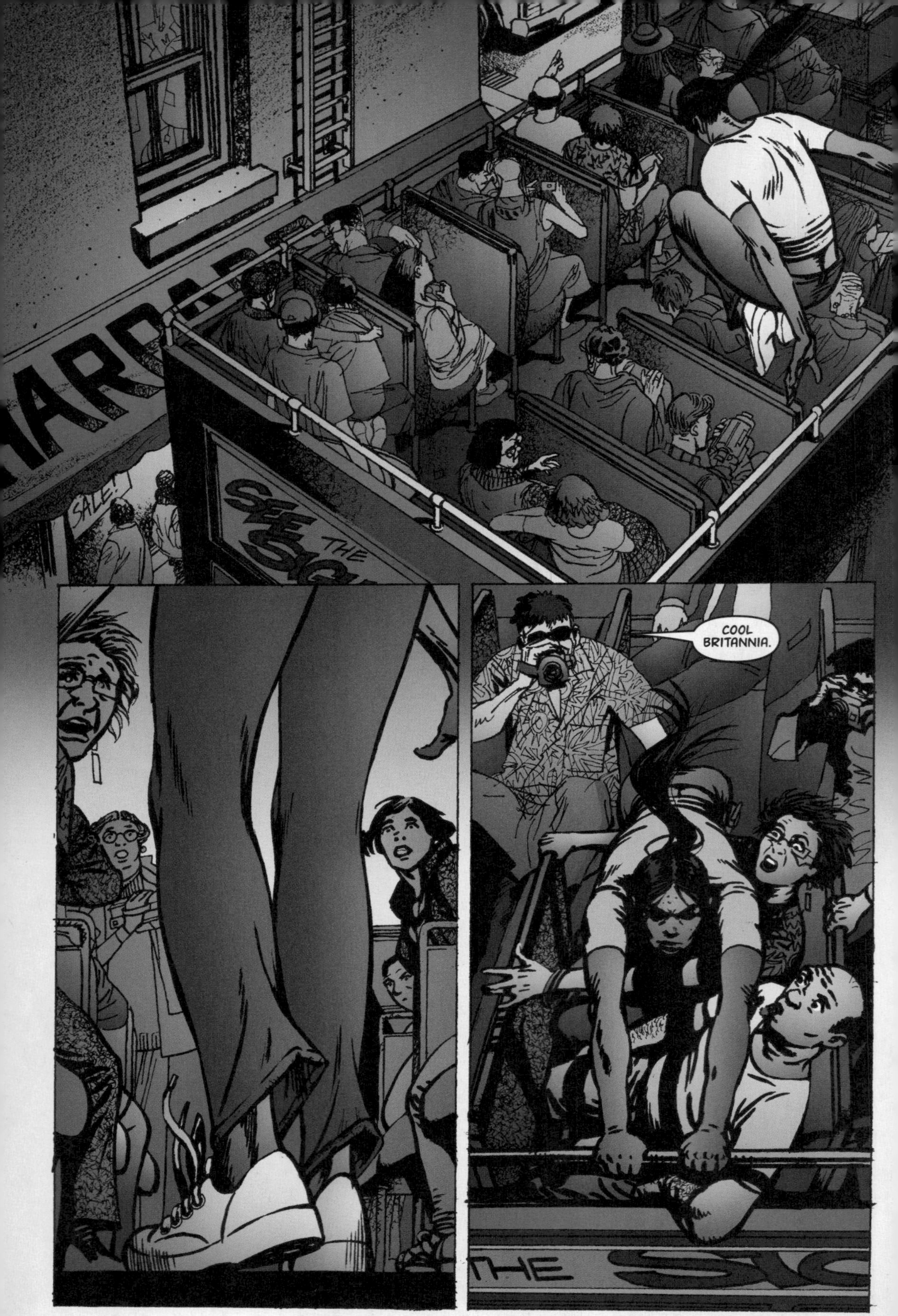
HARRODS
SALE!
SEE THE SIGHTS
COOL BRITANNIA.
THE SIG

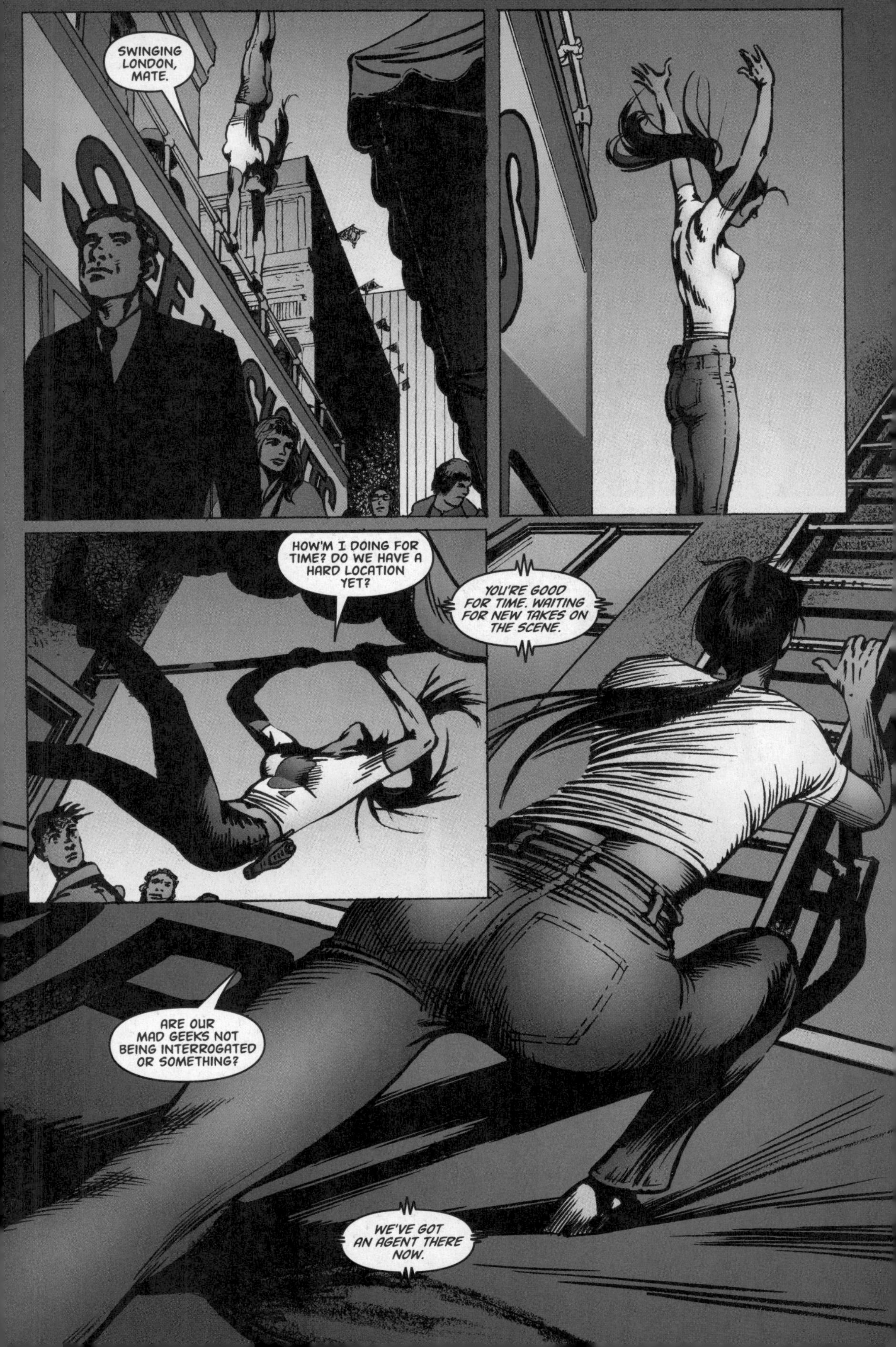
SWINGING LONDON, MATE.
HOW'M I DOING FOR TIME? DO WE HAVE A HARD LOCATION YET?
YOU'RE GOOD FOR TIME. WAITING FOR NEW TAKES ON THE SCENE.
ARE OUR MAD GEEKS NOT BEING INTERROGATED OR SOMETHING?
WE'VE GOT AN AGENT THERE NOW.

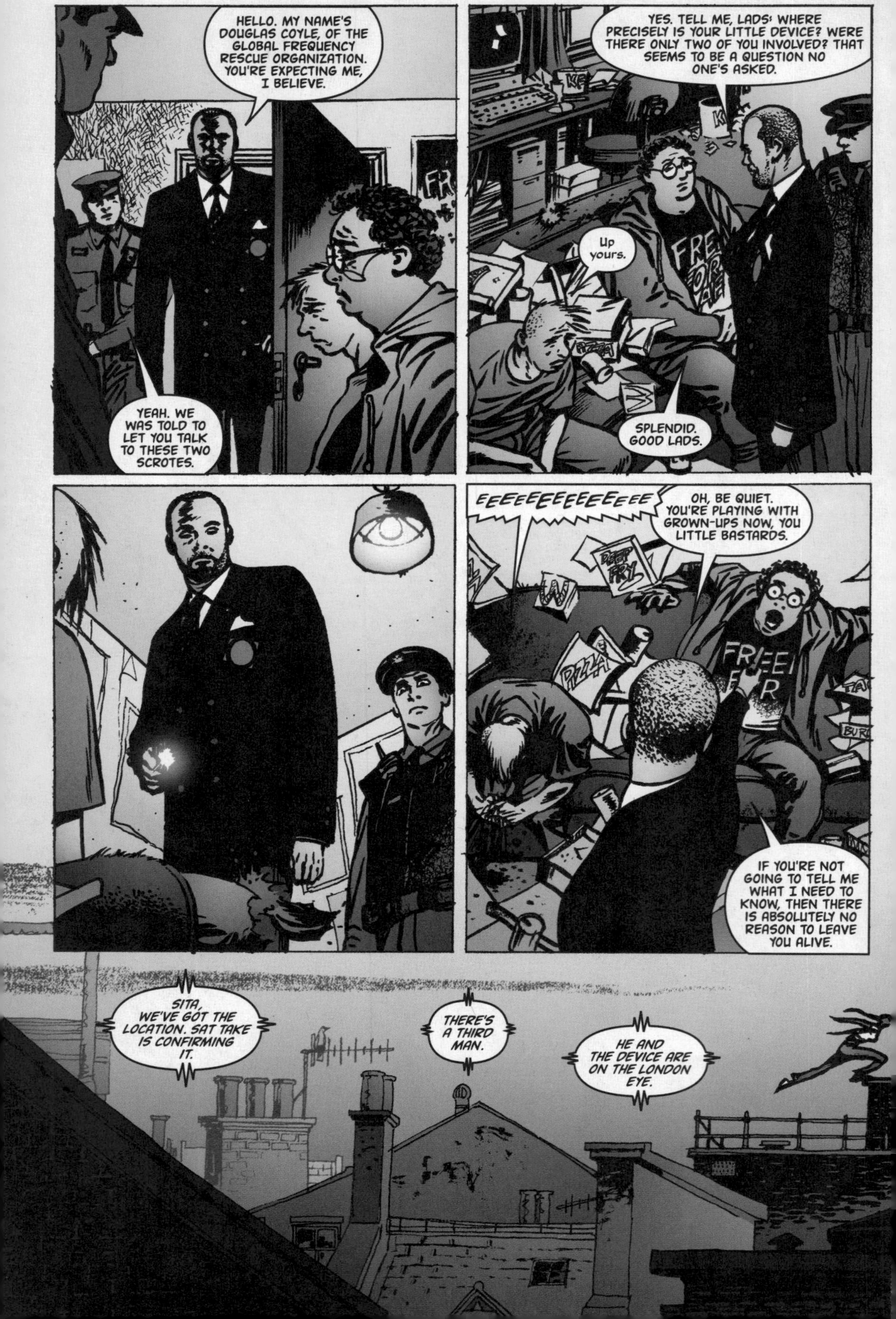
HELLO. MY NAME'S DOUGLAS COYLE, OF THE GLOBAL FREQUENCY RESCUE ORGANIZATION. YOU'RE EXPECTING ME, I BELIEVE.
YEAH. WE WAS TOLD TO LET YOU TALK TO THESE TWO SCROTES.
YES. TELL ME, LADS: WHERE PRECISELY IS YOUR LITTLE DEVICE? WERE THERE ONLY TWO OF YOU INVOLVED? THAT SEEMS TO BE A QUESTION NO ONE'S ASKED.
Up yours.
SPLENDID. GOOD LADS.
EEEEEEEEEEEEEE
OH, BE QUIET. YOU'RE PLAYING WITH GROWN-UPS NOW, YOU LITTLE BASTARDS.
IF YOU'RE NOT GOING TO TELL ME WHAT I NEED TO KNOW, THEN THERE IS ABSOLUTELY NO REASON TO LEAVE YOU ALIVE.
SITA, WE'VE GOT THE LOCATION. SAT TAKE IS CONFIRMING IT.
THERE'S A THIRD MAN.
HE AND THE DEVICE ARE ON THE LONDON EYE.

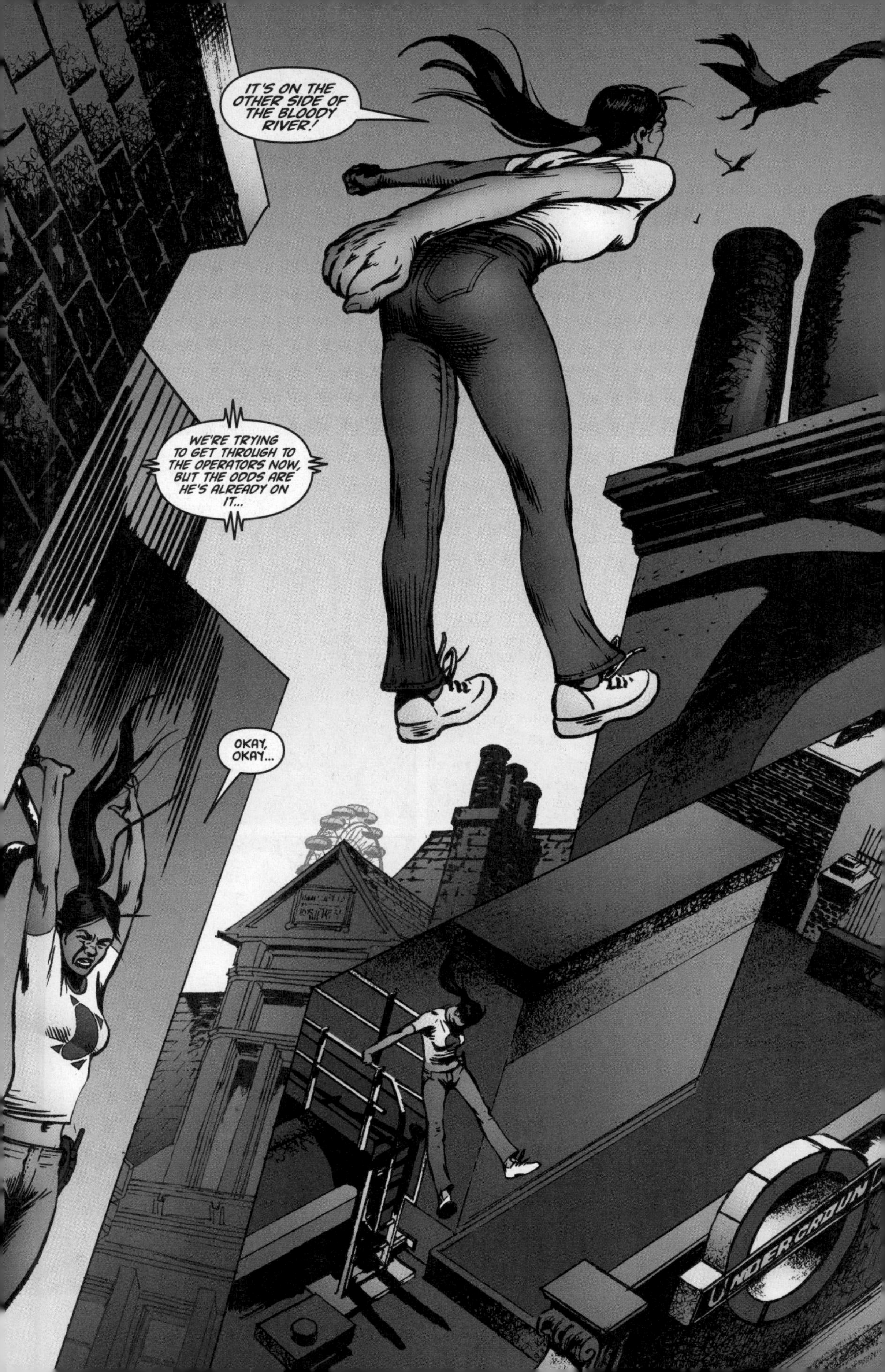
IT'S ON THE OTHER SIDE OF THE BLOODY RIVER!
WE'RE TRYING TO GET THROUGH TO THE OPERATORS NOW, BUT THE ODDS ARE HE'S ALREADY ON IT...
OKAY, OKAY...
UNDERGROUN

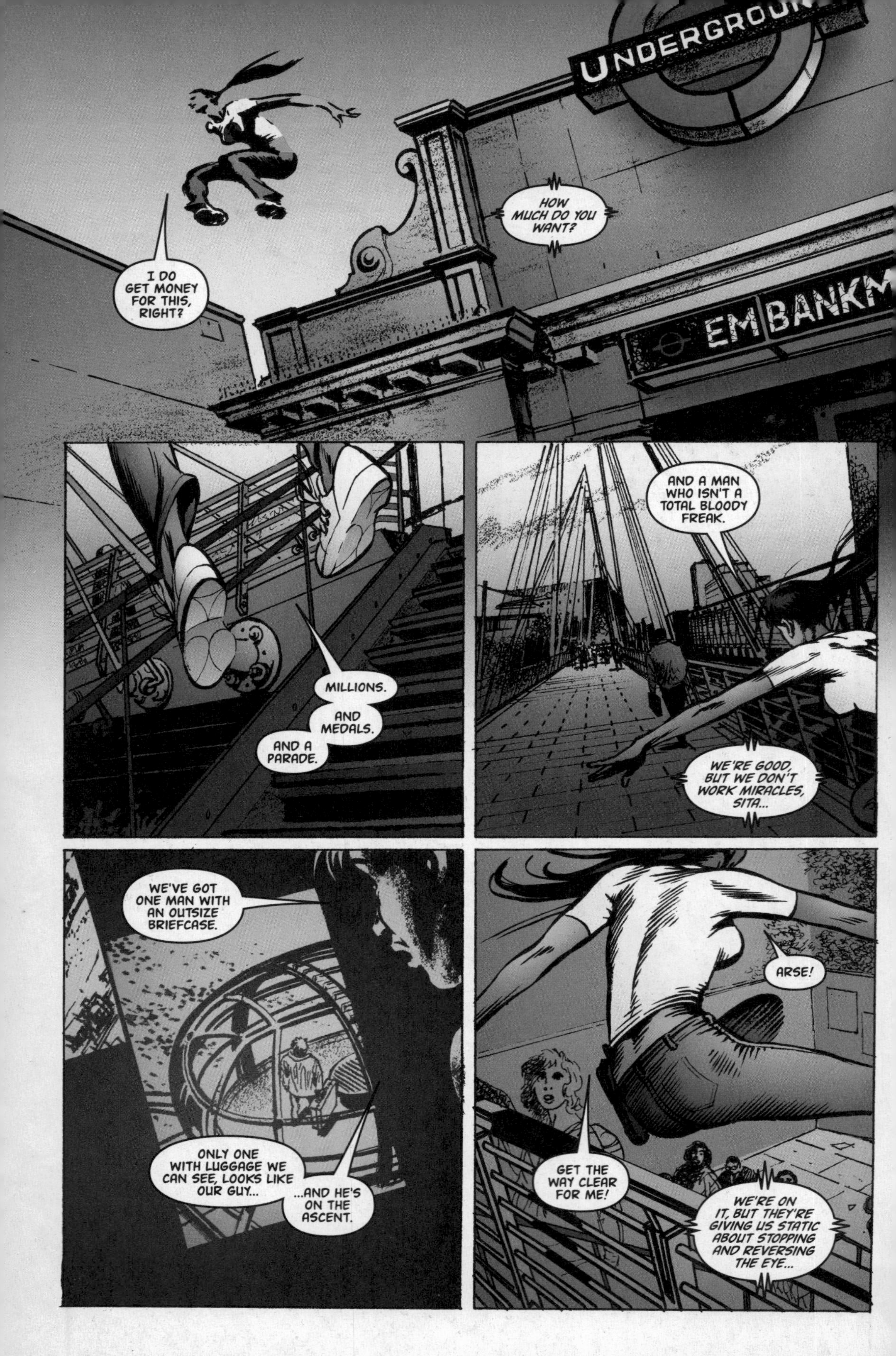
UNDERGROUN
EMBANKM
I DO GET MONEY FOR THIS, RIGHT?
HOW MUCH DO YOU WANT?
MILLIONS.
AND MEDALS.
AND A PARADE.
AND A MAN WHO ISN'T A TOTAL BLOODY FREAK.
WE'RE GOOD, BUT WE DON'T WORK MIRACLES, SITA...
WE'VE GOT ONE MAN WITH AN OUTSIZE BRIEFCASE.
ONLY ONE WITH LUGGAGE WE CAN SEE, LOOKS LIKE OUR GUY...
...AND HE'S ON THE ASCENT.
ARSE!
GET THE WAY CLEAR FOR ME!
WE'RE ON IT, BUT THEY'RE GIVING US STATIC ABOUT STOPPING AND REVERSING THE EYE...

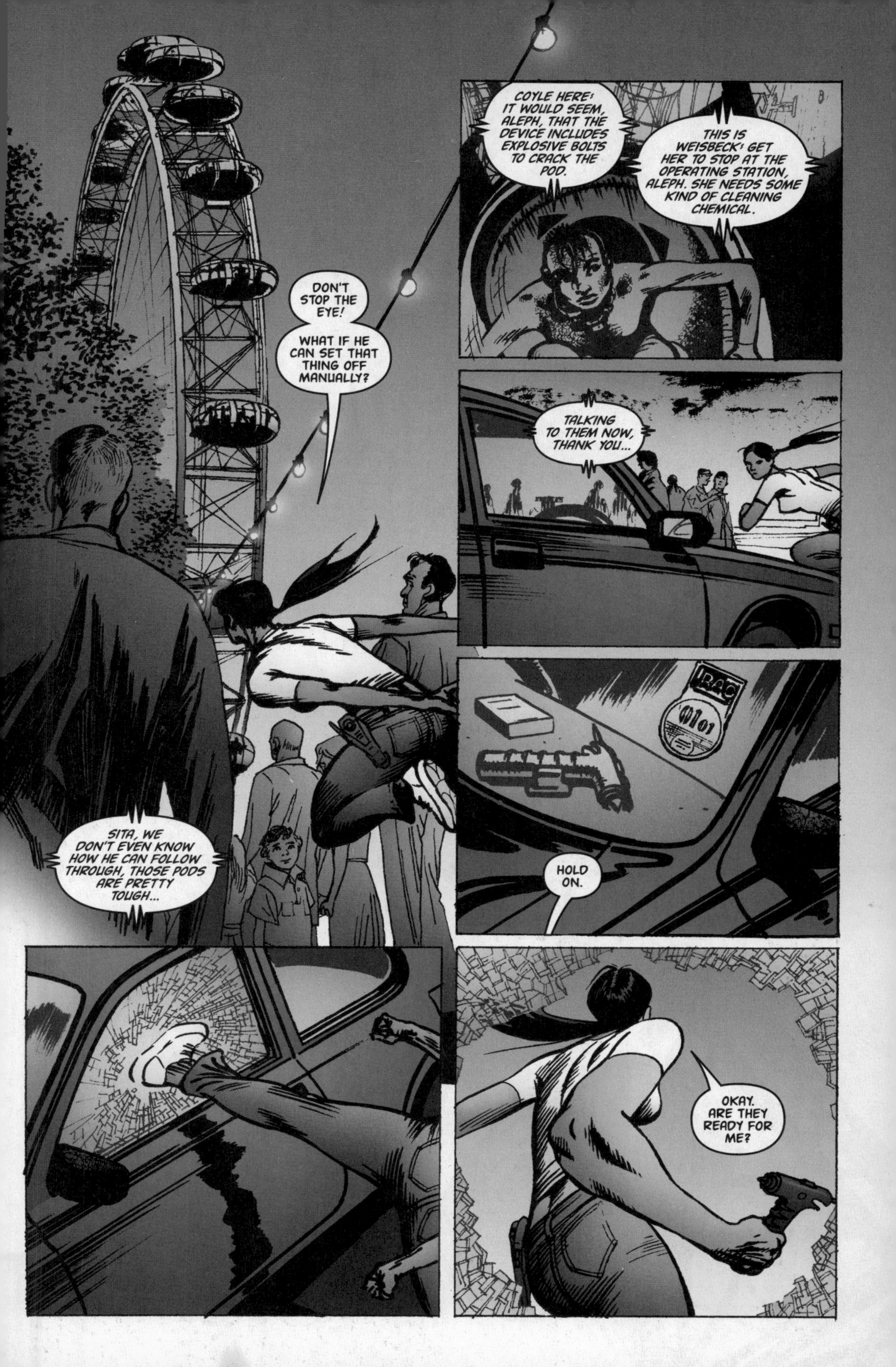
DON'T STOP THE EYE!
WHAT IF HE CAN SET THAT THING OFF MANUALLY?
SITA, WE DON'T EVEN KNOW HOW HE CAN FOLLOW THROUGH, THOSE PODS ARE PRETTY TOUGH...
COYLE HERE: IT WOULD SEEM, ALEPH, THAT THE DEVICE INCLUDES EXPLOSIVE BOLTS TO CRACK THE POD.
THIS IS WEISBECK: GET HER TO STOP AT THE OPERATING STATION, ALEPH. SHE NEEDS SOME KIND OF CLEANING CHEMICAL.
TALKING TO THEM NOW, THANK YOU...
RAC
HOLD ON.
OKAY. ARE THEY READY FOR ME?

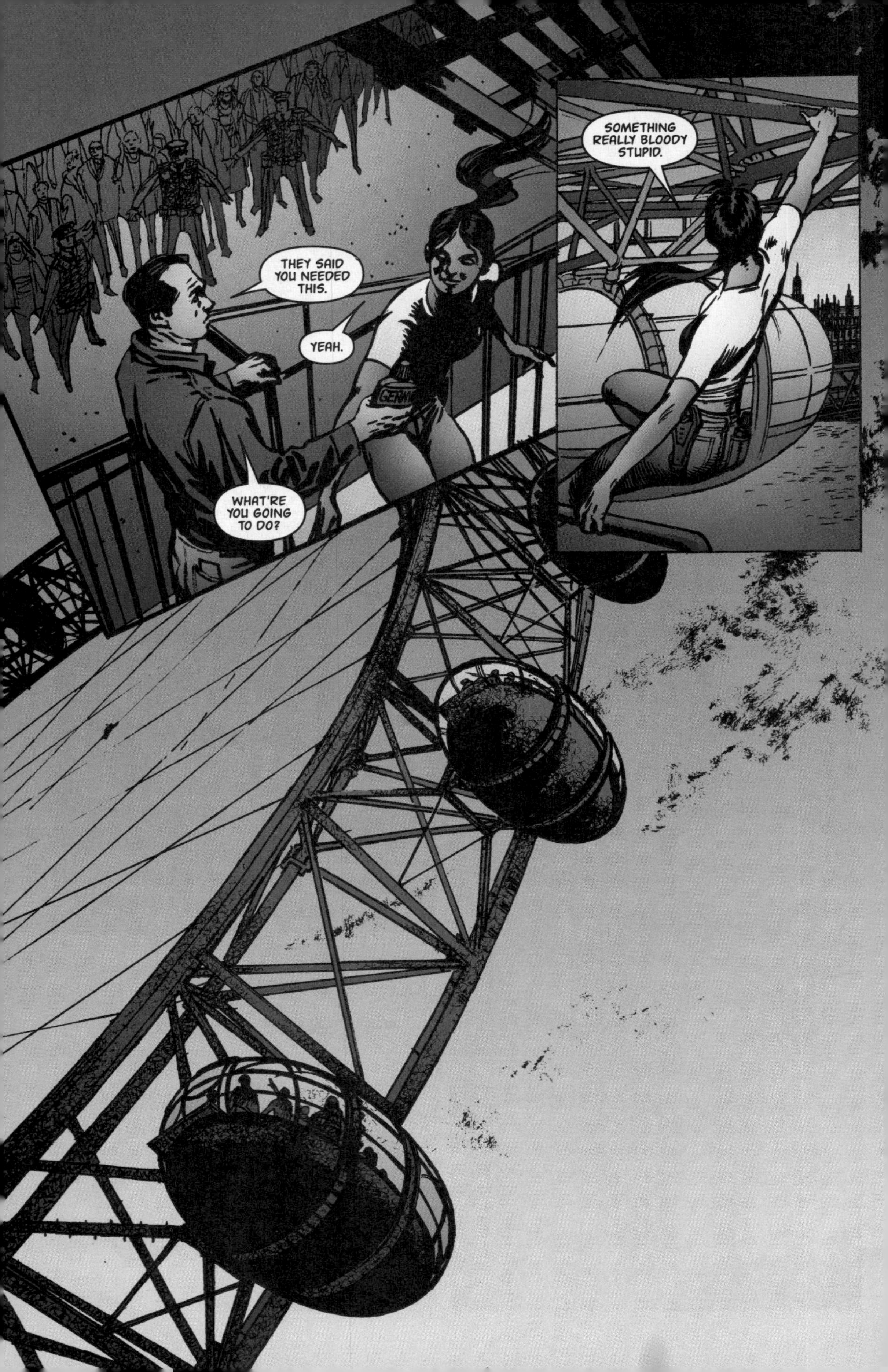
THEY SAID YOU NEEDED THIS.
YEAH.
WHAT'RE YOU GOING TO DO?
SOMETHING REALLY BLOODY STUPID.

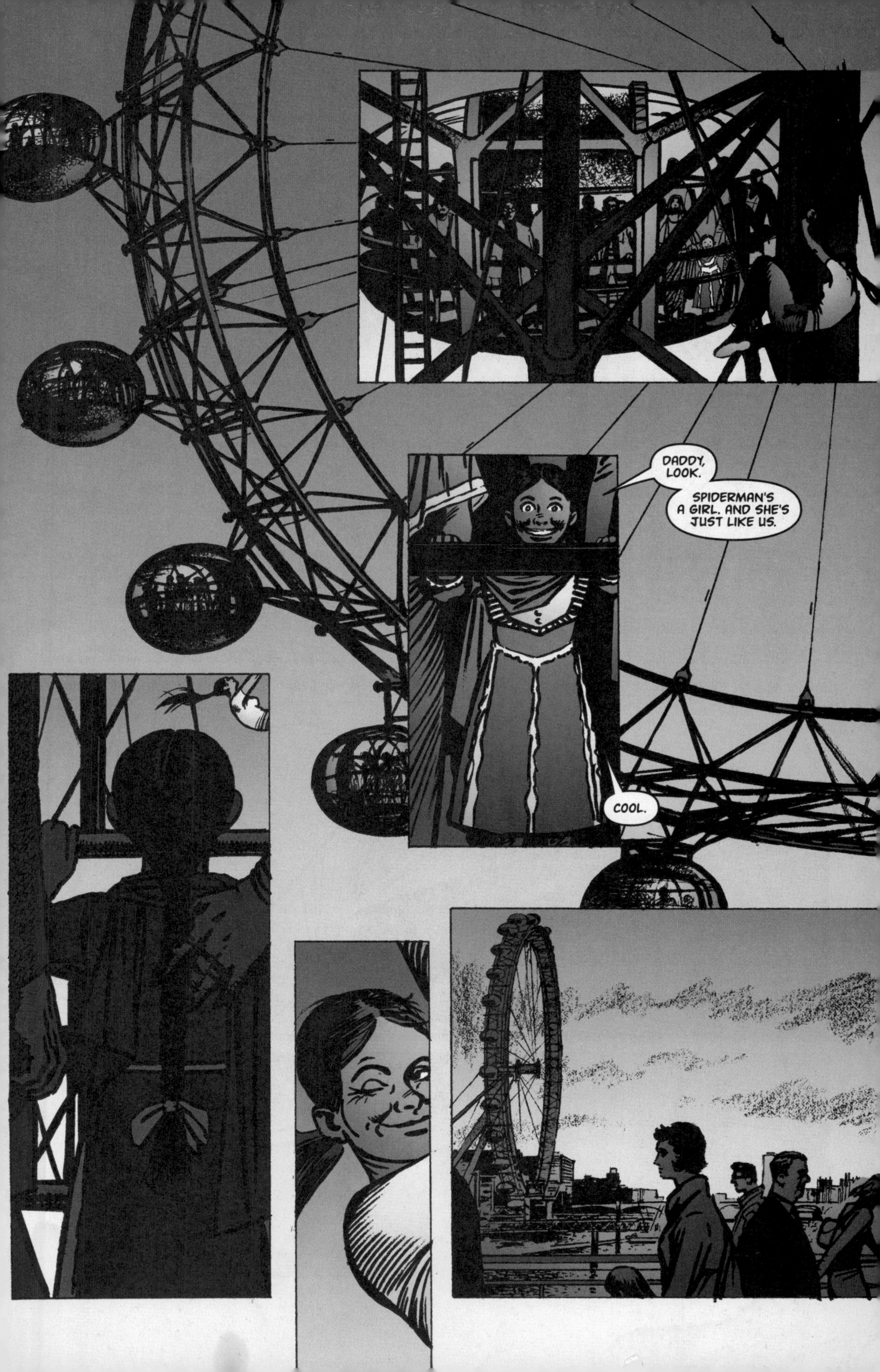
DADDY, LOOK.
SPIDERMAN'S A GIRL. AND SHE'S JUST LIKE US.
COOL.

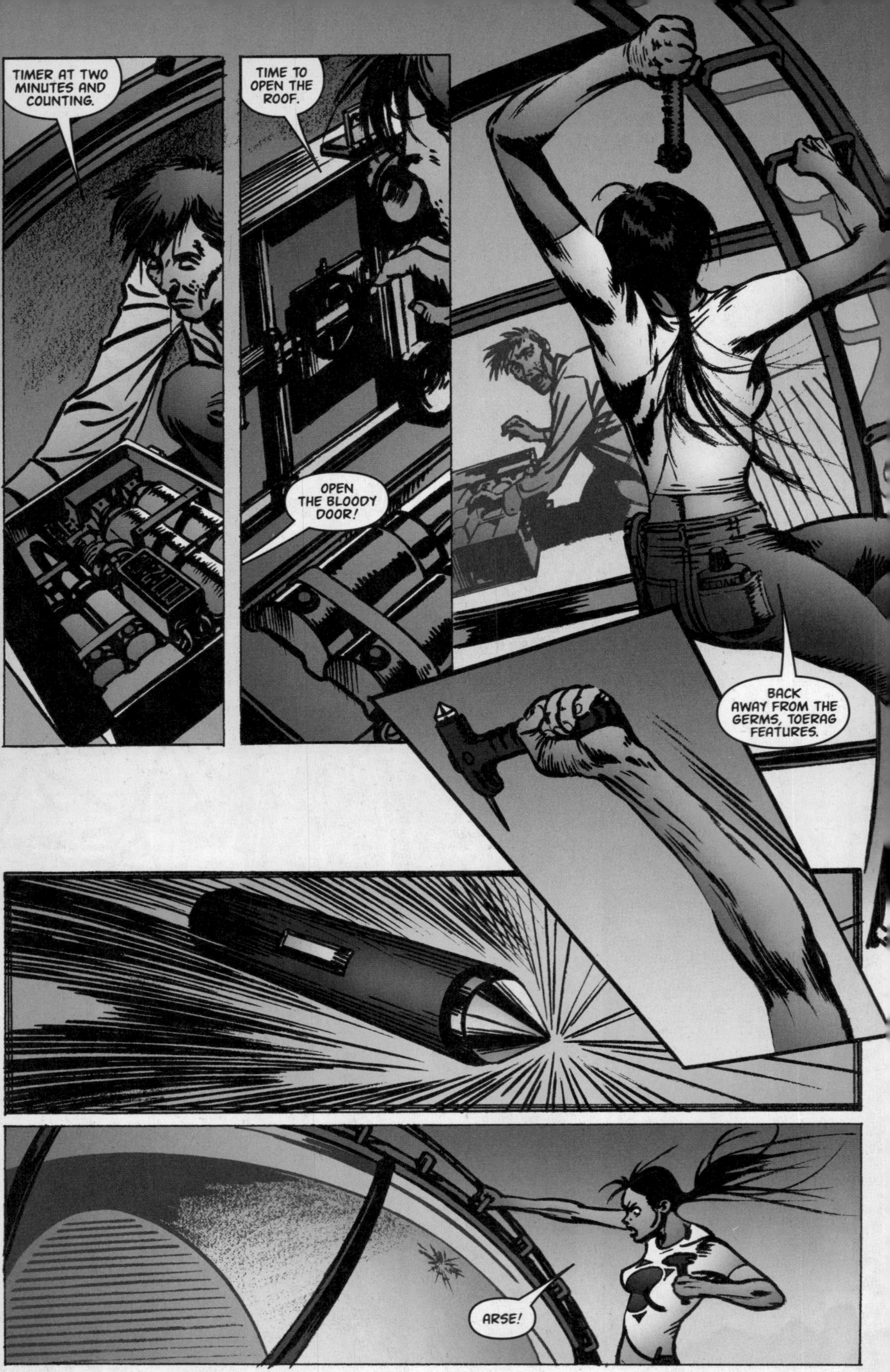
TIMER AT TWO MINUTES AND COUNTING.
TIME TO OPEN THE ROOF.
OPEN THE BLOODY DOOR!
BACK AWAY FROM THE GERMS, TOERAG FEATURES.
ARSE!

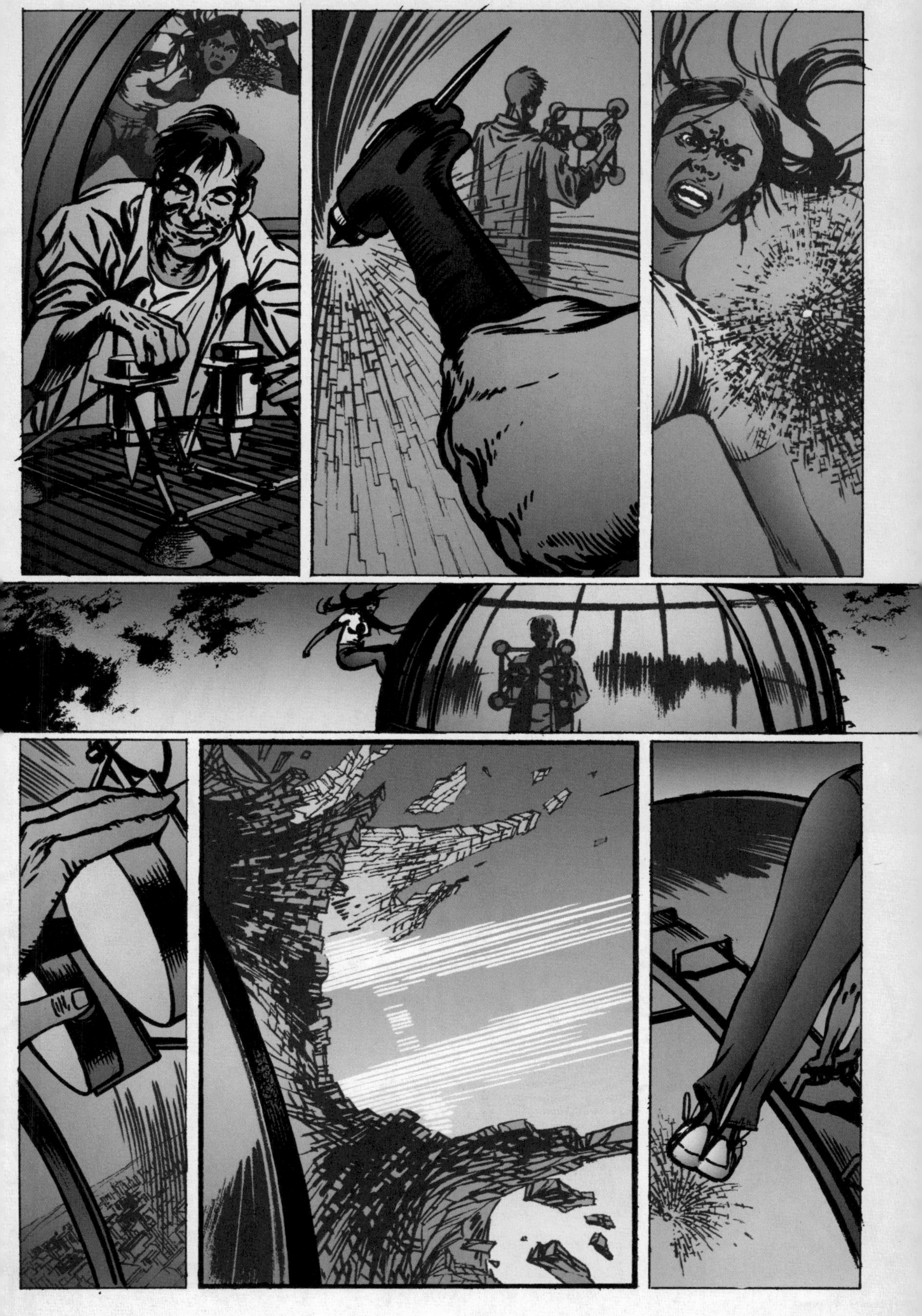

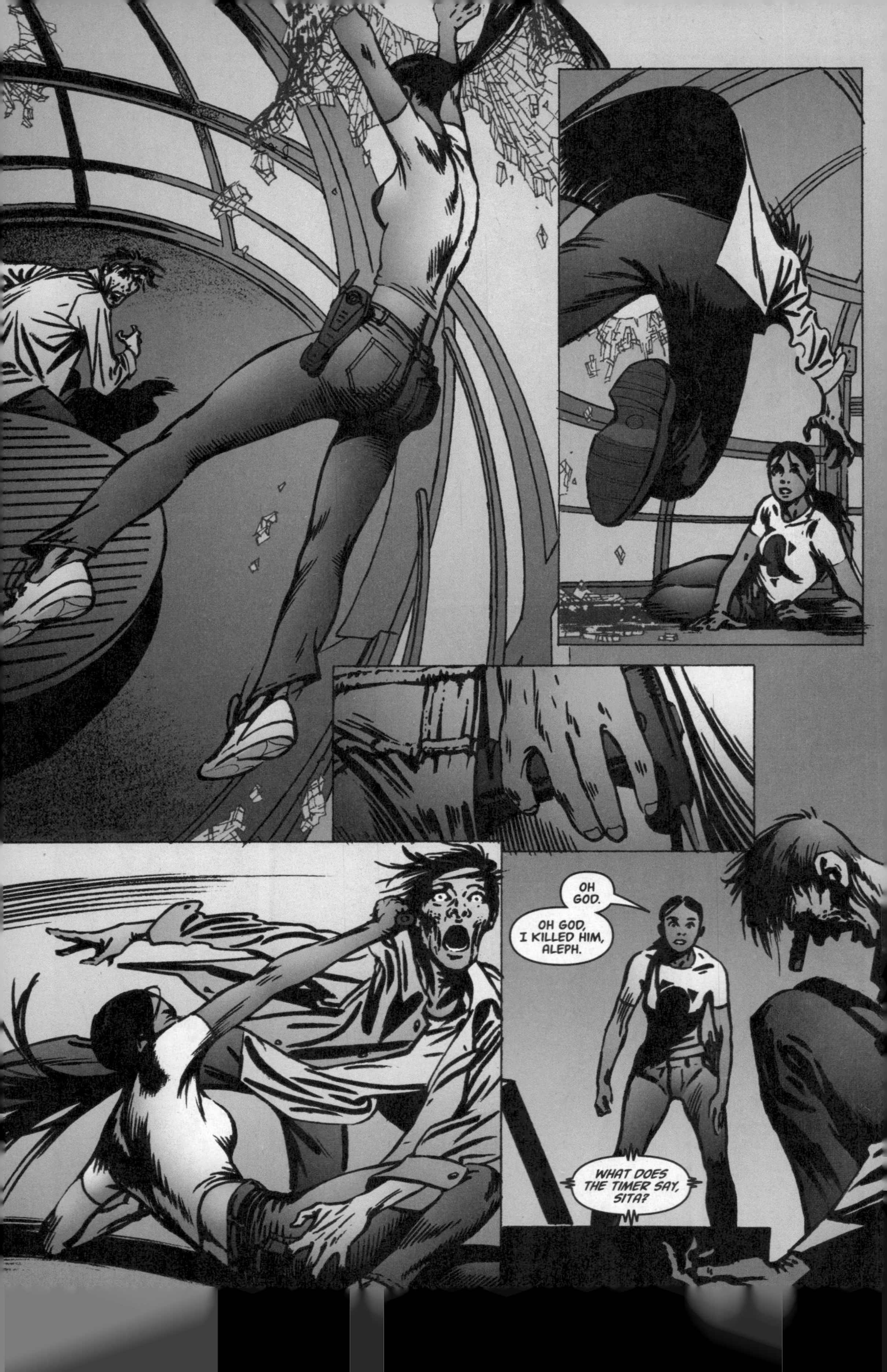
OH GOD.
OH GOD, I KILLED HIM, ALEPH.
WHAT DOES THE TIMER SAY, SITA?

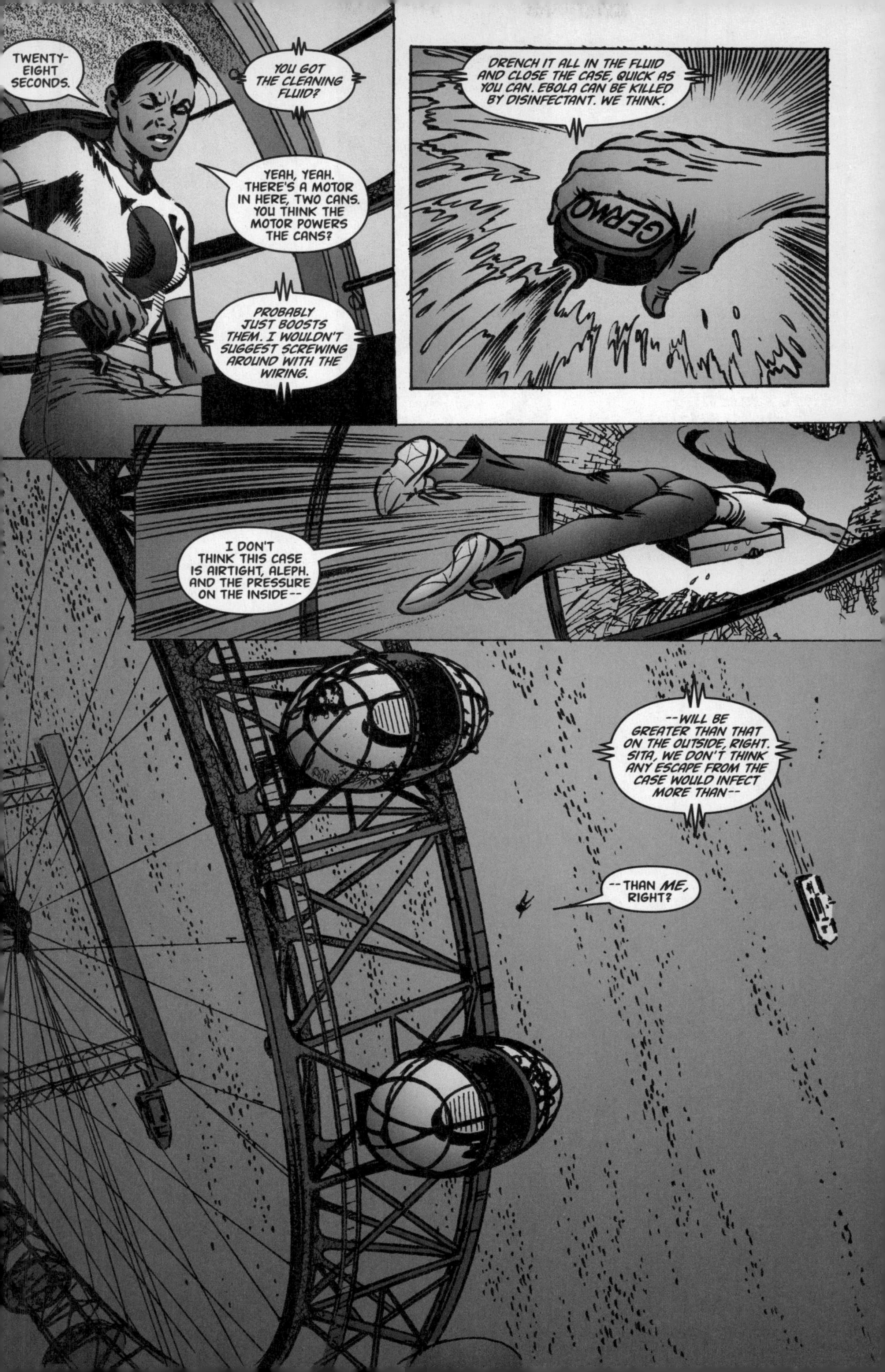
TWENTY-EIGHT SECONDS.
YOU GOT THE CLEANING FLUID?
YEAH, YEAH. THERE'S A MOTOR IN HERE, TWO CANS. YOU THINK THE MOTOR POWERS THE CANS?
PROBABLY JUST BOOSTS THEM. I WOULDN'T SUGGEST SCREWING AROUND WITH THE WIRING.
DRENCH IT ALL IN THE FLUID AND CLOSE THE CASE, QUICK AS YOU CAN. EBOLA CAN BE KILLED BY DISINFECTANT. WE THINK.
GERMO
I DON'T THINK THIS CASE IS AIRTIGHT, ALEPH. AND THE PRESSURE ON THE INSIDE--
--WILL BE GREATER THAN THAT ON THE OUTSIDE, RIGHT. SITA, WE DON'T THINK ANY ESCAPE FROM THE CASE WOULD INFECT MORE THAN--
--THAN *ME*, RIGHT?

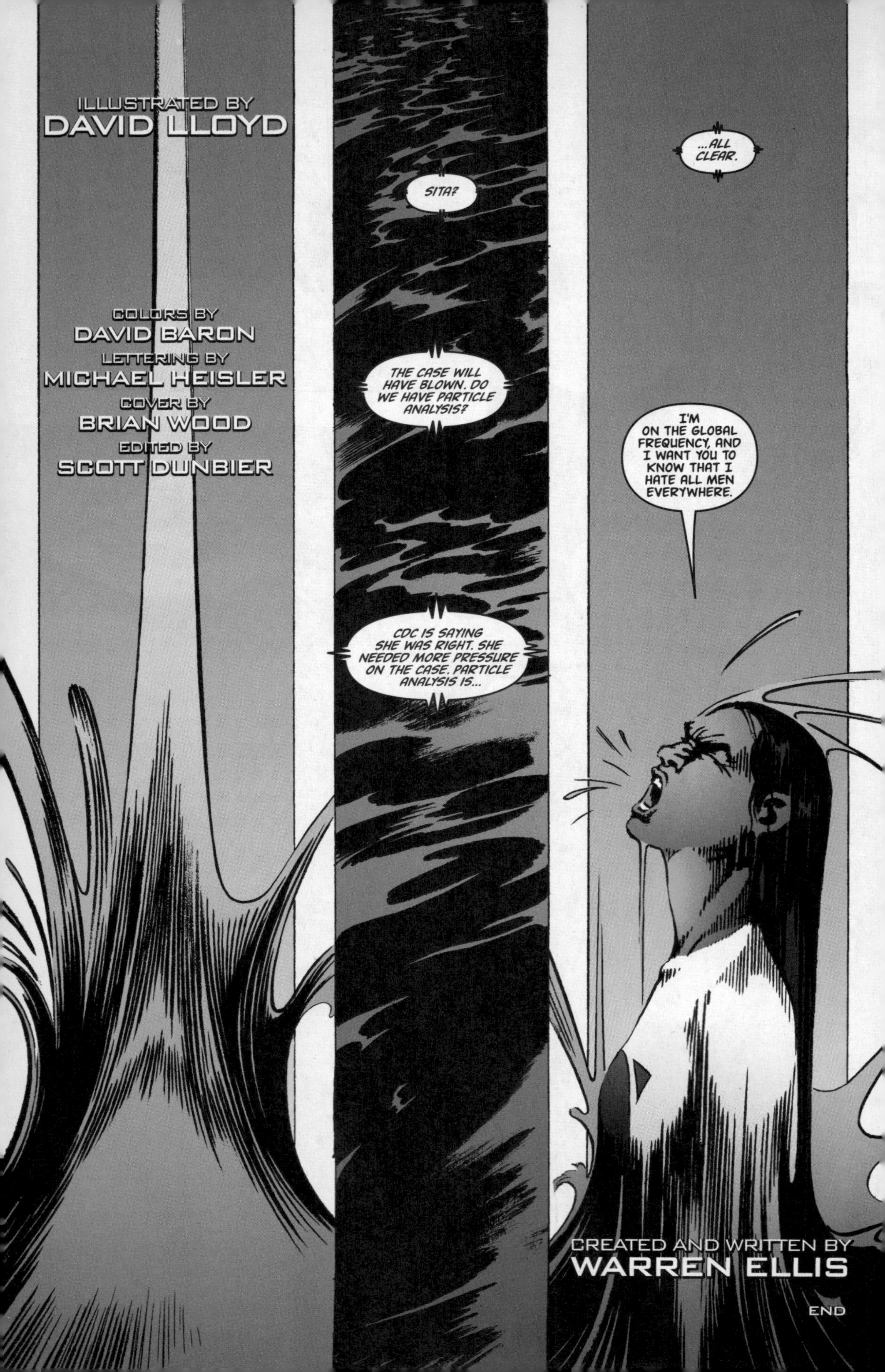
ILLUSTRATED BY
DAVID LLOYD
COLORS BY
DAVID BARON
LETTERING BY
MICHAEL HEISLER
COVER BY
BRIAN WOOD
EDITED BY
SCOTT DUNBIER
SITA?
THE CASE WILL HAVE BLOWN. DO WE HAVE PARTICLE ANALYSIS?
CDC IS SAYING SHE WAS RIGHT. SHE NEEDED MORE PRESSURE ON THE CASE. PARTICLE ANALYSIS IS...
...ALL CLEAR.
I'M ON THE GLOBAL FREQUENCY, AND I WANT YOU TO KNOW THAT I HATE ALL MEN EVERYWHERE.
CREATED AND WRITTEN BY
WARREN ELLIS
END

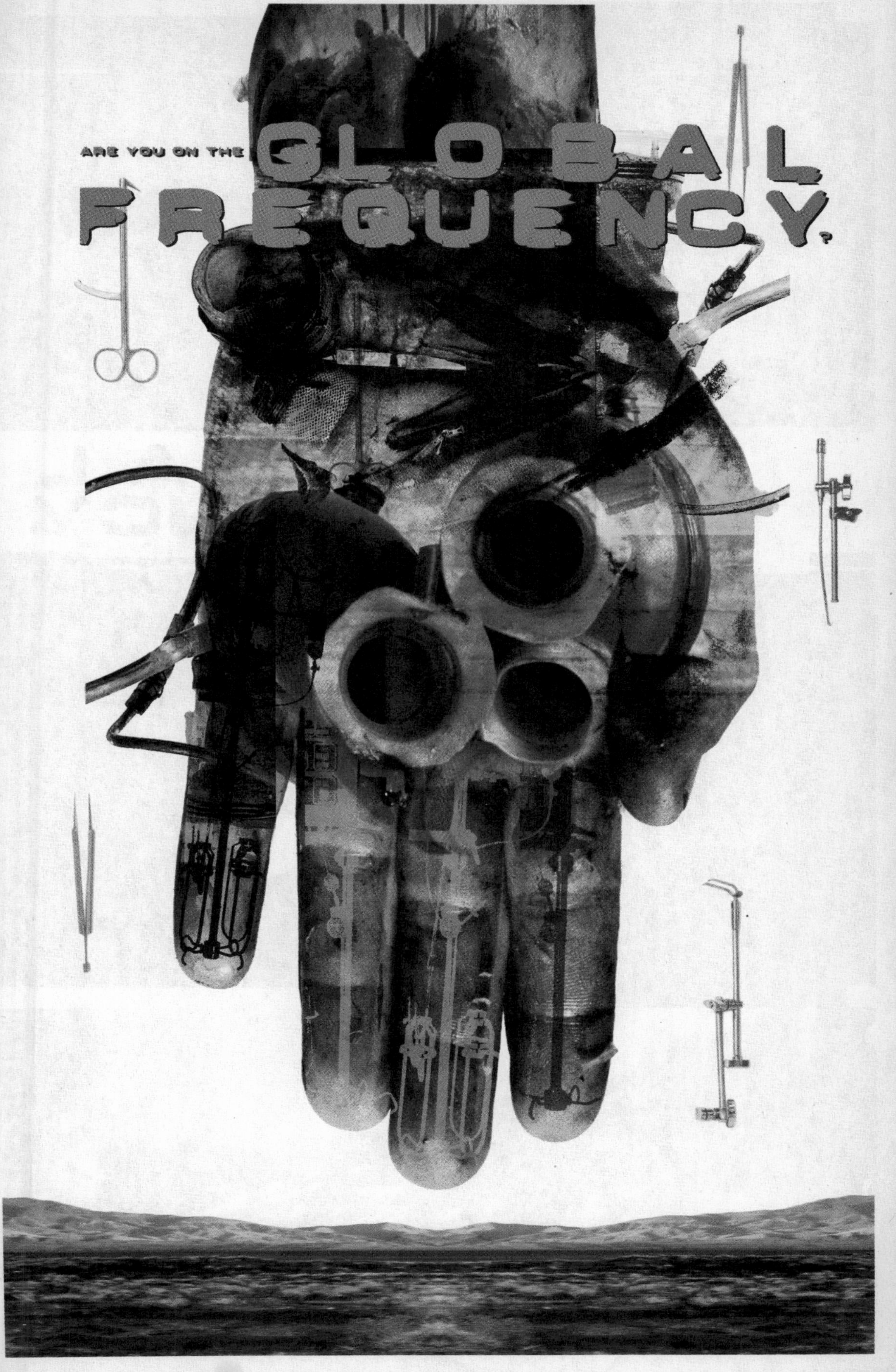
ARE YOU ON THE GLOBAL FREQUENCY?

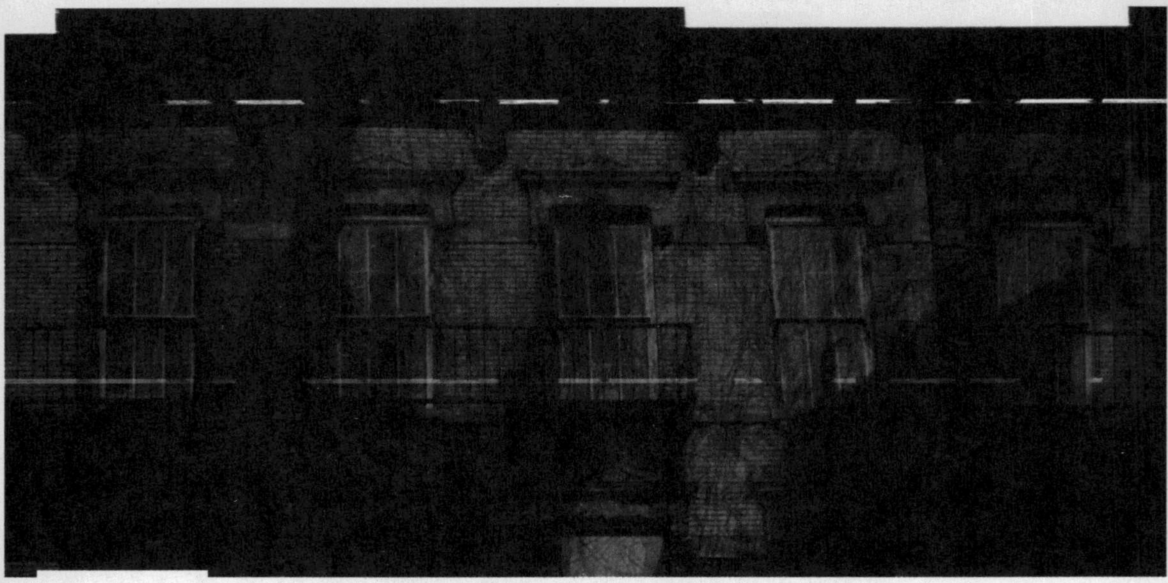

ARE YOU ON THE **GLOBAL FREQUENCY?**

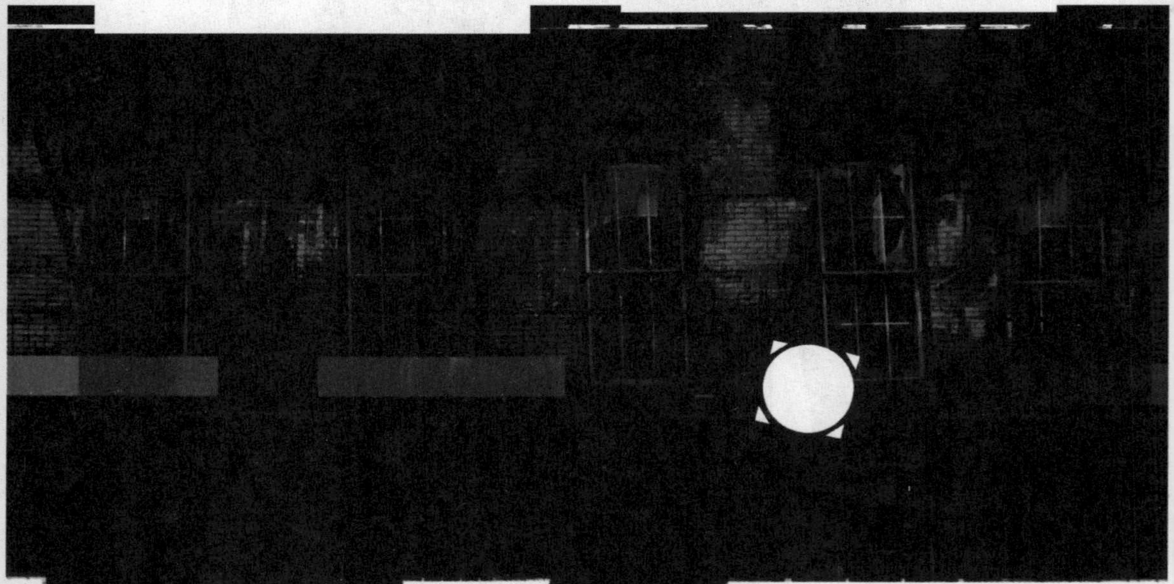

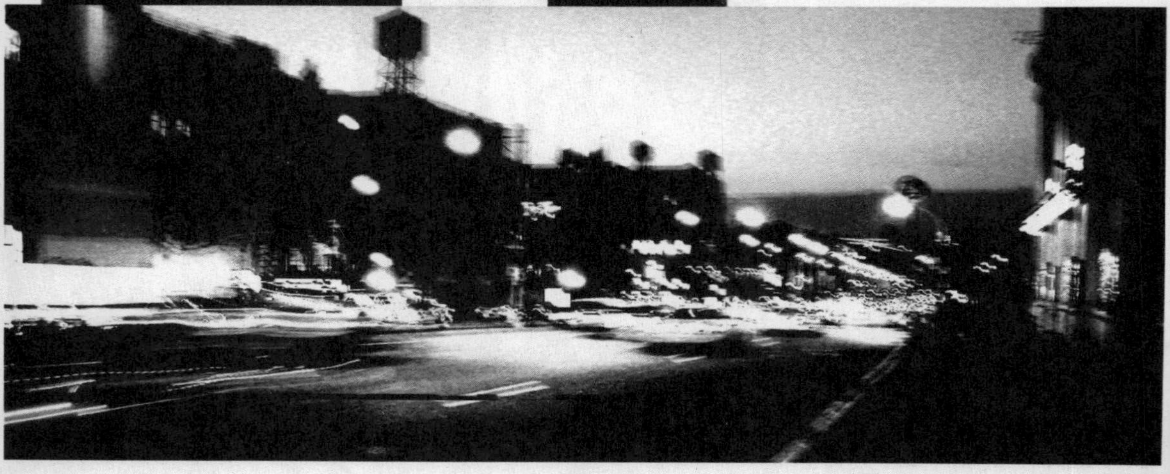

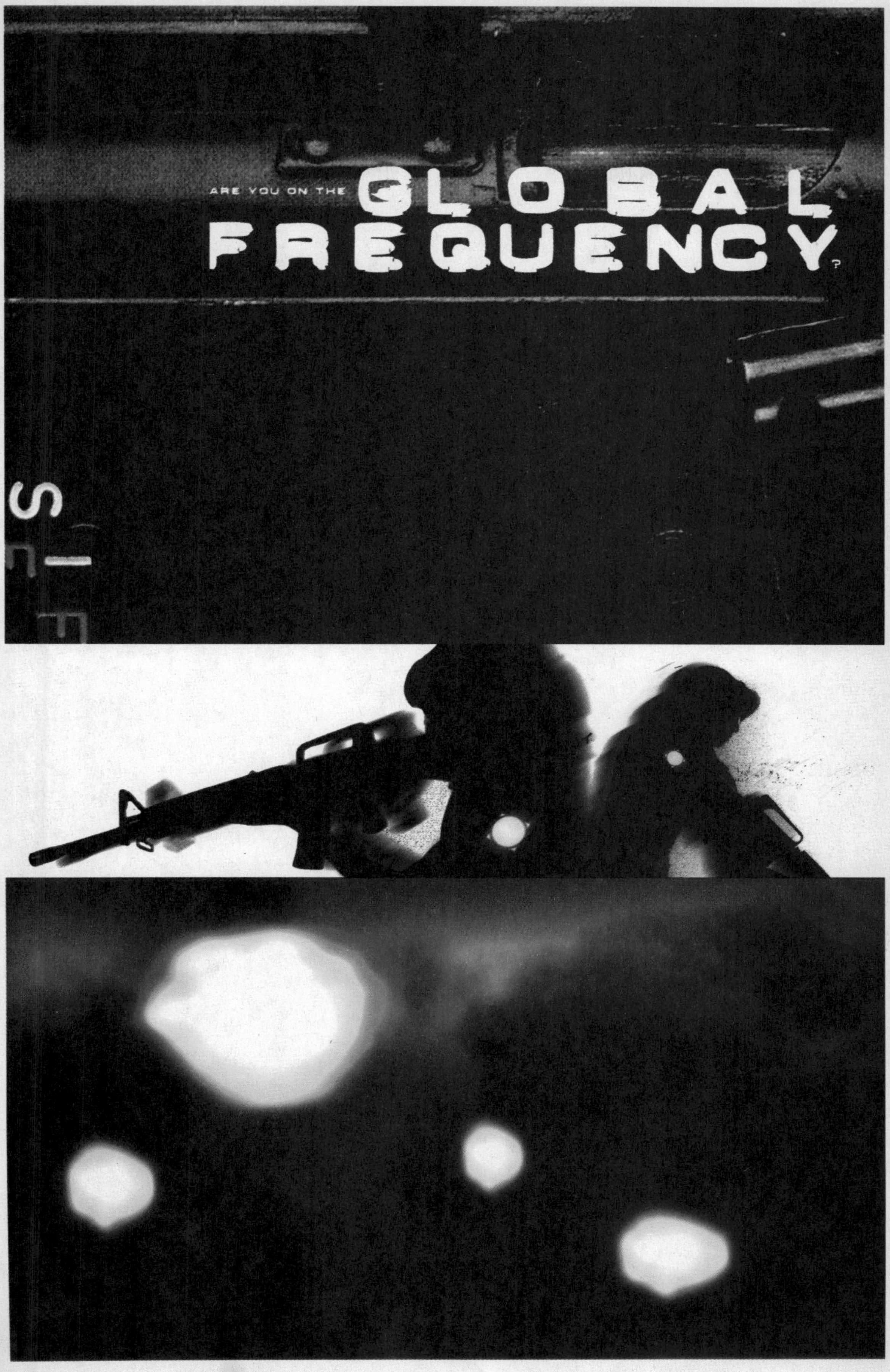

ARE YOU ON THE GLOBAL FREQUENCY?

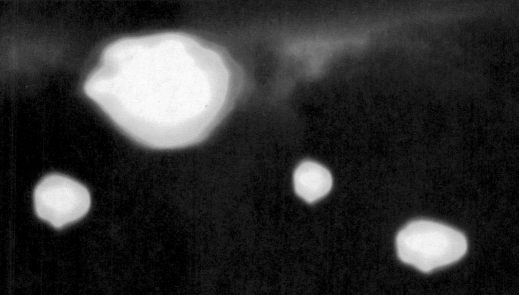

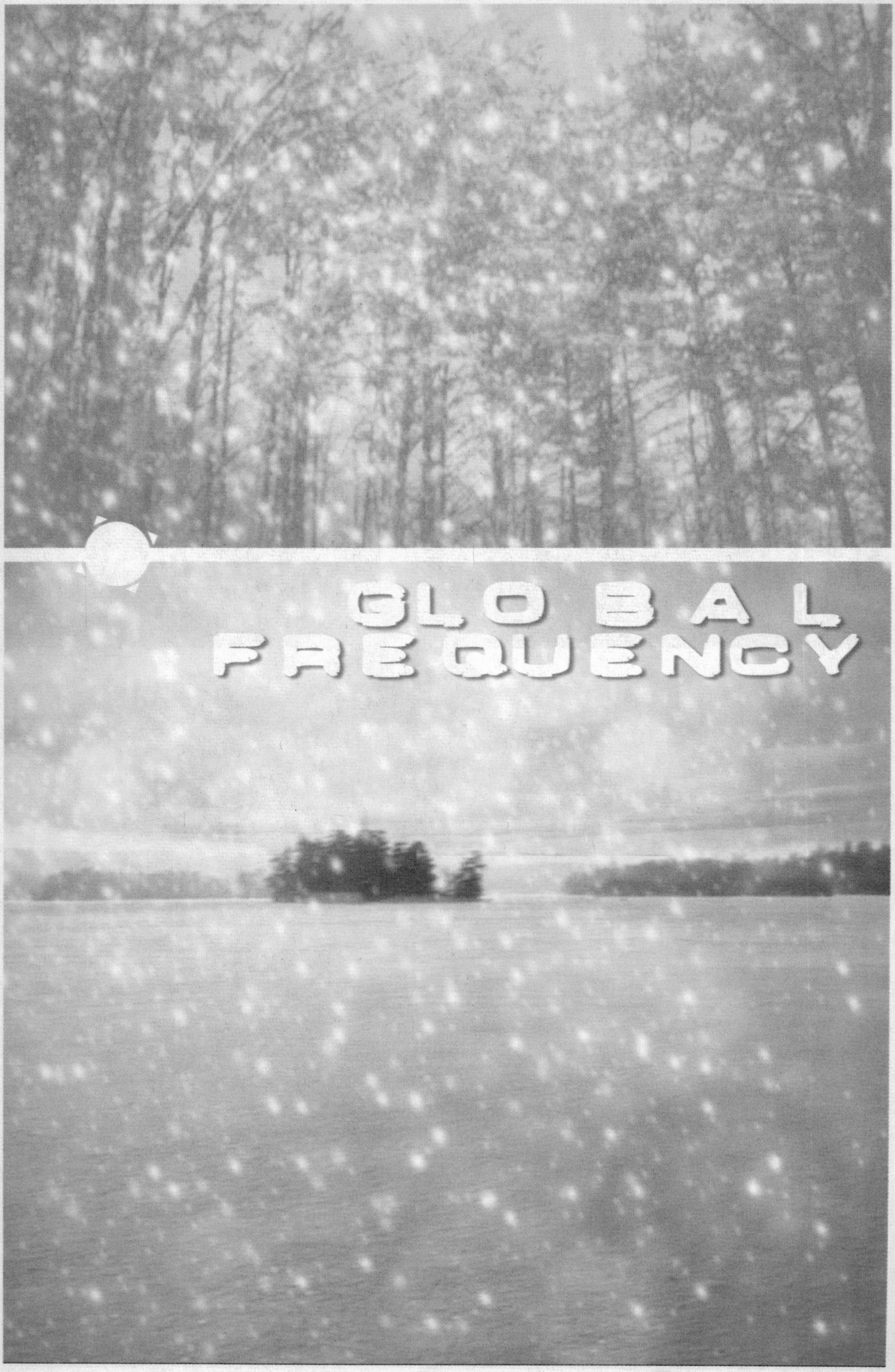
GLOBAL
FREQUENCY

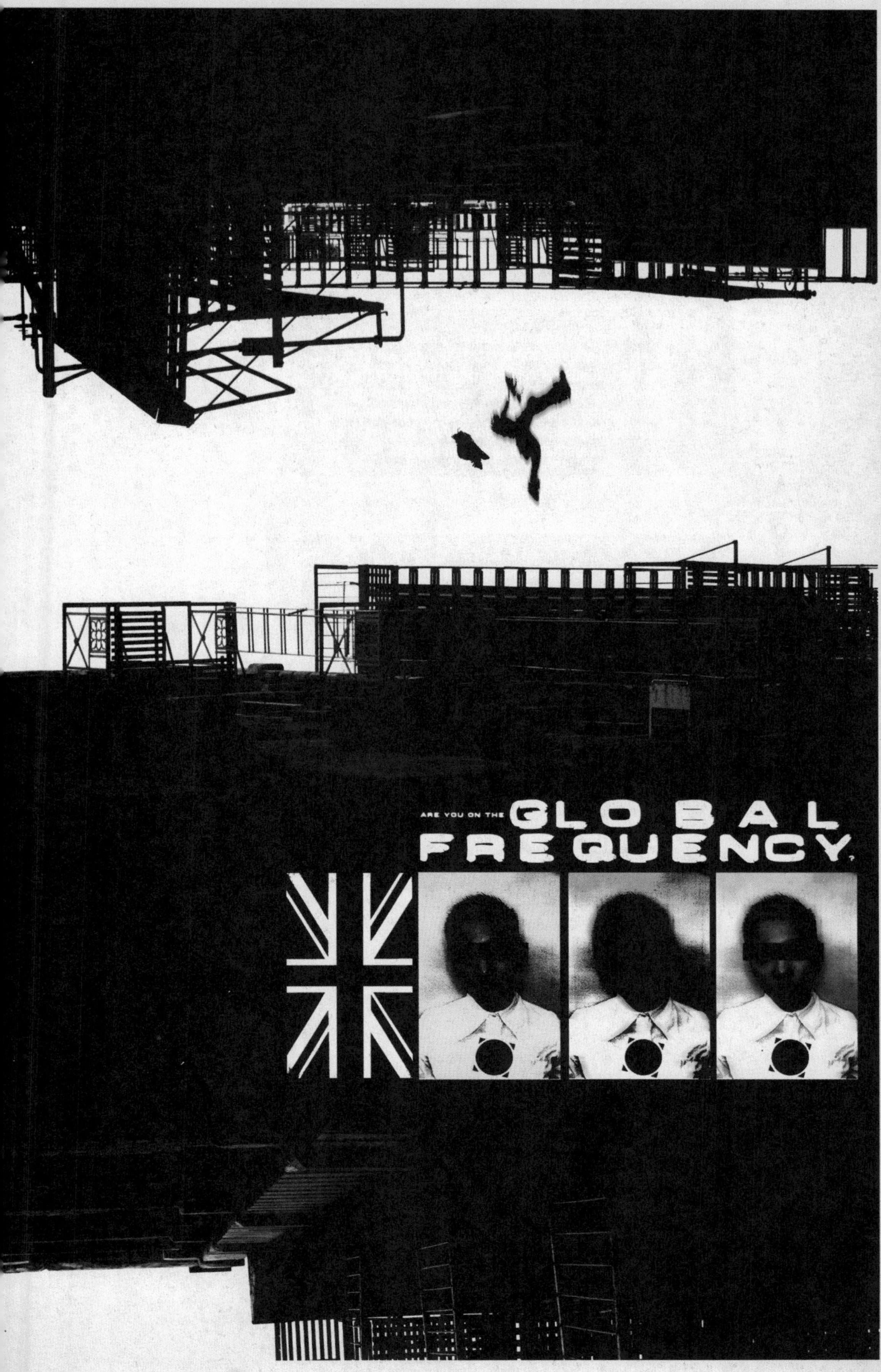
ARE YOU ON THE GLOBAL FREQUENCY?

Global Frequency creator bios

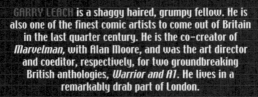

WARREN ELLIS is one of the most acclaimed writers working in comics. He is noted for his work on *STORMWATCH, THE AUTHORITY, PLANETARY,* and *TRANSMETROPOLITAN,* among others. His upcoming schedule includes more work for WILDSTORM— if he knows what's good for him!

GARRY LEACH is a shaggy haired, grumpy fellow. He is also one of the finest comic artists to come out of Britain in the last quarter century. He is the co-creator of *Marvelman,* with Alan Moore, and was the art director and coeditor, respectively, for two groundbreaking British anthologies, *Warrior and A1.* He lives in a remarkably drab part of London.

GLENN FABRY is a painter of extraordinary talent. His work has graced many a comic cover, including the entire run of *PREACHER.* Aside from his painting skills, Glenn is also a master of pen & ink, as his entry here deftly shows. He lives with his family near the English shore...we think.

STEVE DILLON is renowned for his masterful storytelling ability. He is considered by many writers to be the perfect collaborator because of his ability to put everything the story calls for on the page, in the right order, and with enough room left over for the word balloons —not as common a virtue as you may think! He lives a short ways from London and knows where all the best Irish pubs are in New York.

ROY A. MARTINEZ is our first non–Brit artist on the Global Frequency, but we try not to hold it against him. He hails from the other side of the globe and, when keeping his cell phone charged, is aces with us.

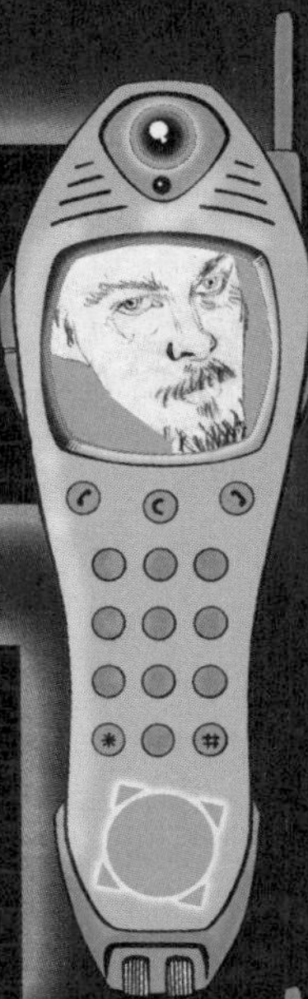

JON J MUTH insists we leave off the period after his middle initial so don't send us letters correcting our editorial blunder. Muth is famed for his painted comic series such as *Moonshadow & M,* as well as for his traditional pen and ink comic work. He currently resides in the northeastern United States.

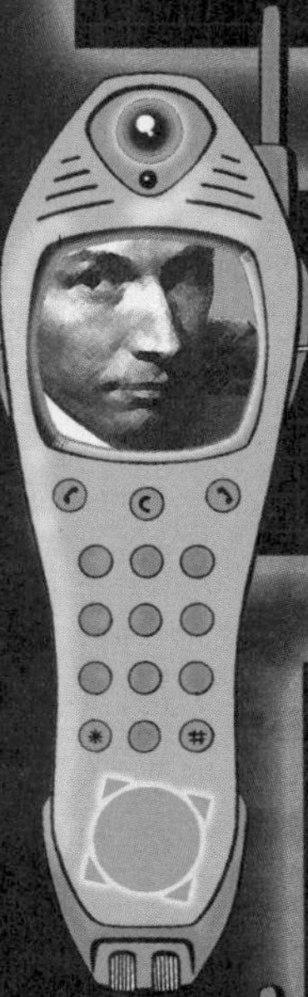

DAVID LLOYD is the esteemed artist and co-creator, with Alan Moore, of V FOR VENDETTA. His more recent work includes chapters of Garth Ennis' WAR STORIES: NIGHTINGALE and J FOR JENNY, and an adaptation of Raymond Chandler's story *The Pencil in Marlowe: The Graphic Novel.*

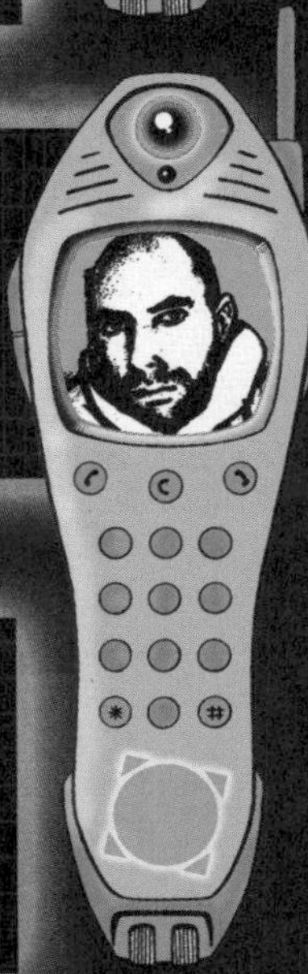

BRIAN WOOD, besides providing GLOBAL FREQUENCY with stunning graphic cover designs, is an accomplished comics creator. His *Channel Zero* has won him critical praise from many quarters—he says that while he appreciates the quarters, he prefers dollars.

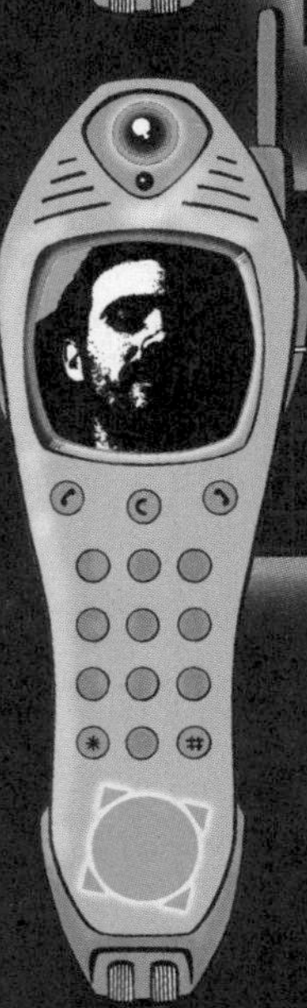

DAVID BARON has been a first-rate colorist at WildStorm Productions since he was 16 years old, thanks to the corrupting influence of John and Clydene Nee. He is also a good pool player and is okay at poker, thereby giving credence to the old adage about being the product of a misspent youth.